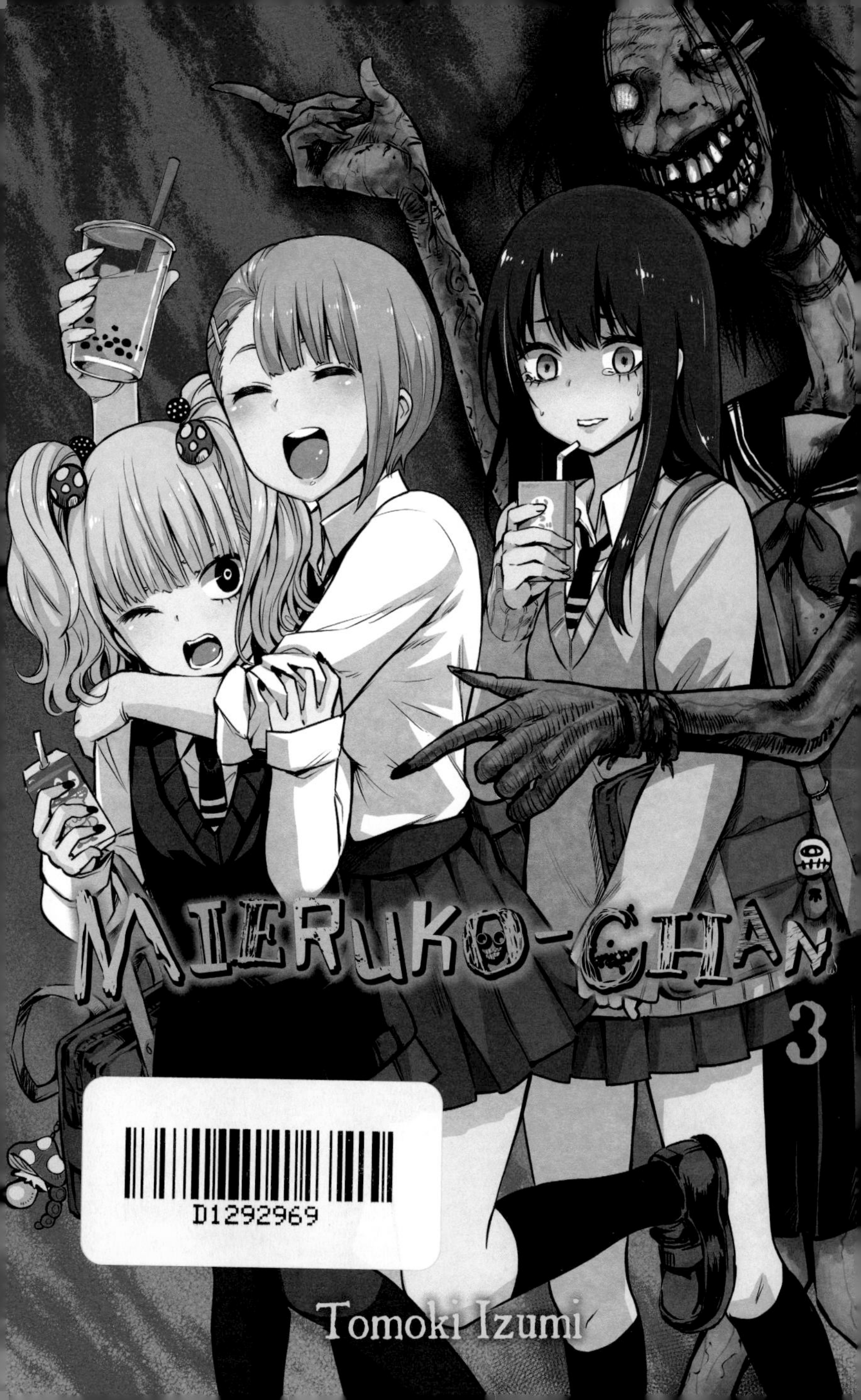
MIERUKO-CHAN
3
Tomoki Izumi

CONTENTS

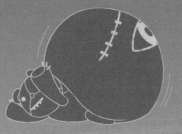

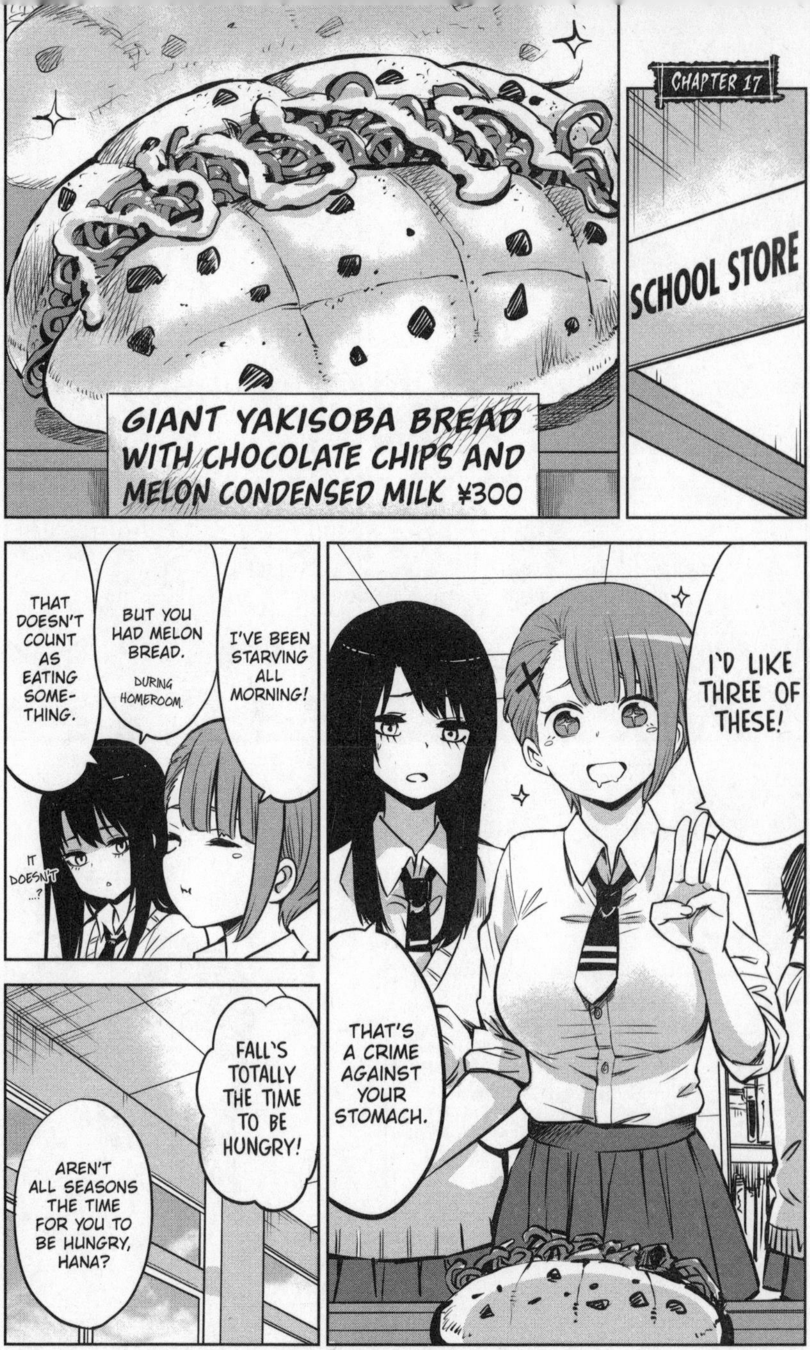
CHAPTER 17
SCHOOL STORE
GIANT YAKISOBA BREAD WITH CHOCOLATE CHIPS AND MELON CONDENSED MILK ¥300
I'D LIKE THREE OF THESE!
I'VE BEEN STARVING ALL MORNING!
BUT YOU HAD MELON BREAD.
DURING HOMEROOM.
THAT DOESN'T COUNT AS EATING SOME-THING.
IT DOESN'T ...?
THAT'S A CRIME AGAINST YOUR STOMACH.
FALL'S TOTALLY THE TIME TO BE HUNGRY!
AREN'T ALL SEASONS THE TIME FOR YOU TO BE HUNGRY, HANA?

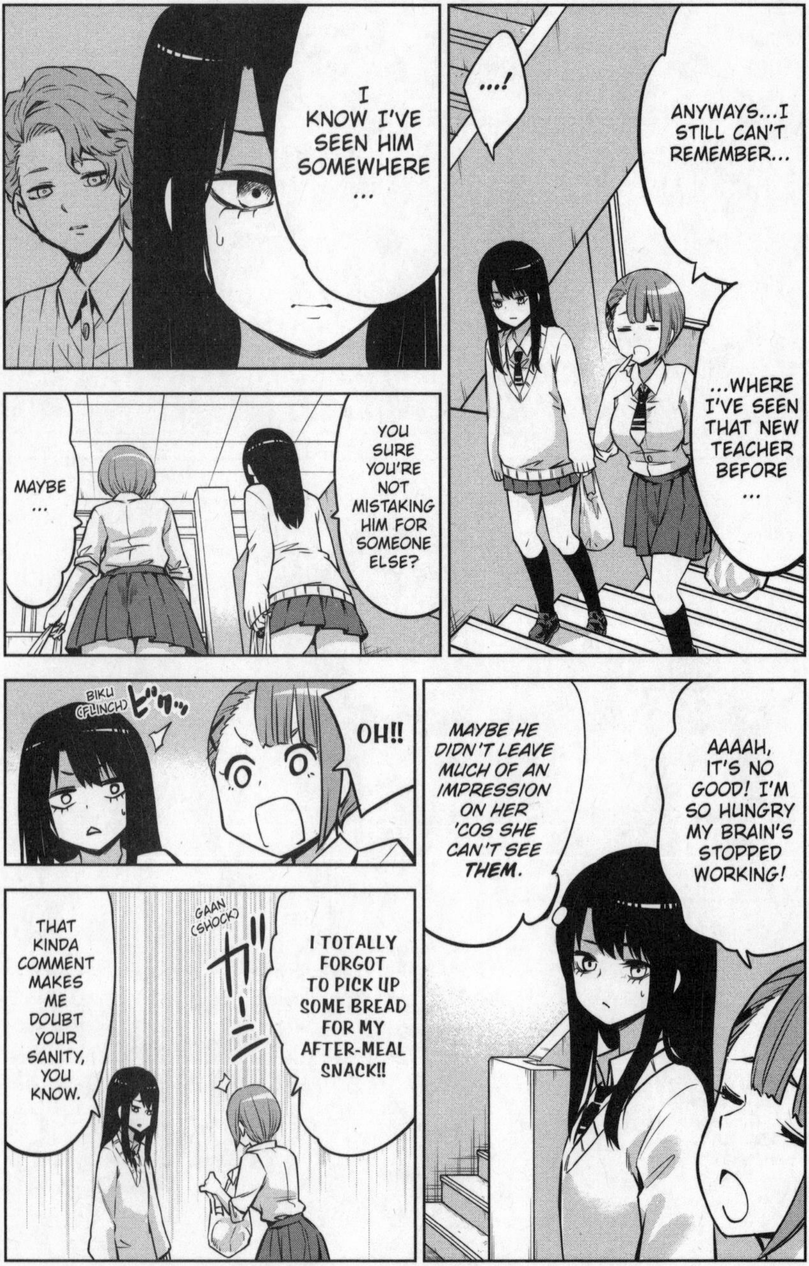
ANYWAYS...I STILL CAN'T REMEMBER...
...WHERE I'VE SEEN THAT NEW TEACHER BEFORE...
...!
I KNOW I'VE SEEN HIM SOMEWHERE...
YOU SURE YOU'RE NOT MISTAKING HIM FOR SOMEONE ELSE?
MAYBE...
AAAAH, IT'S NO GOOD! I'M SO HUNGRY MY BRAIN'S STOPPED WORKING!
MAYBE HE DIDN'T LEAVE MUCH OF AN IMPRESSION ON HER 'COS SHE CAN'T SEE THEM.
OH!!
BIKU (FLINCH)
GAAN (SHOCK)
I TOTALLY FORGOT TO PICK UP SOME BREAD FOR MY AFTER-MEAL SNACK!!
THAT KINDA COMMENT MAKES ME DOUBT YOUR SANITY, YOU KNOW.

HEY—

SORRY! GO ON AHEAD!! I'LL BE RIGHT BACK!

SHUBA (WHOOSH)

MRS. D...

...COU-PONS...

I NEED TO FIND A WAY TO DISTRACT HER...

WELL, IT WOULD GET PRETTY AWKWARD IF SHE DID REMEMBER HIM...

OH...

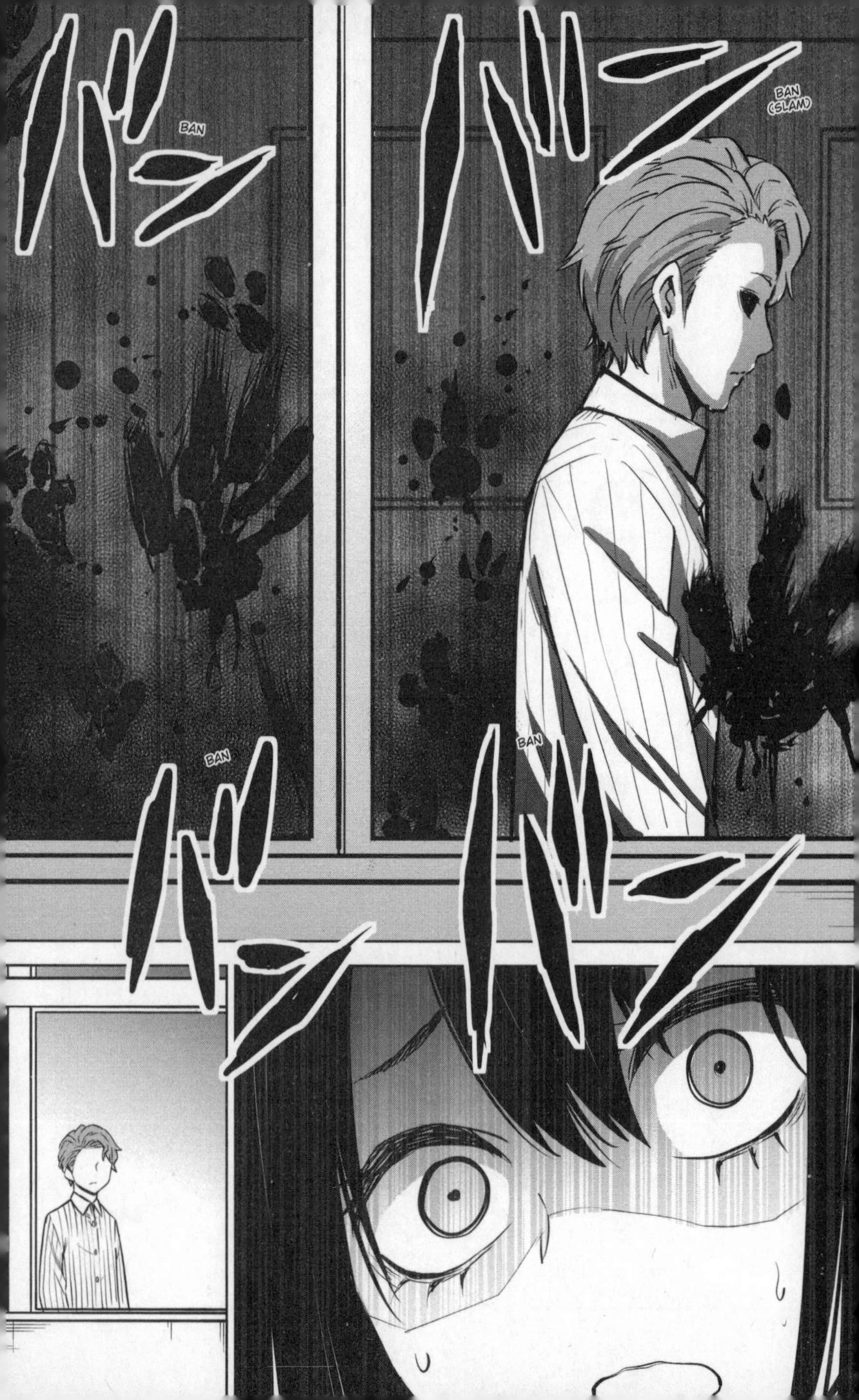
BAN (SLAM)
BAN
BAN
BAN

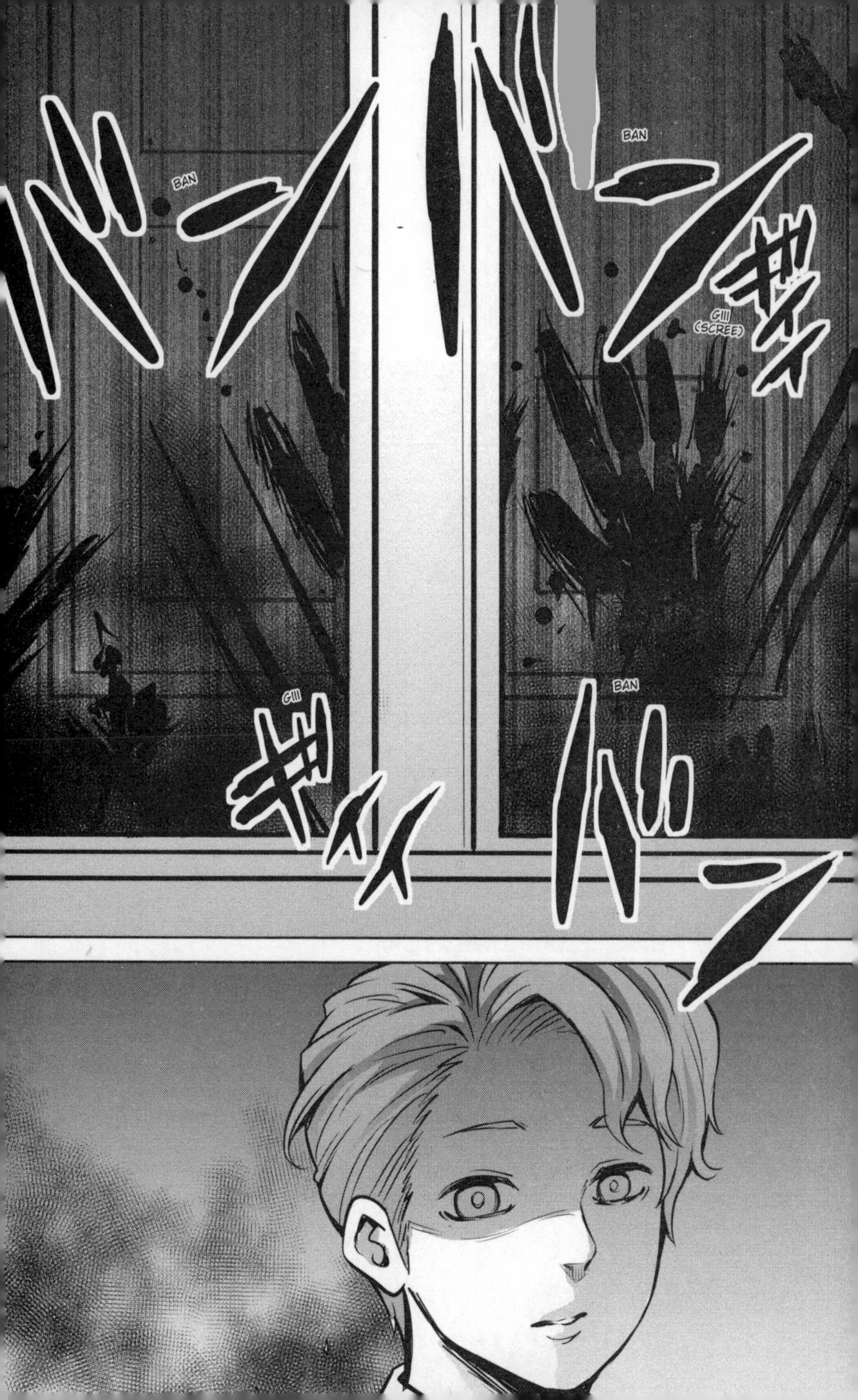
BAN
GIII (SCREE)
BAN
BAN
GIII

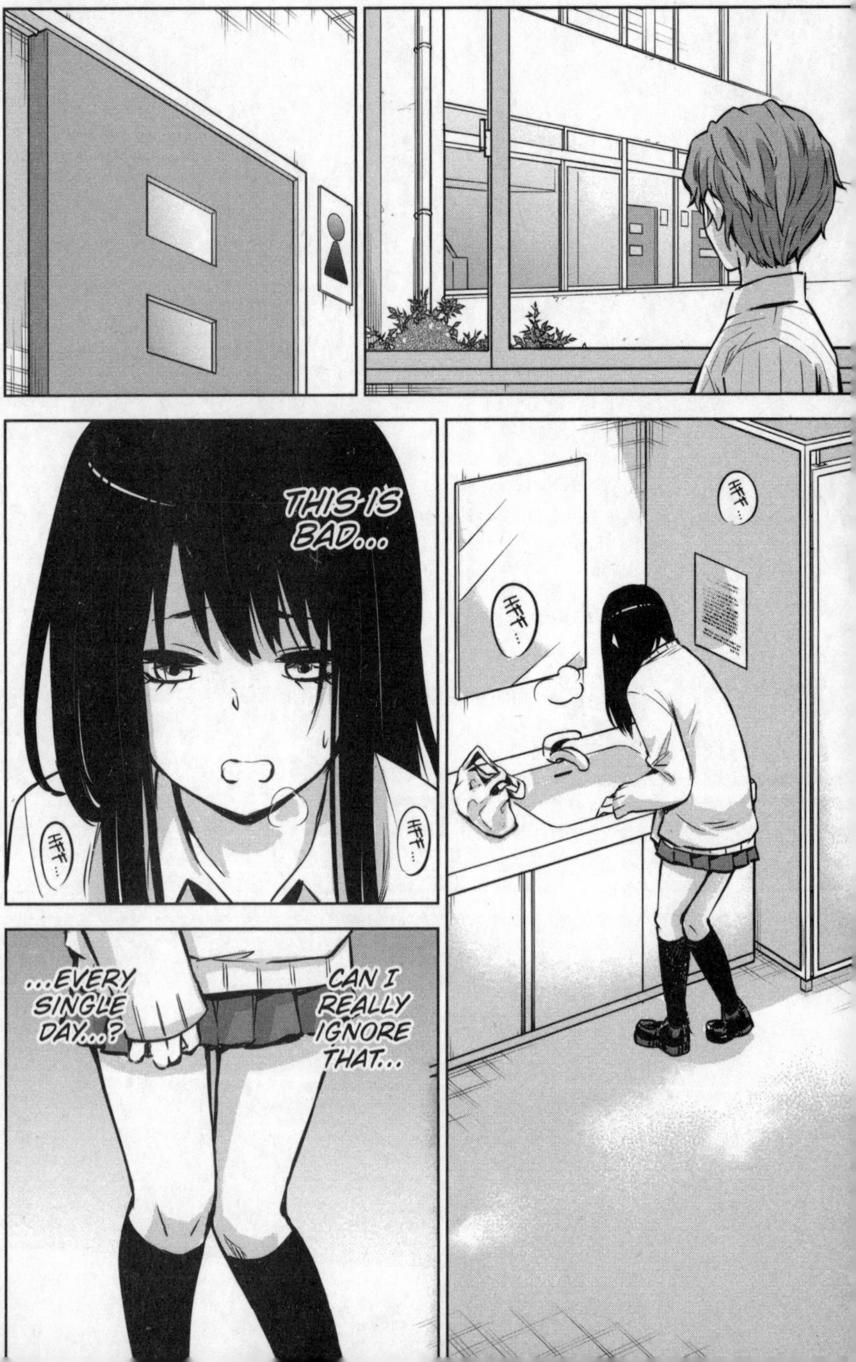
HFF...
HFF...
THIS IS BAD...
HFF...
HFF...
CAN I REALLY IGNORE THAT...
...EVERY SINGLE DAY...?

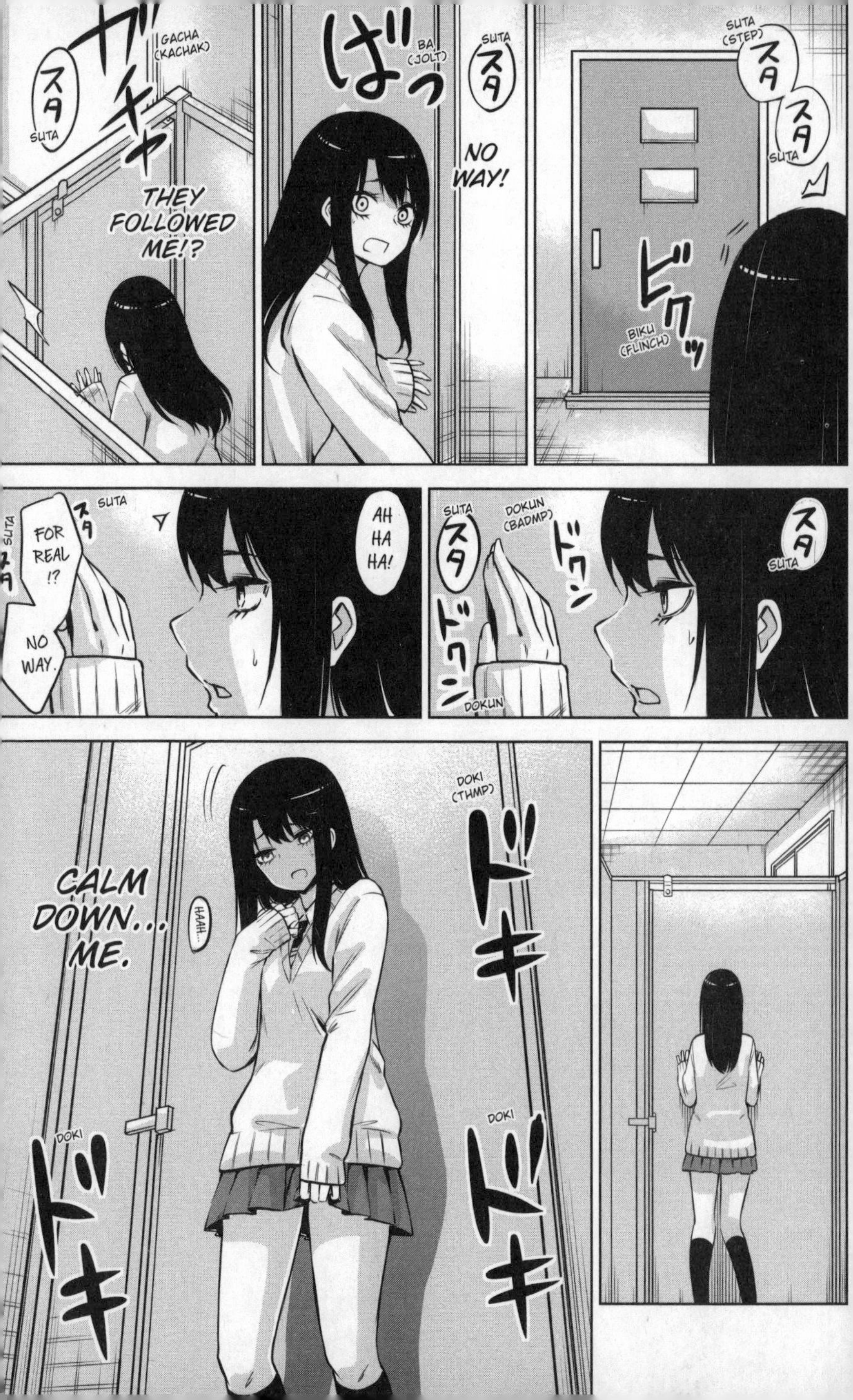
SUTA (STEP)
スタ
スタ
SUTA
ビクッ
BIKU (FLINCH)
ばっ
BA (JOLT)
SUTA
スタ
NO WAY!
ガチャ
GACHA (KACHAK)
スタ
SUTA
THEY FOLLOWED ME!?
スタ
SUTA
SUTA
スタ
DOKUN (BADMP)
ドクン
ドクン
DOKUN
AH HA HA!
SUTA
スタ
FOR REAL!?
NO WAY.
SUTA
スタ
DOKI (THMP)
ドキ
DOKI
ドキ
CALM DOWN... ME.
HAAH...
DOKI
ドキ

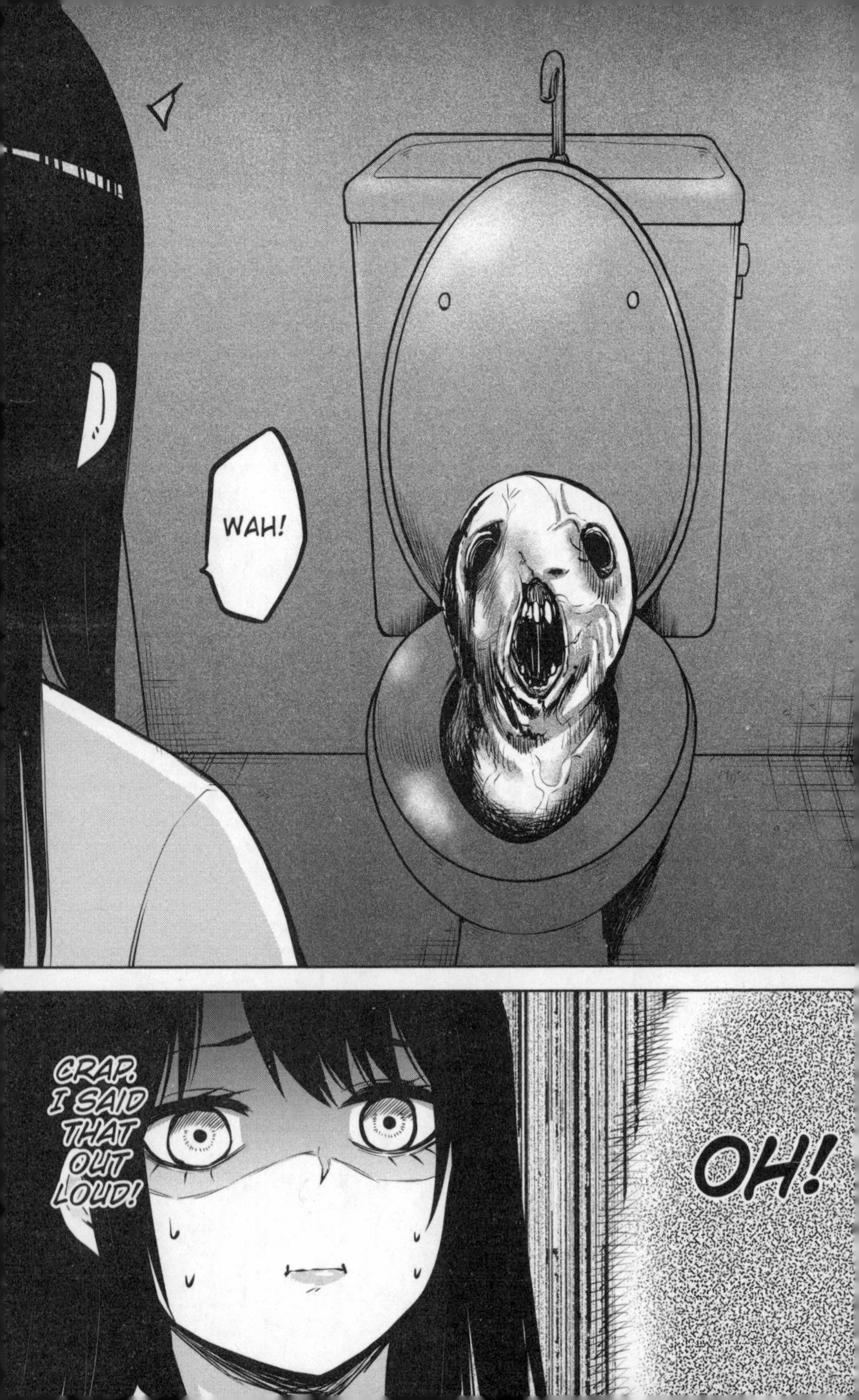
WAH!
OH!
CRAP. I SAID THAT OUT LOUD!

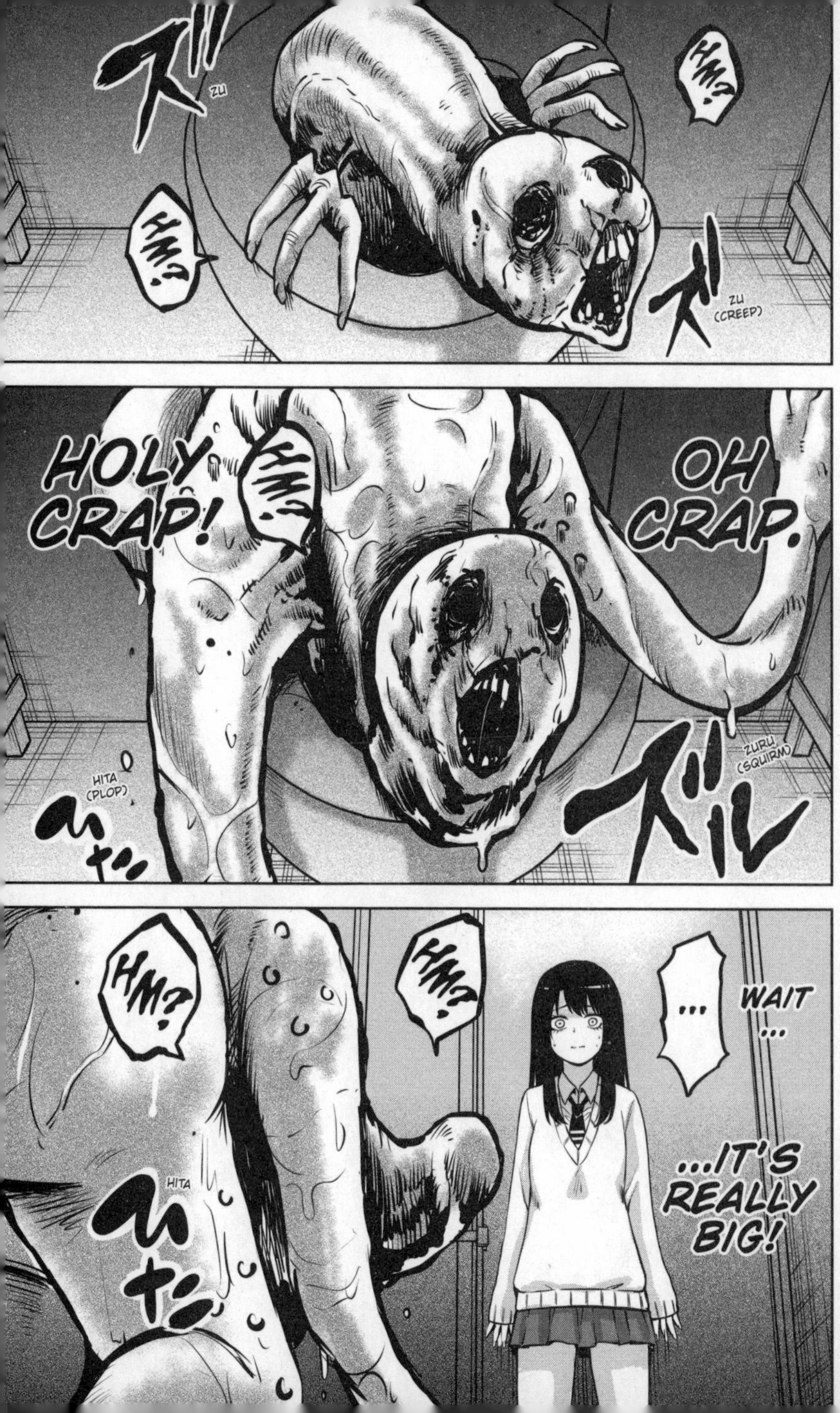
HM?
ZU (CREEP)
ZU
HM?
OH CRAP.
ZURU (SQUIRM)
HM?
HOLY CRAP!
HITA (PLOP)
WAIT...
...
...IT'S REALLY BIG!
HM?
HM?
HITA

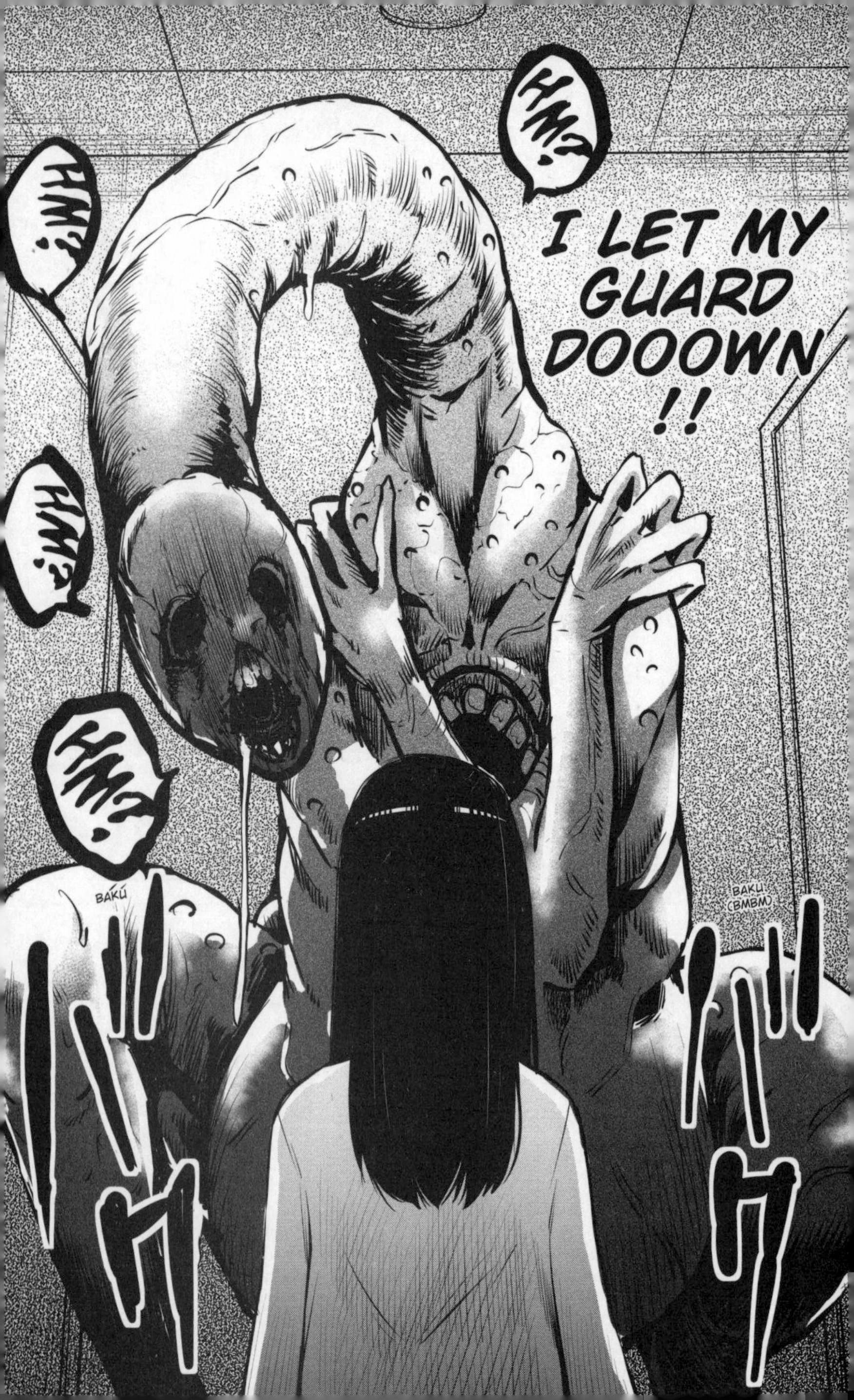
HM?
I LET MY GUARD DOOOWN !!
HM?
HM?
HM?
BAKU (BMBM)
BAKU

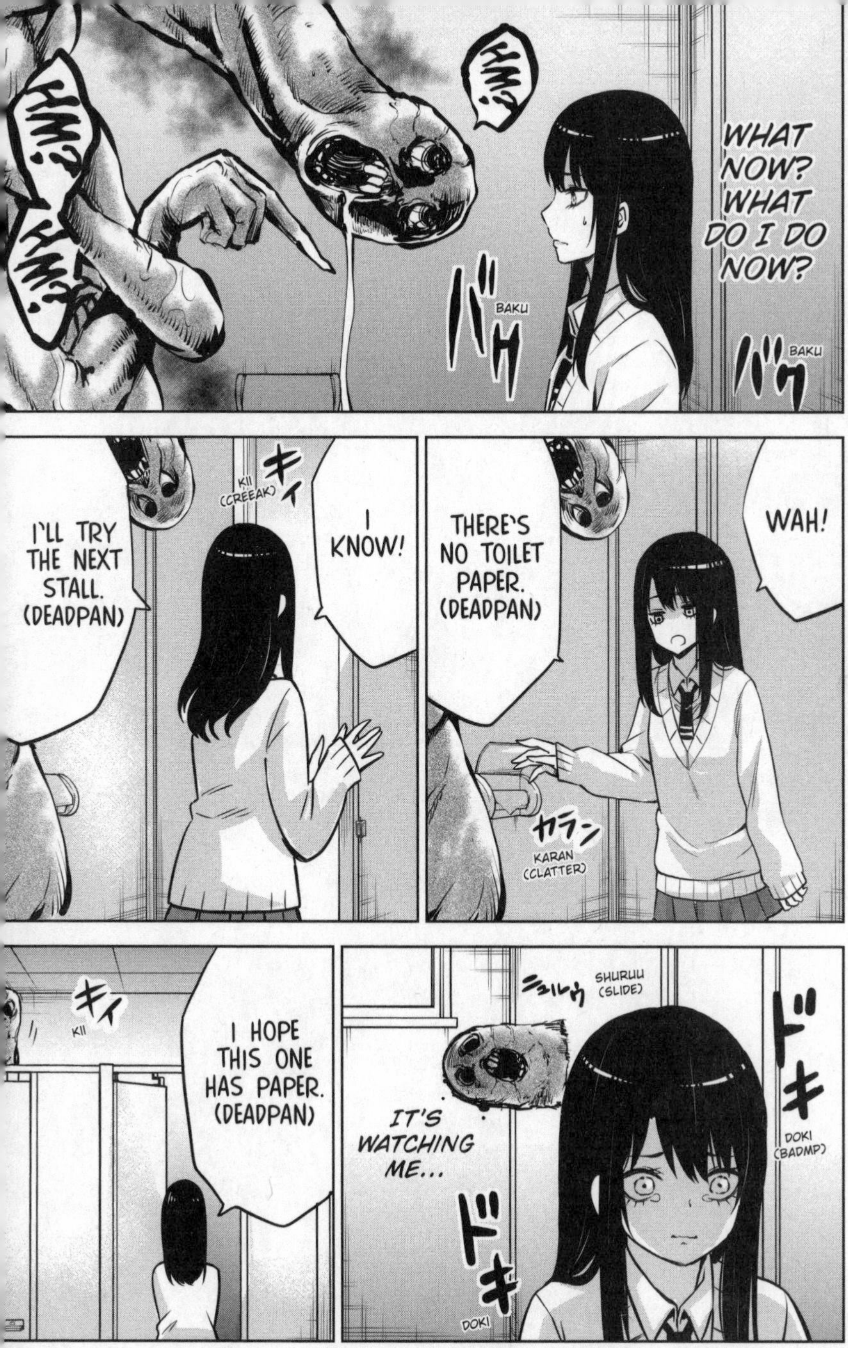
WHAT NOW? WHAT DO I DO NOW?
バク
BAKU
バク
BAKU
HM?
HM? HM? HM?
WAH!
THERE'S NO TOILET PAPER. (DEADPAN)
カラン
KARAN (CLATTER)
I KNOW!
キィ
KII (CREEAK)
I'LL TRY THE NEXT STALL. (DEADPAN)
シュルゥ
SHURUU (SLIDE)
ドキ
DOKI (BADMP)
IT'S WATCHING ME...
ドキ
DOKI
キィ
KII
I HOPE THIS ONE HAS PAPER. (DEADPAN)

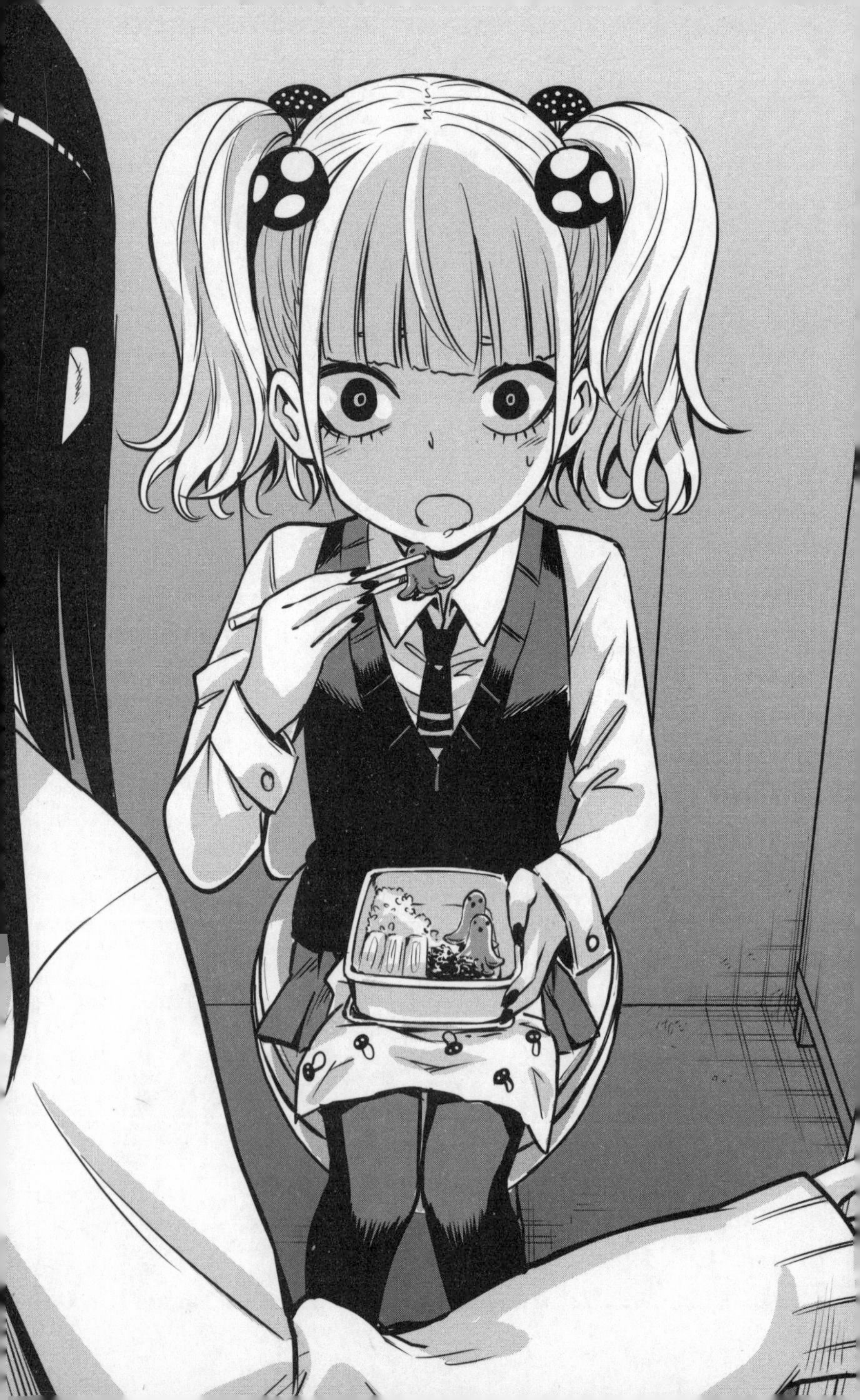

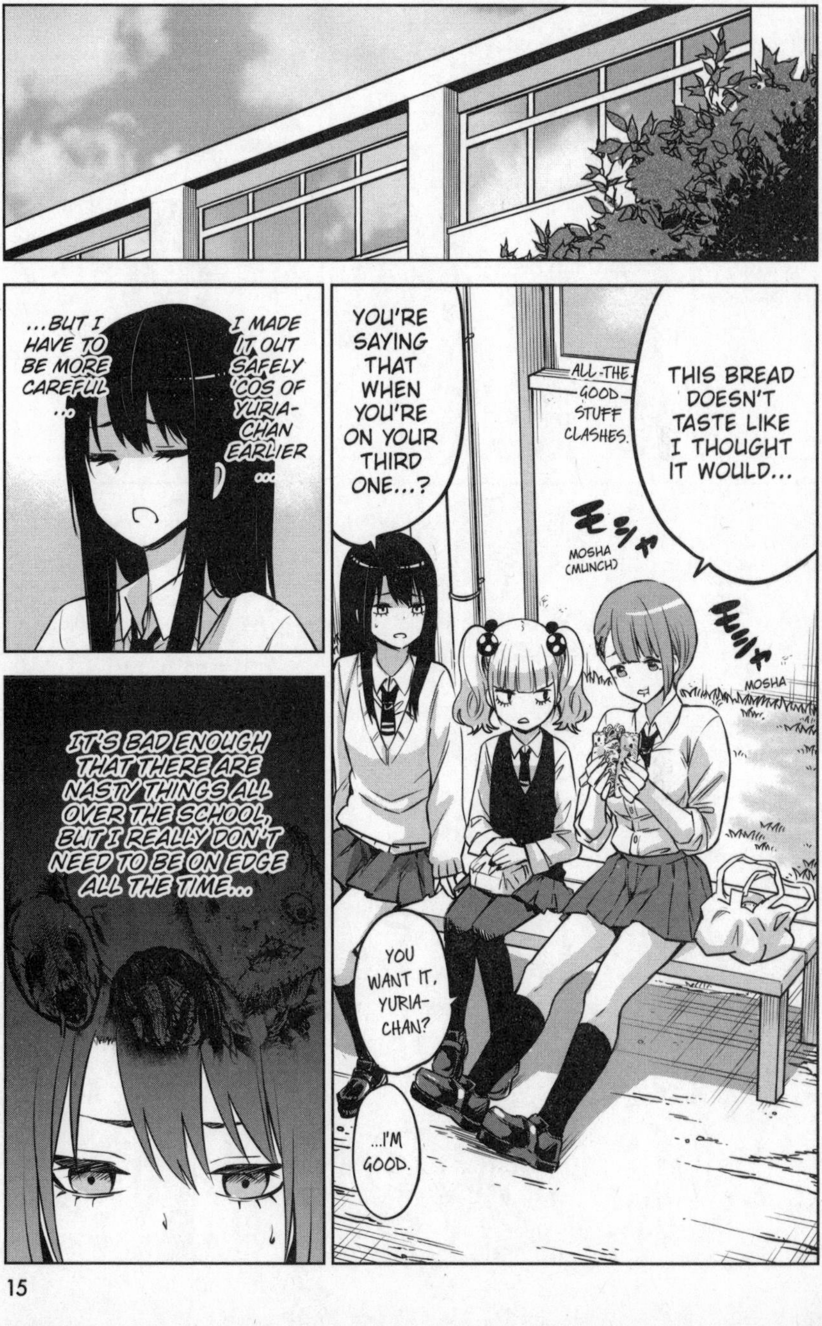
THIS BREAD DOESN'T TASTE LIKE I THOUGHT IT WOULD...
ALL-THE-GOOD-STUFF CLASHES.
MOSHA (MUNCH)
MOSHA
YOU'RE SAYING THAT WHEN YOU'RE ON YOUR THIRD ONE...?
YOU WANT IT, YURIA-CHAN?
...I'M GOOD.
I MADE IT OUT SAFELY 'COS OF YURIA-CHAN EARLIER...
...BUT I HAVE TO BE MORE CAREFUL...
IT'S BAD ENOUGH THAT THERE ARE NASTY THINGS ALL OVER THE SCHOOL, BUT I REALLY DON'T NEED TO BE ON EDGE ALL THE TIME...

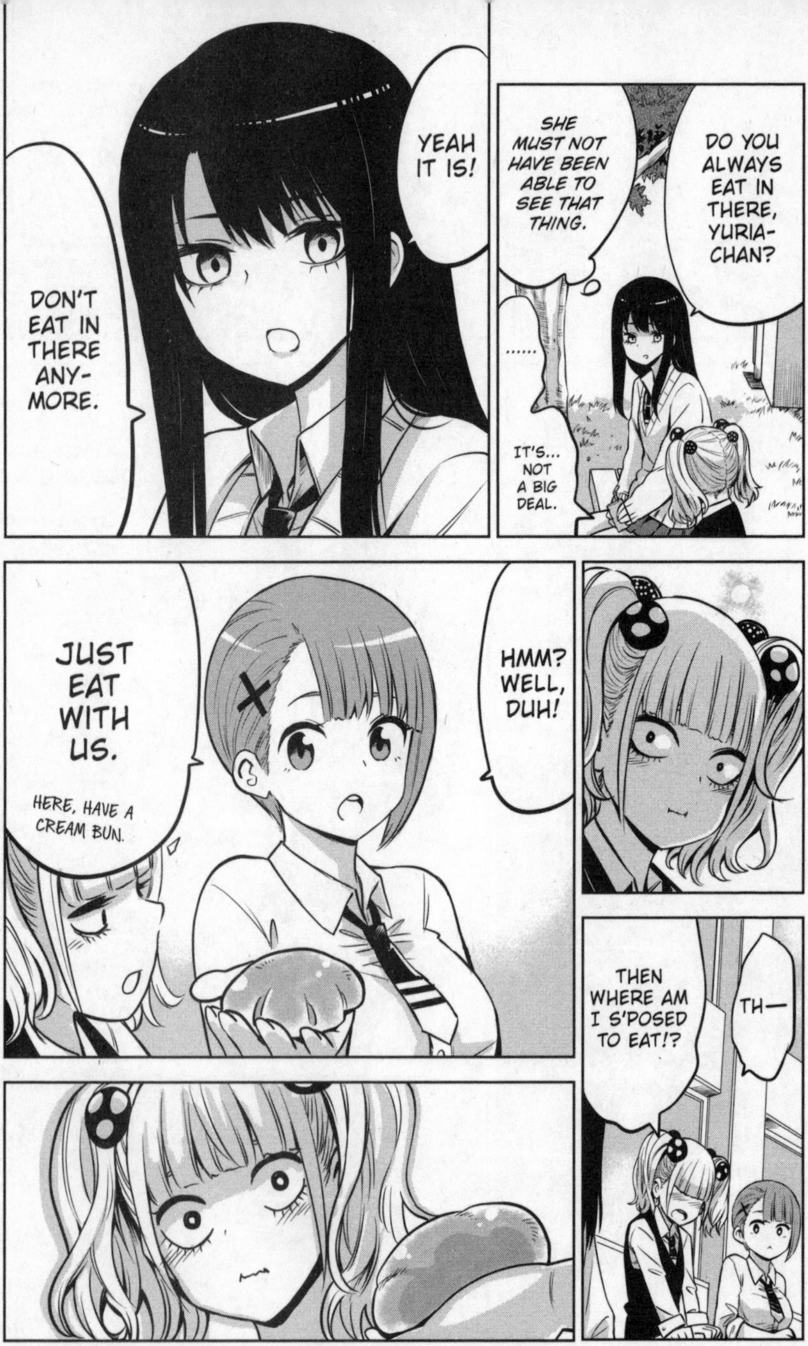
DO YOU ALWAYS EAT IN THERE, YURIA-CHAN?
SHE MUST NOT HAVE BEEN ABLE TO SEE THAT THING.
......
IT'S... NOT A BIG DEAL.
YEAH IT IS!
DON'T EAT IN THERE ANYMORE.
TH—
THEN WHERE AM I S'POSED TO EAT!?
HMM? WELL, DUH!
JUST EAT WITH US.
HERE, HAVE A CREAM BUN.

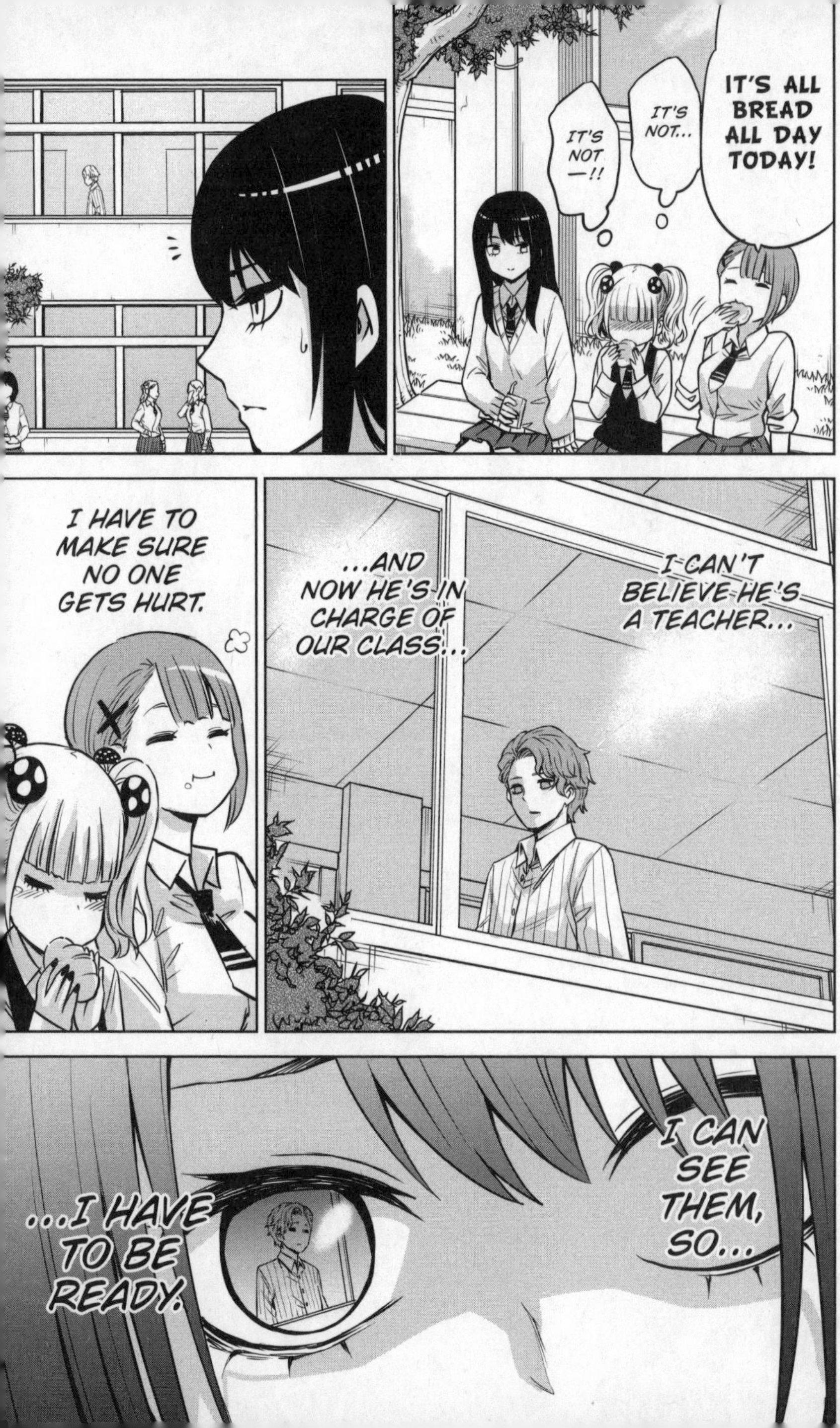
IT'S ALL BREAD ALL DAY TODAY!
IT'S NOT...
IT'S NOT—!!
I CAN'T BELIEVE HE'S A TEACHER...
...AND NOW HE'S IN CHARGE OF OUR CLASS...
I HAVE TO MAKE SURE NO ONE GETS HURT.
I CAN SEE THEM, SO...
...I HAVE TO BE READY.

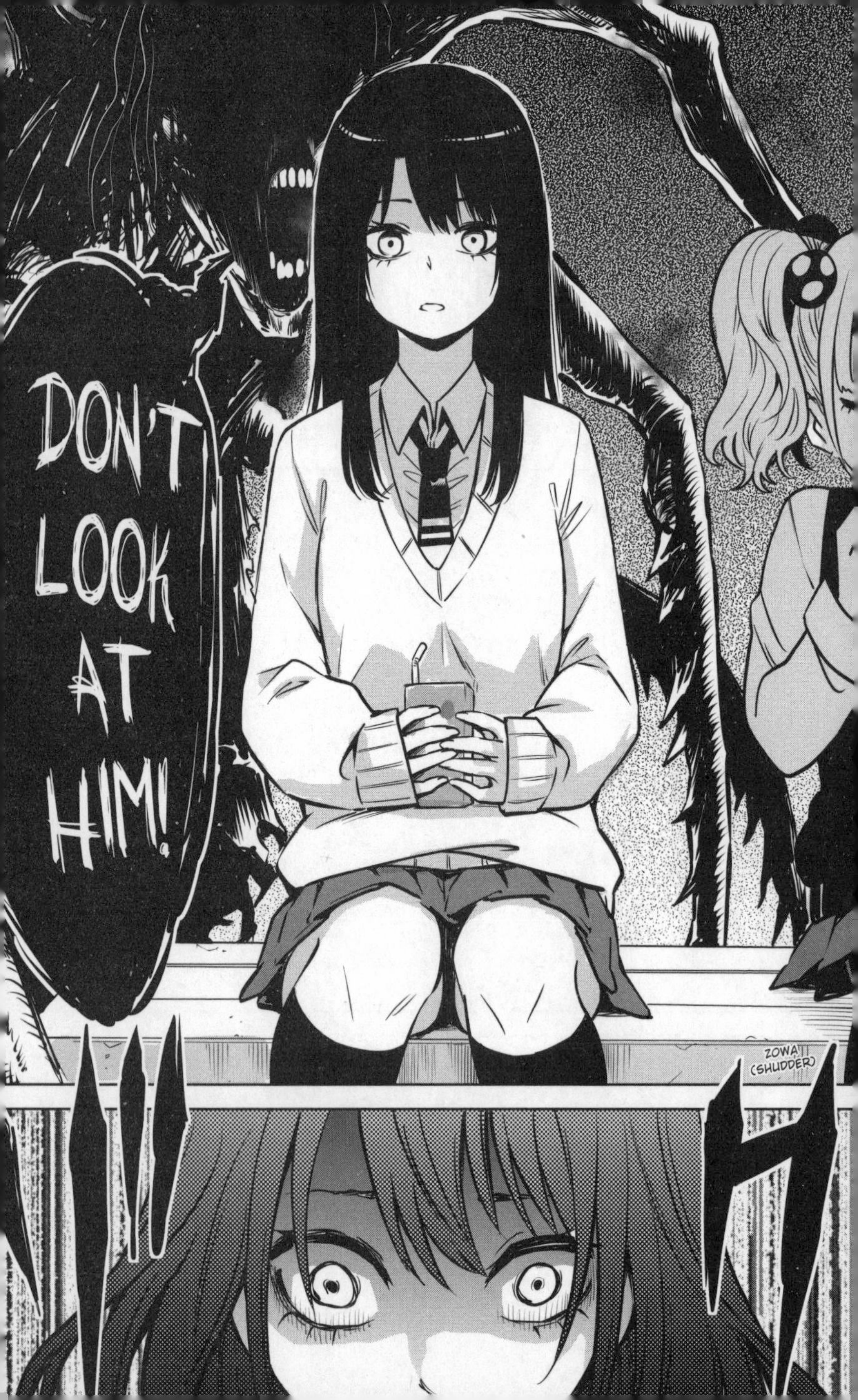
DON'T LOOK AT HIM!
ZOWA!
(SHUDDER)

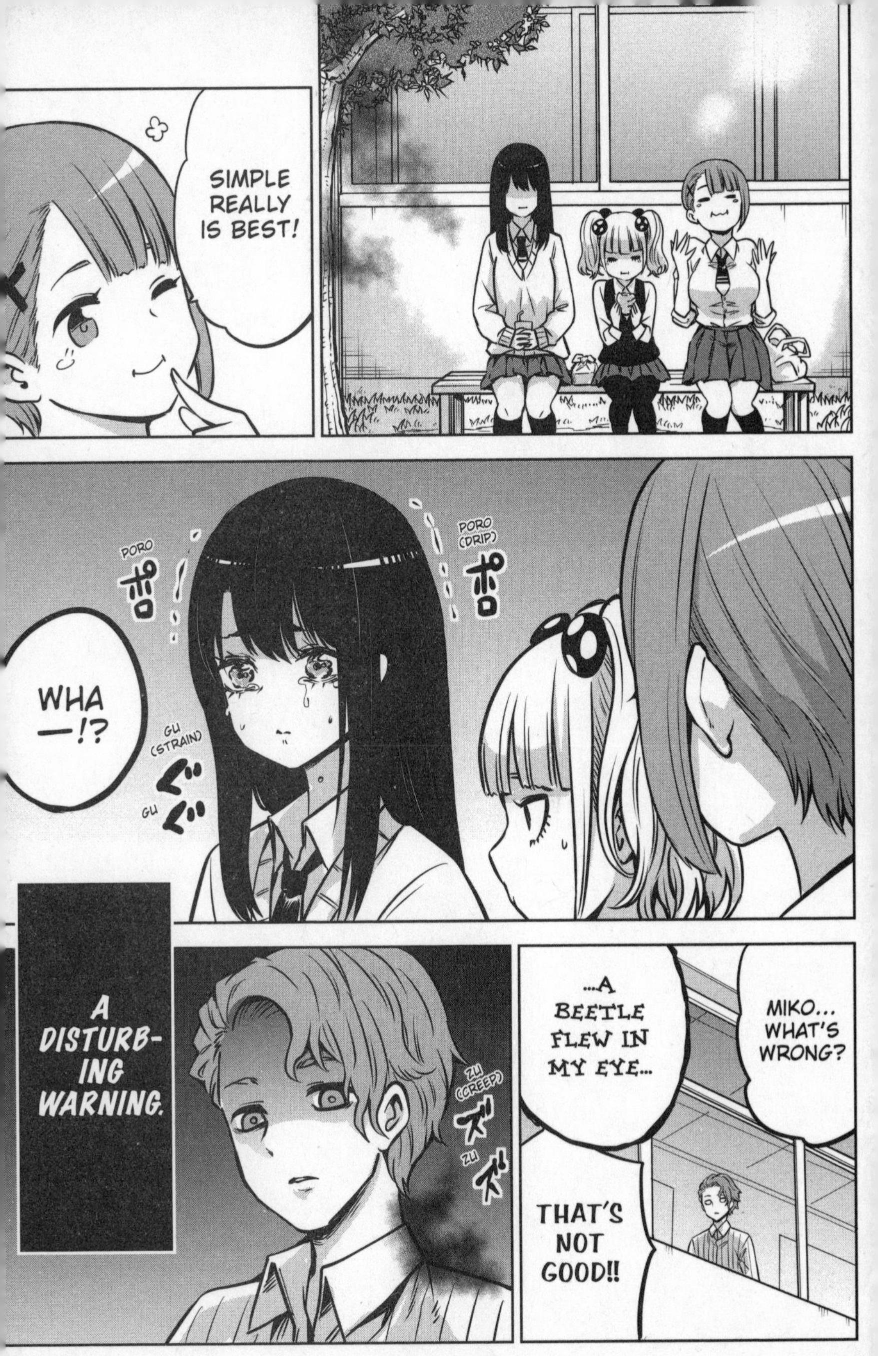
SIMPLE REALLY IS BEST!
PORO (DRIP) ポロ
PORO ポロ
GU (STRAIN) ぐ
GU ぐ
WHA—!?
MIKO... WHAT'S WRONG?
...A BEETLE FLEW IN MY EYE...
THAT'S NOT GOOD!!
ZU (CREEP) ズ
ZU ズ
A DISTURB-ING WARNING.

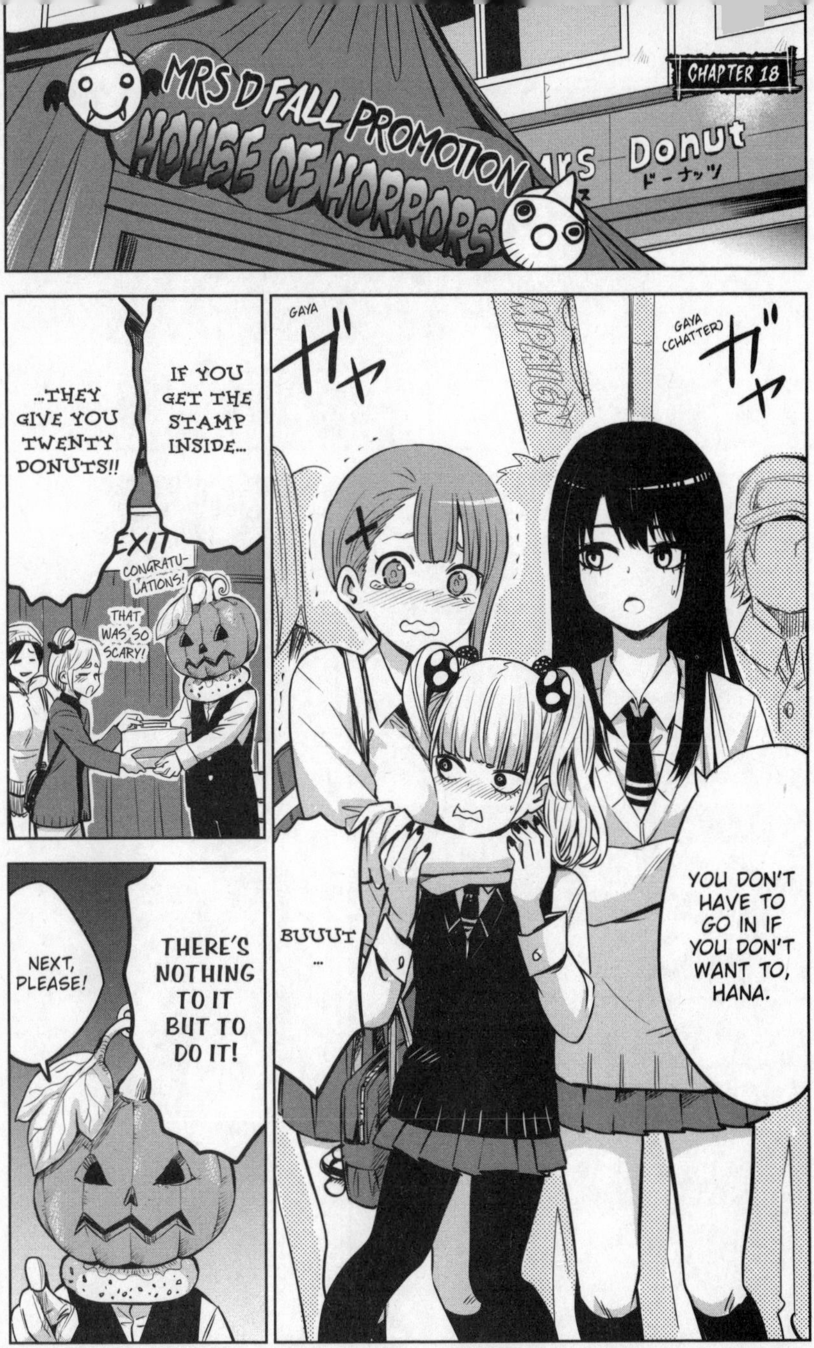
CHAPTER 18
MRS D FALL PROMOTION
HOUSE OF HORRORS
Mrs Donut
ドーナッツ
GAYA (CHATTER)
ガヤ
GAYA
ガヤ
YOU DON'T HAVE TO GO IN IF YOU DON'T WANT TO, HANA.
BUUUT...
IF YOU GET THE STAMP INSIDE...
...THEY GIVE YOU TWENTY DONUTS!!
EXIT
CONGRATULATIONS!
THAT WAS SO SCARY!
THERE'S NOTHING TO IT BUT TO DO IT!
NEXT, PLEASE!

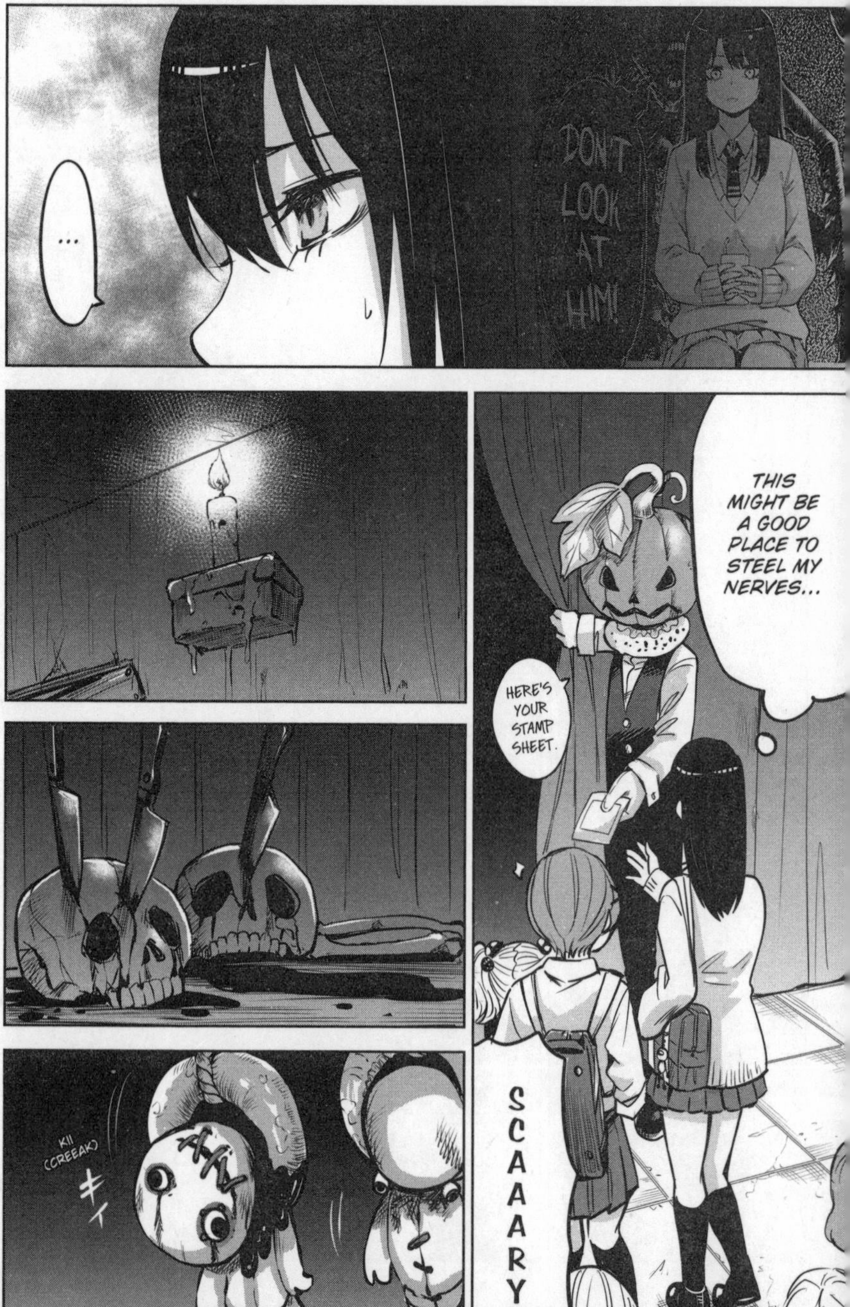
DON'T LOOK AT HIM!
...
THIS MIGHT BE A GOOD PLACE TO STEEL MY NERVES...
HERE'S YOUR STAMP SHEET.
SCAAAARY!!
KII (CREEAK)
キイ

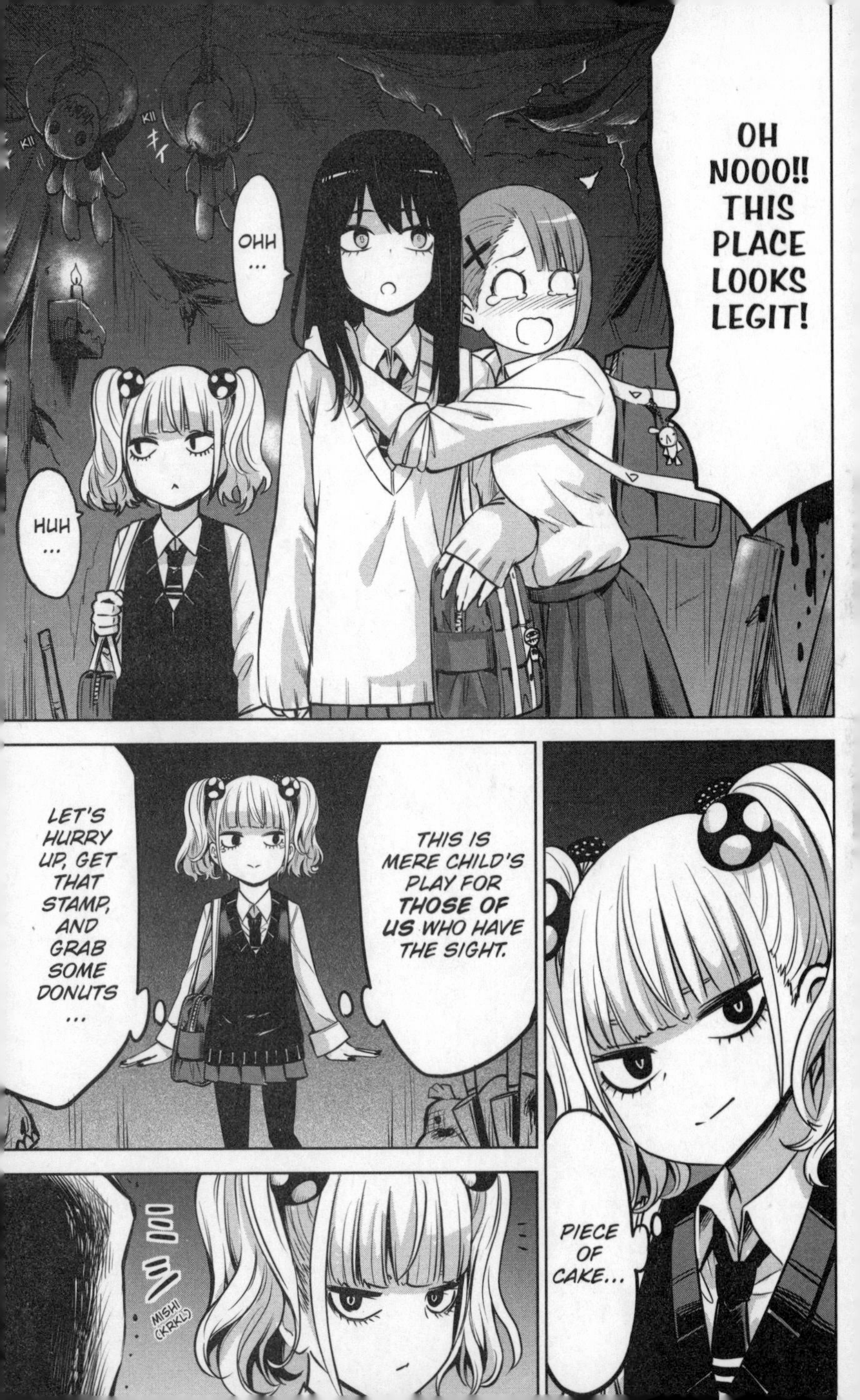
OH NOOO!! THIS PLACE LOOKS LEGIT!
KII
キイ
KII
OHH ...
HUH ...
PIECE OF CAKE...
THIS IS MERE CHILD'S PLAY FOR THOSE OF US WHO HAVE THE SIGHT.
LET'S HURRY UP, GET THAT STAMP, AND GRAB SOME DONUTS ...
MISHI (KRKL)

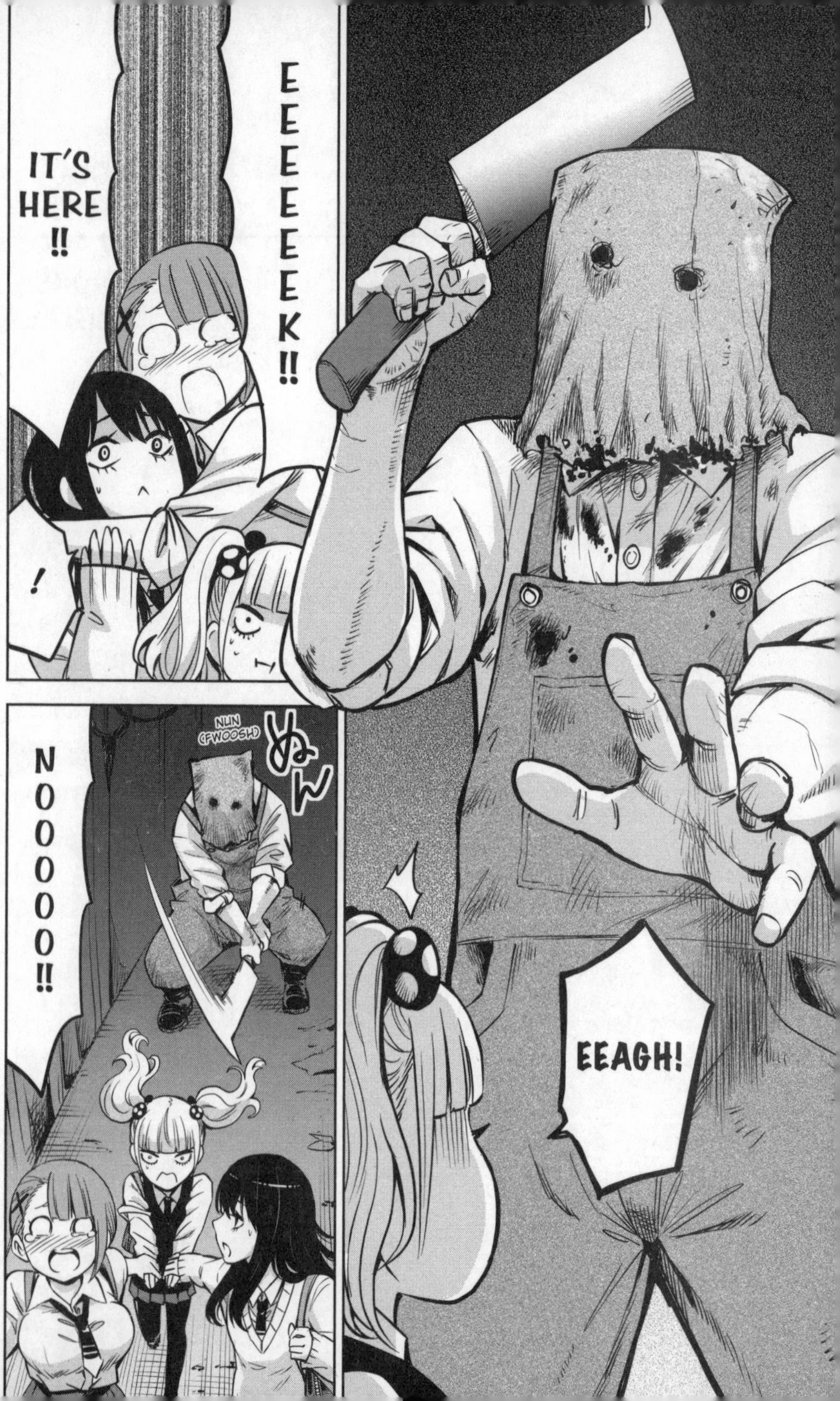
EEAGH!
EEEEEEK!!
IT'S HERE!!
!
ぬん
NUN (FWOOSH)
NOOOOO!!

THIS IS WAY TOO HIGH-LEVEL FOR A DONUT SHOP!!

IT'S TOO SCARY!!

CURSE YOU!

THAT WAS A WESTERN MONSTER... THE PHYSICAL TYPE.

THIS ISN'T WHAT I EXPECTED...!

DOKI (BADMP)

DOKI

I GUESS IT'S NOT REALLY THE SAME SORT OF SCARY I USUALLY RUN INTO...

HMM... SO THIS IS WHAT IT'S LIKE.

I CAN'T HELP IT...!

DOKI

DOKI

...YOUR SCREAMS ARE KINDA SCARING ME, HANA...

EEEEEEK!

BAN (BAND)

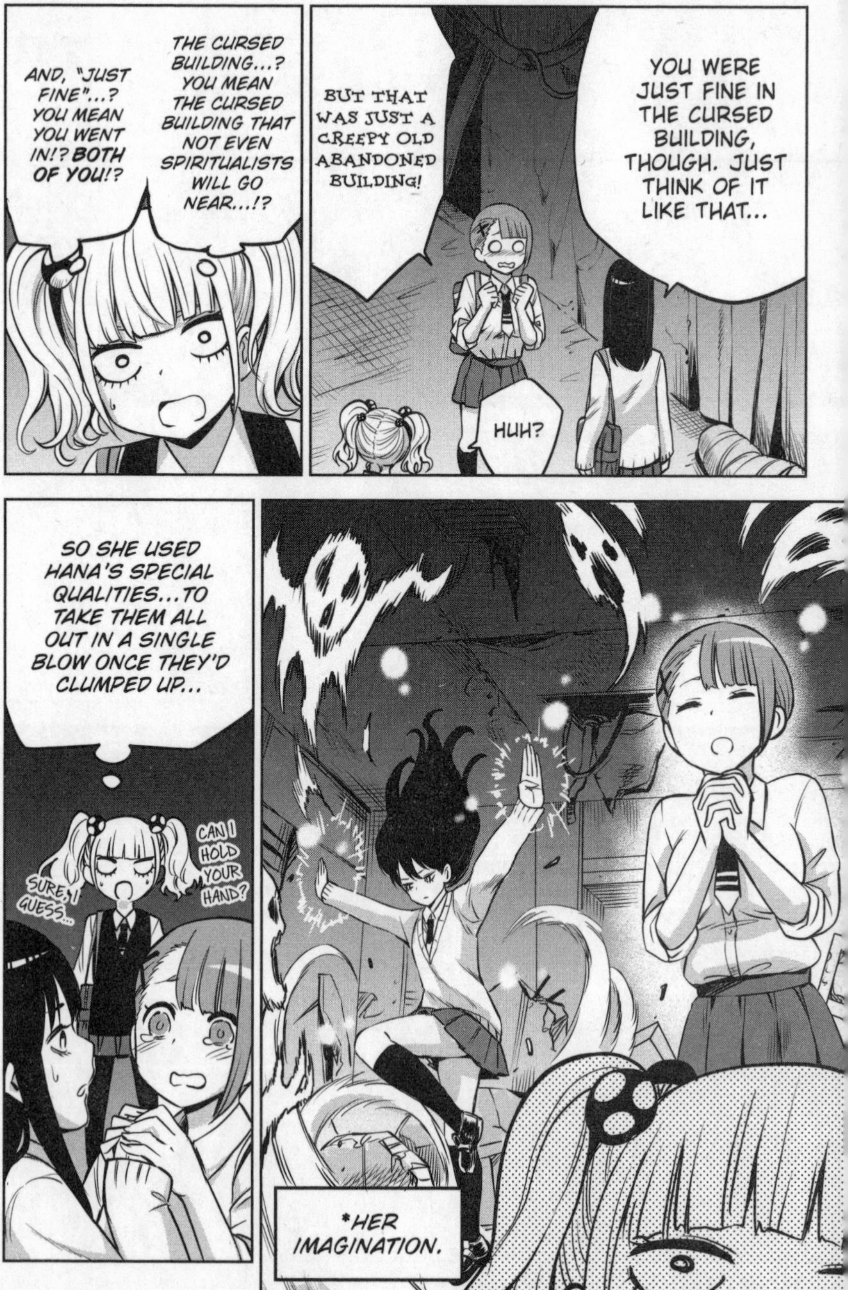
YOU WERE JUST FINE IN THE CURSED BUILDING, THOUGH. JUST THINK OF IT LIKE THAT...
BUT THAT WAS JUST A CREEPY OLD ABANDONED BUILDING!
HUH?
THE CURSED BUILDING...? YOU MEAN THE CURSED BUILDING THAT NOT EVEN SPIRITUALISTS WILL GO NEAR...!?
AND, "JUST FINE"...? YOU MEAN YOU WENT IN!? BOTH OF YOU!?
*HER IMAGINATION.
SO SHE USED HANA'S SPECIAL QUALITIES...TO TAKE THEM ALL OUT IN A SINGLE BLOW ONCE THEY'D CLUMPED UP...
CAN I HOLD YOUR HAND?
SURE, I GUESS...

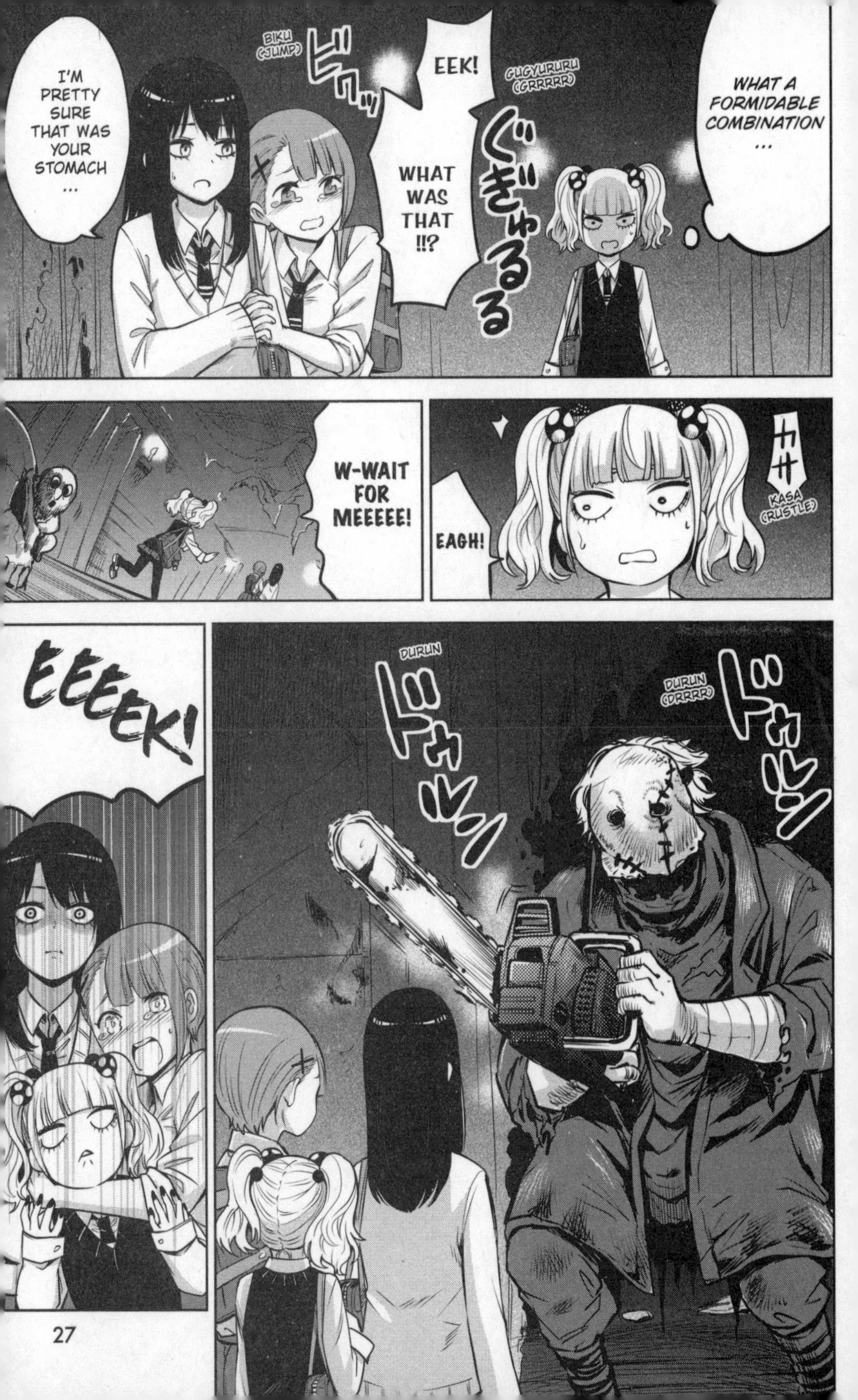
WHAT A FORMIDABLE COMBINATION ...
GUGYURURU (GRRRRR)
ぐぎゅるる
EEK!
WHAT WAS THAT !!?
BIKU (JUMP)
ビクッ
I'M PRETTY SURE THAT WAS YOUR STOMACH ...
カサ
KASA (RUSTLE)
EAGH!
W-WAIT FOR MEEEEE!
DURUN (DRRRR)
ドゥルン
DURUN
ドゥルン
EEEEEK!

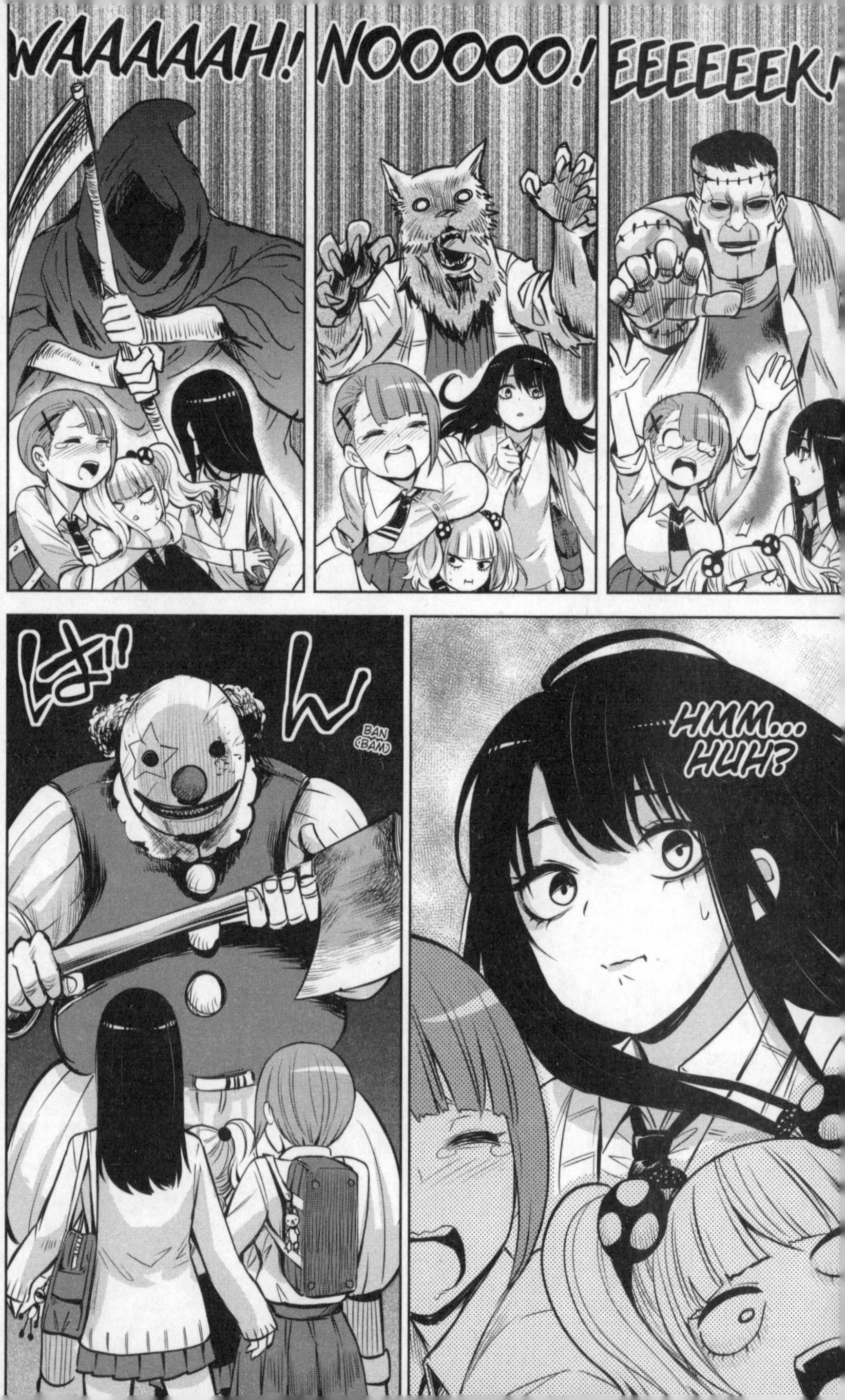
EEEEEEK!
NOOOOO!
WAAAAAH!
HMM... HUH?
ば!!
ん
BAN (BAM)

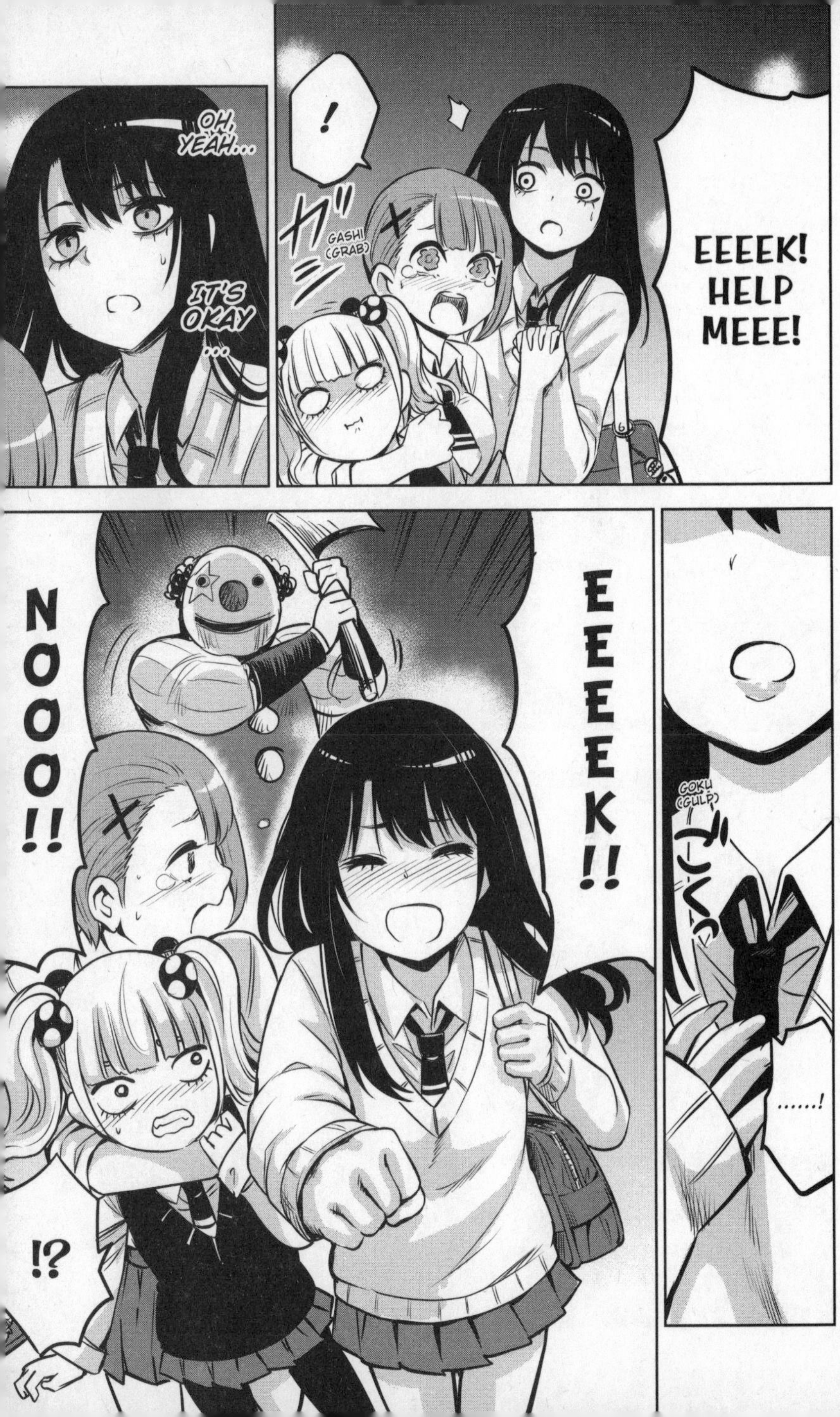
EEEEK! HELP MEEE!
!
GASHI (GRAB)
OH, YEAH...
IT'S OKAY...
GOKU (GULP)
......!
EEEEEK!!
NOOOO!!
!?

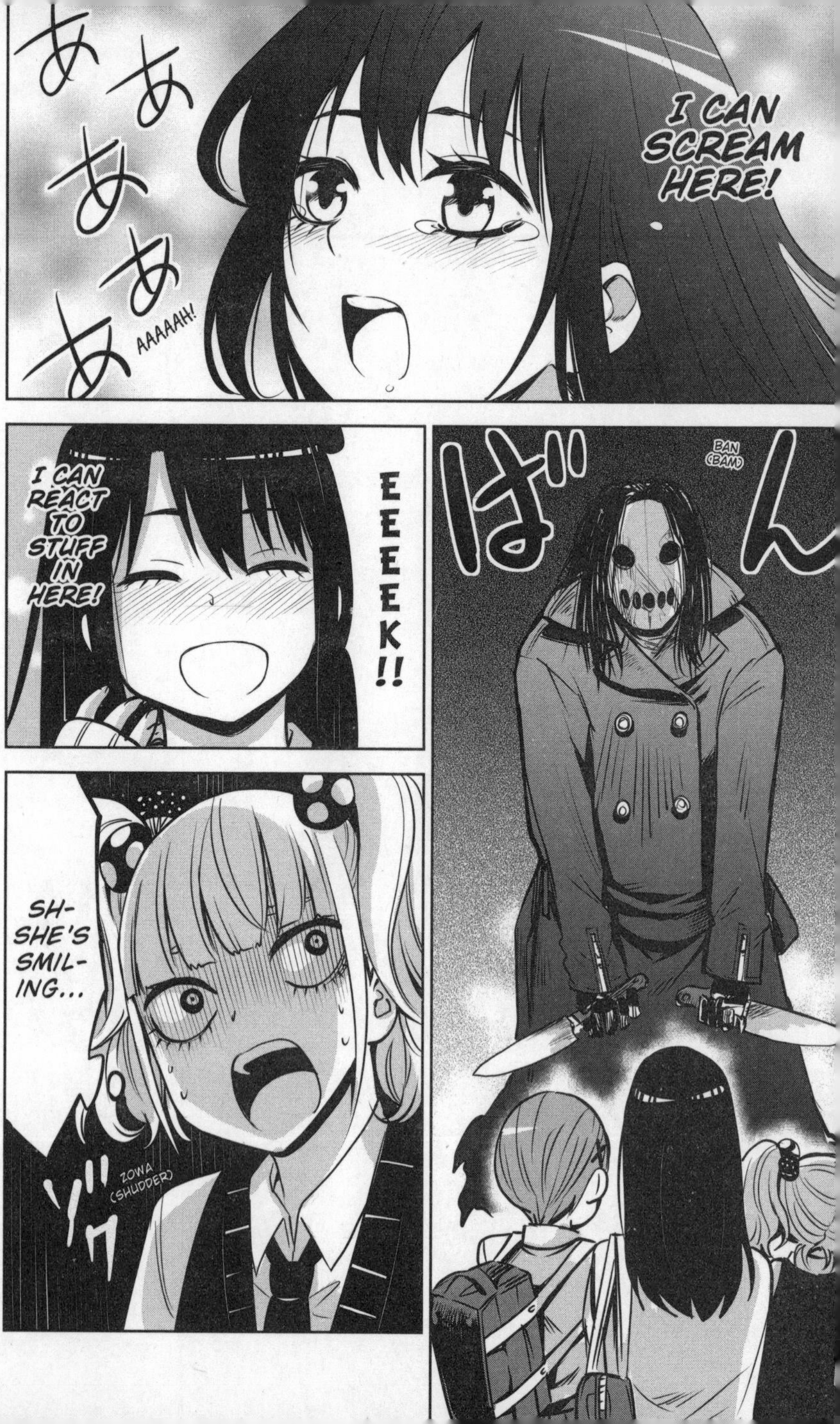
I CAN SCREAM HERE!
AAAAAH!
ばん
BAN (BAM)
EEEEEK!!
I CAN REACT TO STUFF IN HERE!
SH-SHE'S SMIL-ING...
ゾワッ
ZOWA (SHUDDER)

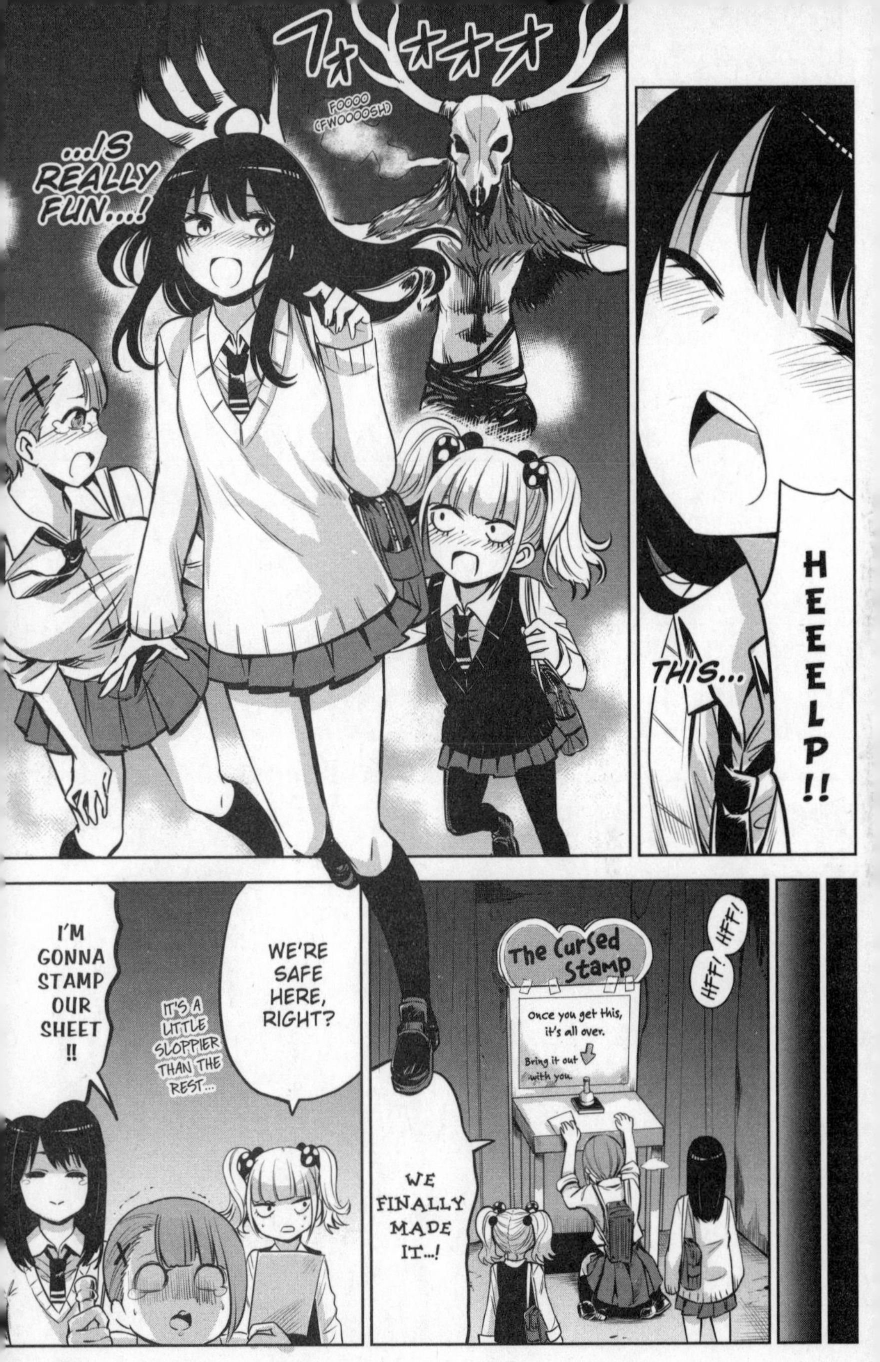
HEEELP!!
THIS...
フォオオオ
FOOOO (FWOOOOSH)
...IS REALLY FUN...!
HFF! HFF!
The Cursed Stamp
Once you get this, it's all over.
Bring it out with you.
WE FINALLY MADE IT...!
WE'RE SAFE HERE, RIGHT?
IT'S A LITTLE SLOPPIER THAN THE REST...
I'M GONNA STAMP OUR SHEET!!

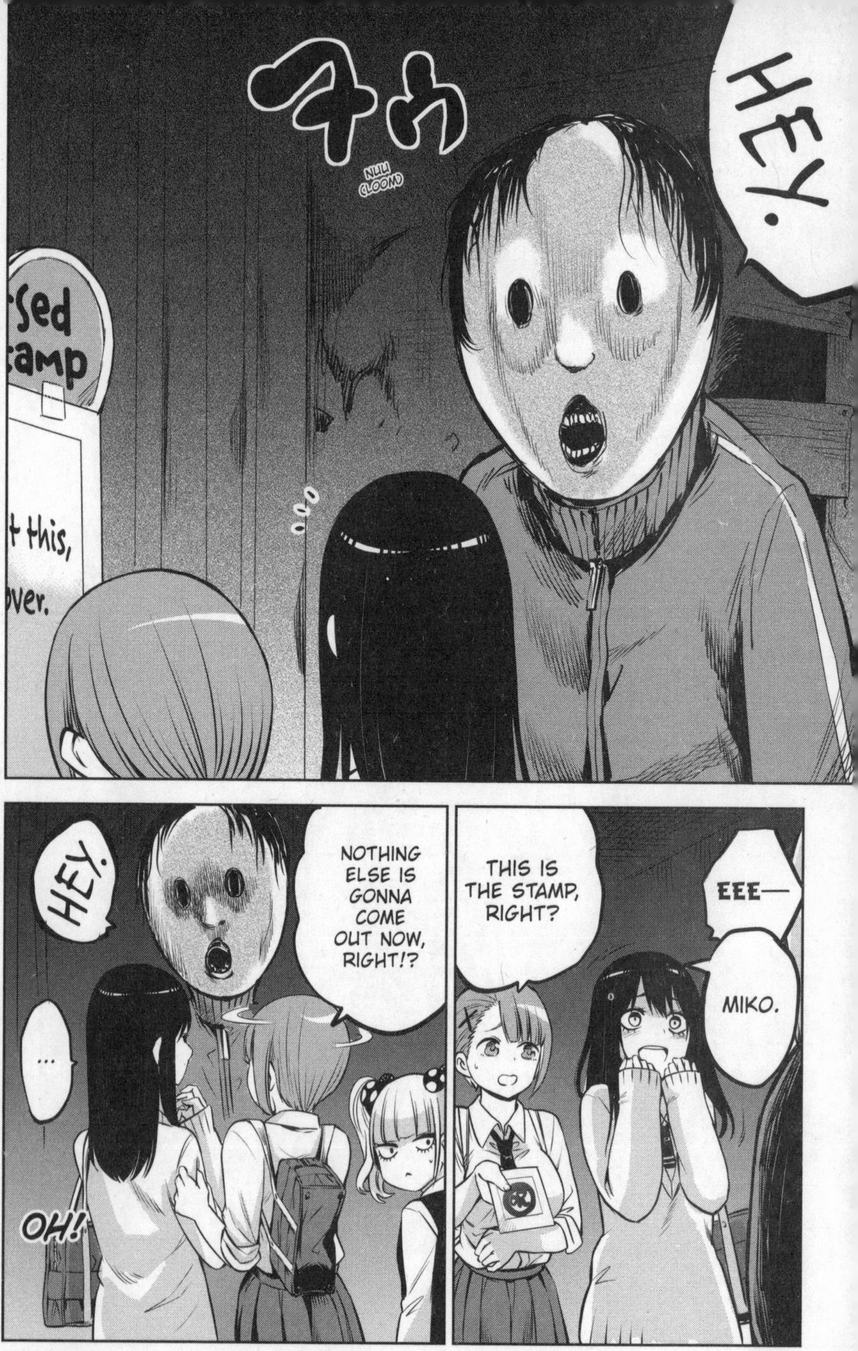
HEY.
ぬぅ
NUU (LOOM)
EEE—
MIKO.
THIS IS THE STAMP, RIGHT?
NOTHING ELSE IS GONNA COME OUT NOW, RIGHT!?
HEY.
...
OH!

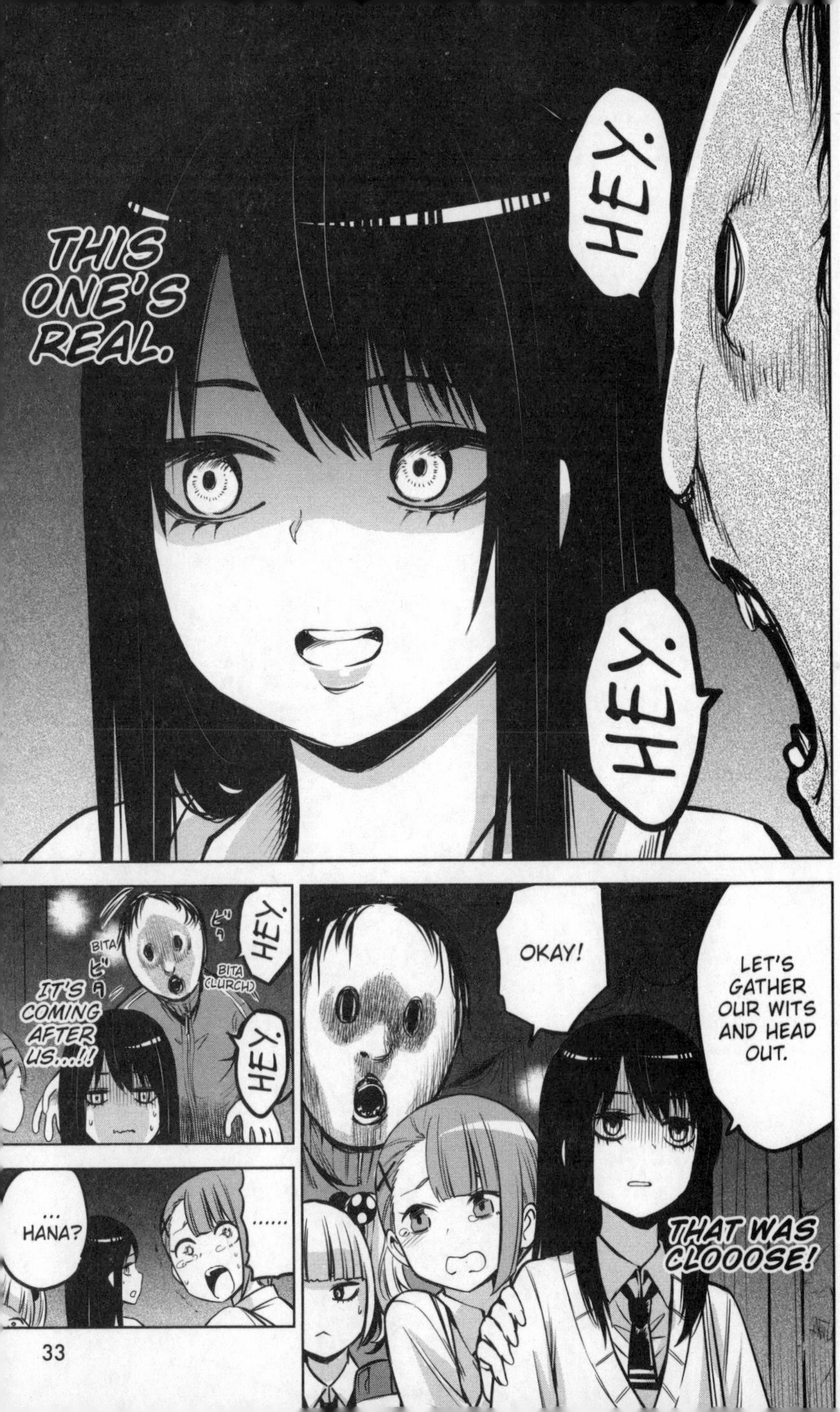

HEY.
HEY.
THIS ONE'S REAL.
LET'S GATHER OUR WITS AND HEAD OUT.
OKAY!
THAT WAS CLOOOSE!
HEY.
BITA
BITA (LURCH)
HEY.
IT'S COMING AFTER US...!!
......
... HANA?

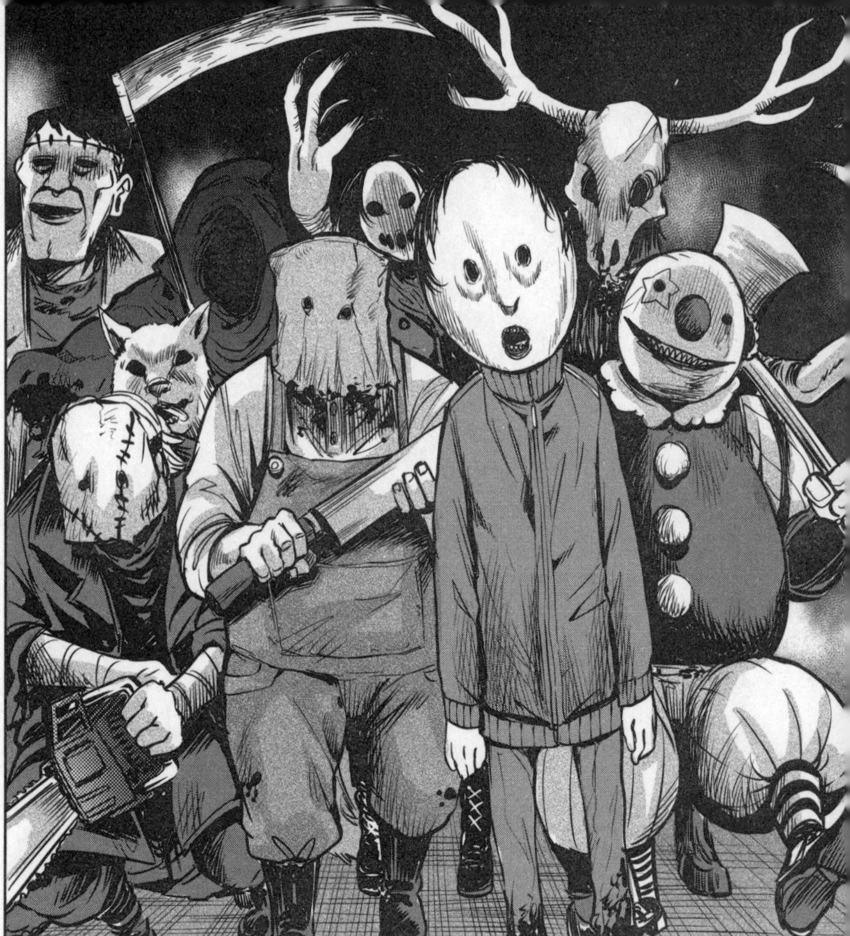
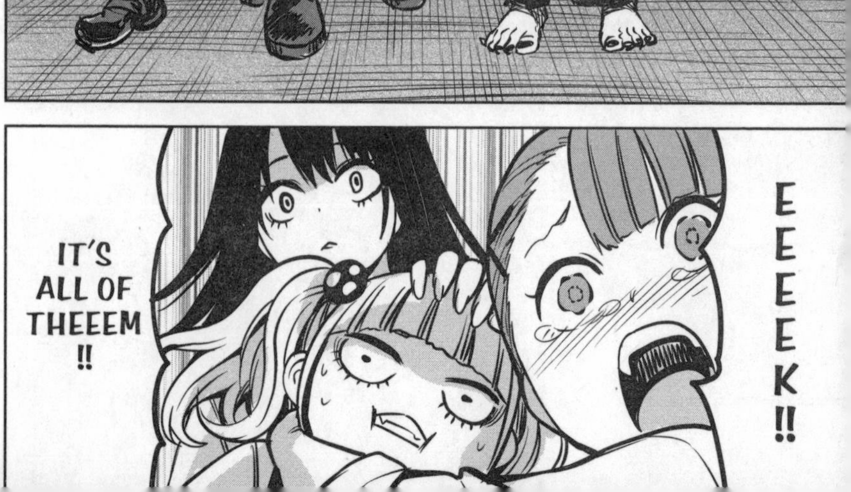
EEEEEK!!
IT'S ALL OF THEEEM!!

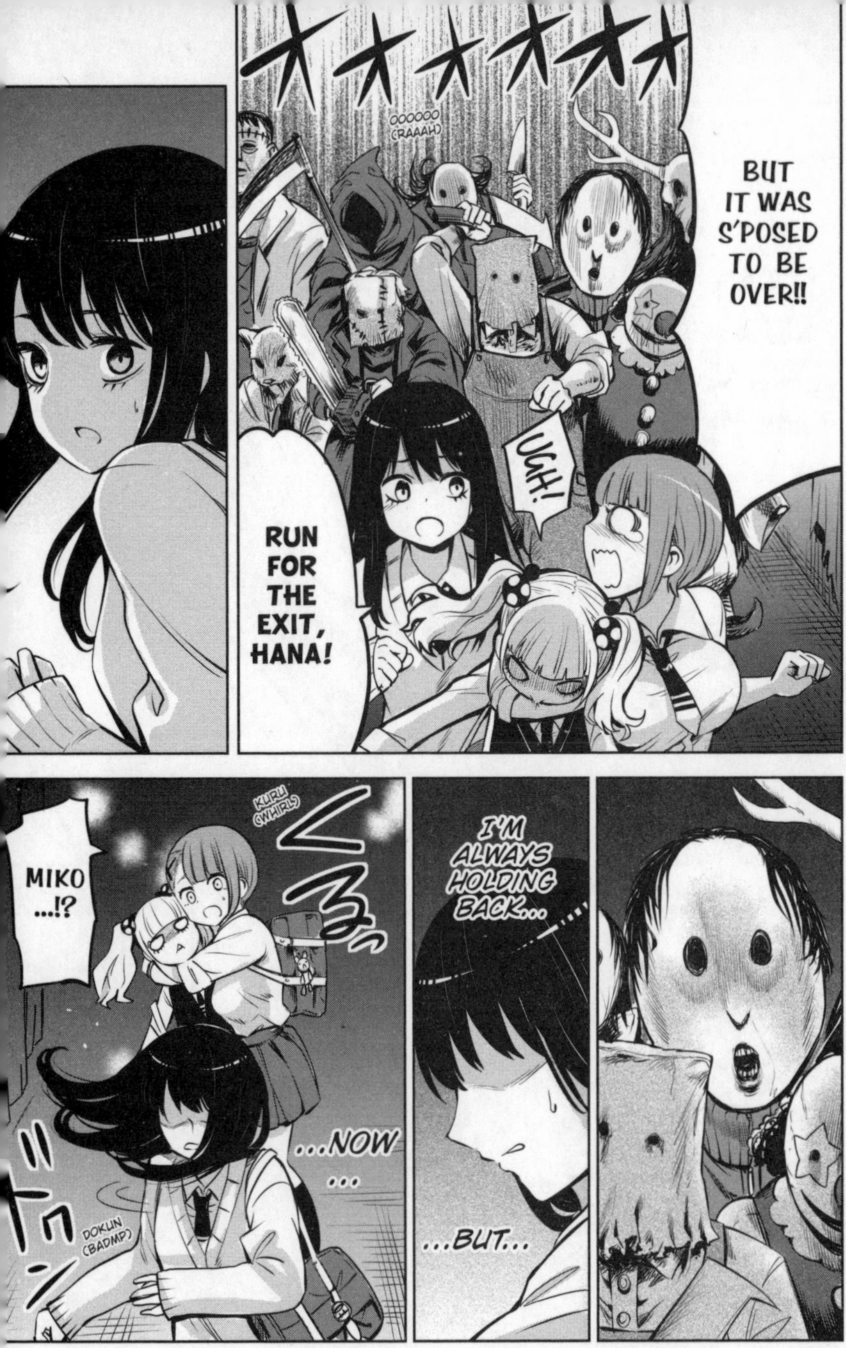
OOOOOO (RAAAH)
BUT IT WAS S'POSED TO BE OVER!!
UGH!
RUN FOR THE EXIT, HANA!
I'M ALWAYS HOLDING BACK...
...BUT...
KURU (WHIRL)
MIKO ...!?
...NOW ...
DOKUN (BADMP)

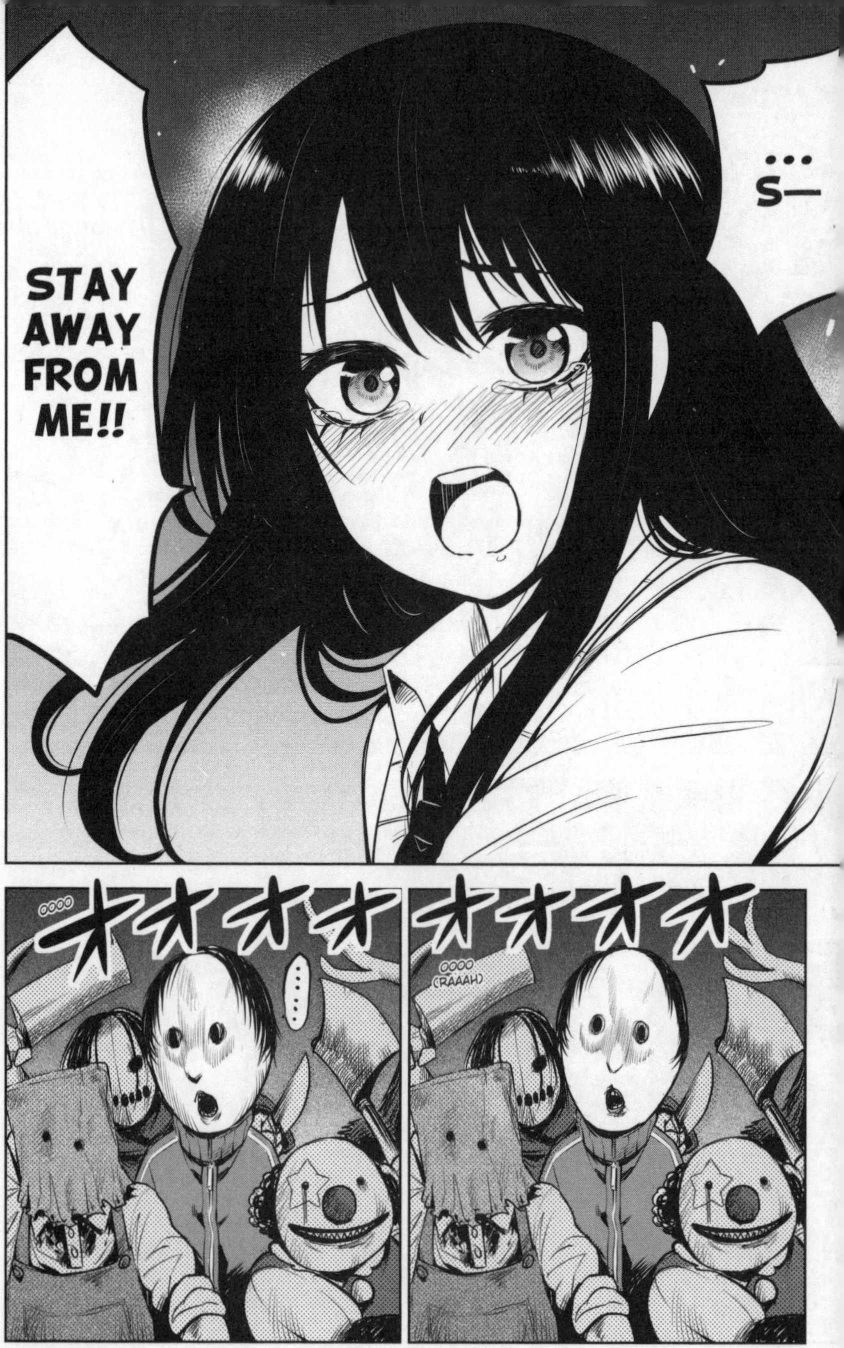

...
S—
STAY AWAY FROM ME!!
オオオオオ
OOOO (RAAAH)
OOOO
オオオオ
......

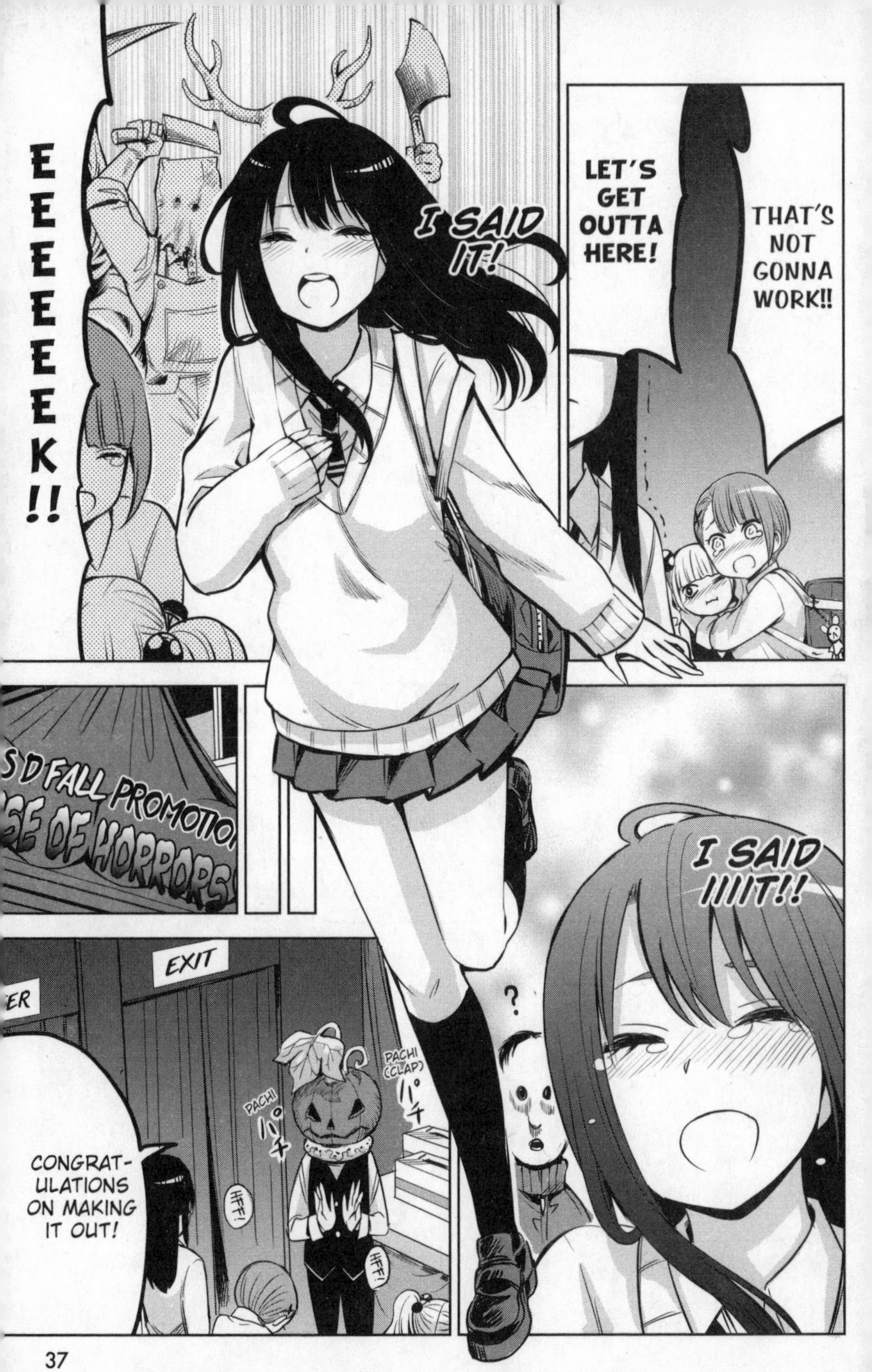
LET'S GET OUTTA HERE!
THAT'S NOT GONNA WORK!!
EEEEEEEK!!
I SAID IT!
I SAID IIIIT!!
S D FALL PROMOTIO
SE OF HORRORS
?
PACHI (CLAP) パチ
PACHI パチ
HFF!
HFF!
EXIT
ER
CONGRAT-ULATIONS ON MAKING IT OUT!

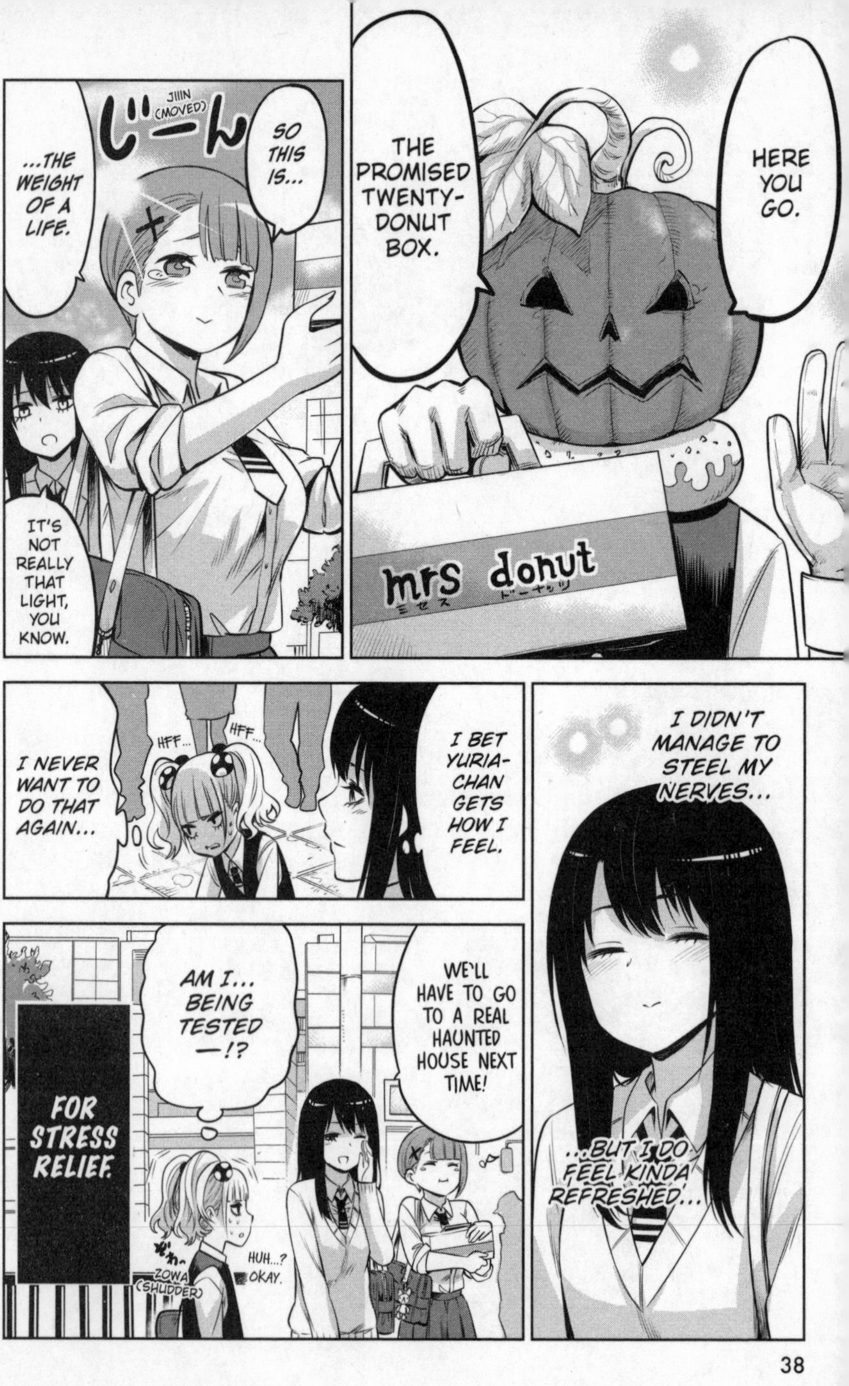
HERE YOU GO.
THE PROMISED TWENTY-DONUT BOX.
mrs donut
SO THIS IS...
じーん
JIIN (MOVED)
...THE WEIGHT OF A LIFE.
IT'S NOT REALLY THAT LIGHT, YOU KNOW.
I DIDN'T MANAGE TO STEEL MY NERVES...
...BUT I DO FEEL KINDA REFRESHED...
I BET YURIA-CHAN GETS HOW I FEEL.
HFF...
HFF...
I NEVER WANT TO DO THAT AGAIN...
WE'LL HAVE TO GO TO A REAL HAUNTED HOUSE NEXT TIME!
HUH...? OKAY.
AM I... BEING TESTED—!?
ZOWA (SHUDDER)
FOR STRESS RELIEF.

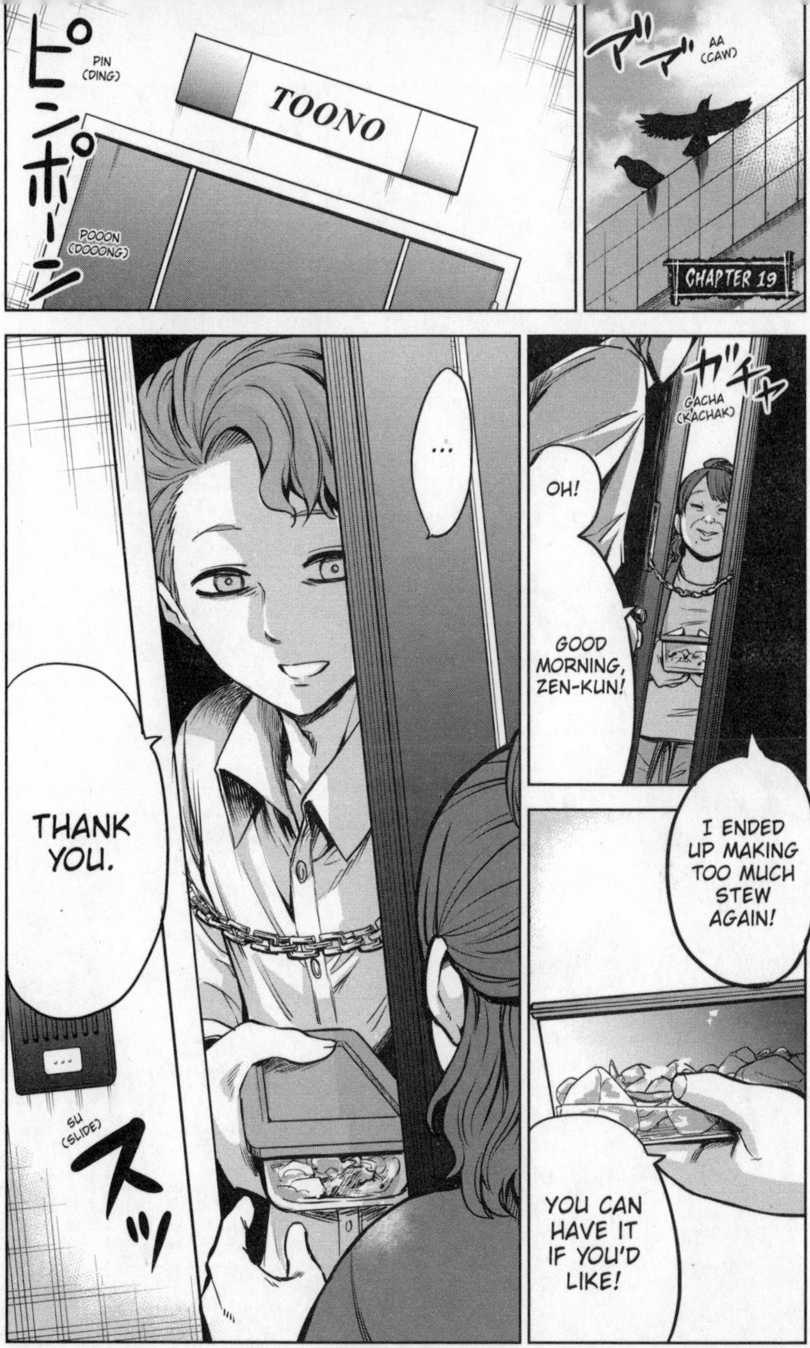
ア゛ア゛
AA (CAW)
CHAPTER 19
ピンポーン
PIN (DING)
TOONO
POOON (DOOONG)
ガチャ
GACHA (KACHAK)
OH!
GOOD MORNING, ZEN-KUN!
I ENDED UP MAKING TOO MUCH STEW AGAIN!
YOU CAN HAVE IT IF YOU'D LIKE!
...
THANK YOU.
スッ
SU (SLIDE)

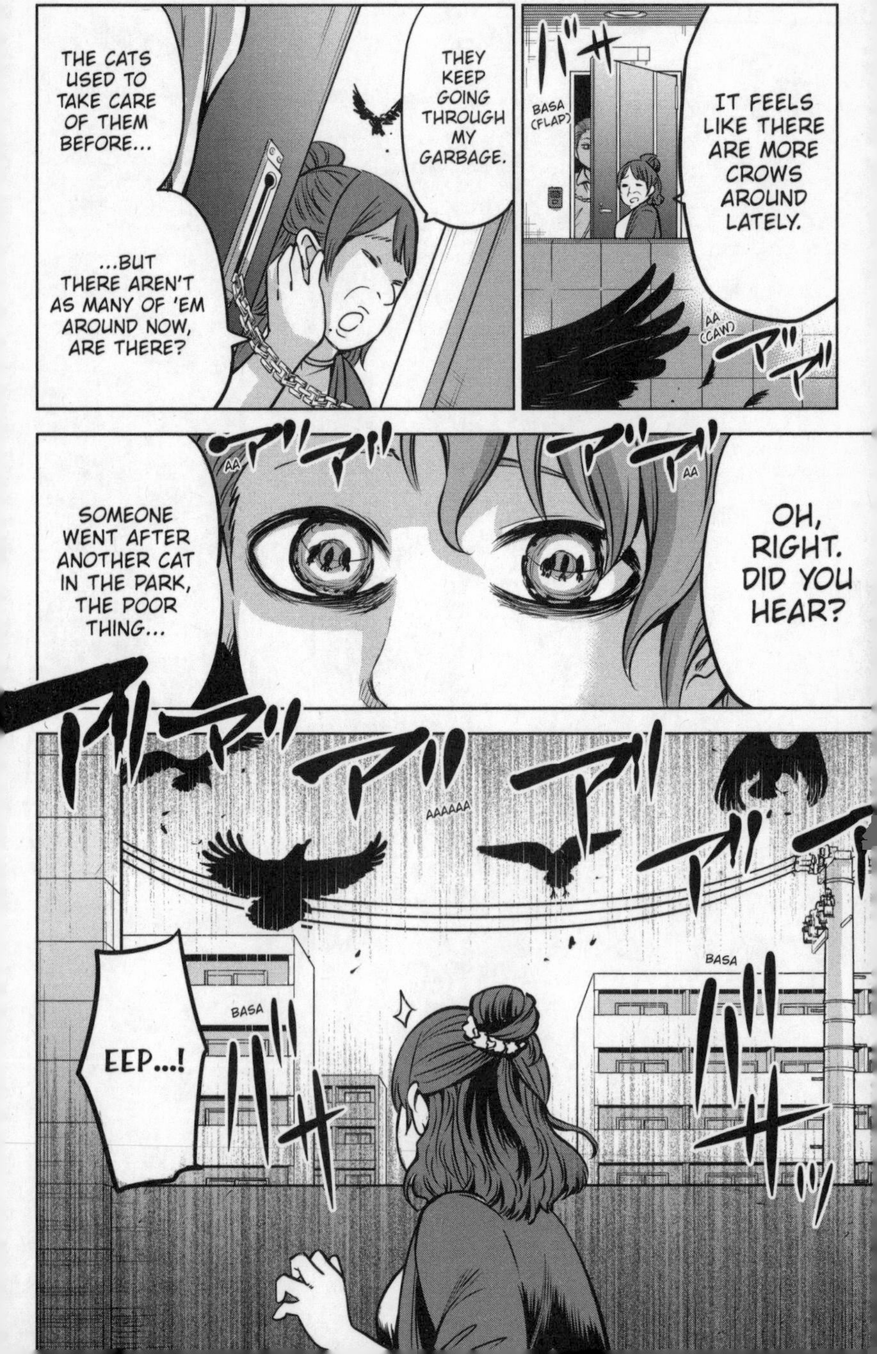

IT FEELS LIKE THERE ARE MORE CROWS AROUND LATELY.
BASA (FLAP)
AA (CAW)
THEY KEEP GOING THROUGH MY GARBAGE.
THE CATS USED TO TAKE CARE OF THEM BEFORE...
...BUT THERE AREN'T AS MANY OF 'EM AROUND NOW, ARE THERE?
AA
AA
OH, RIGHT. DID YOU HEAR?
SOMEONE WENT AFTER ANOTHER CAT IN THE PARK, THE POOR THING...
AAAAAA
BASA
BASA
EEP...!

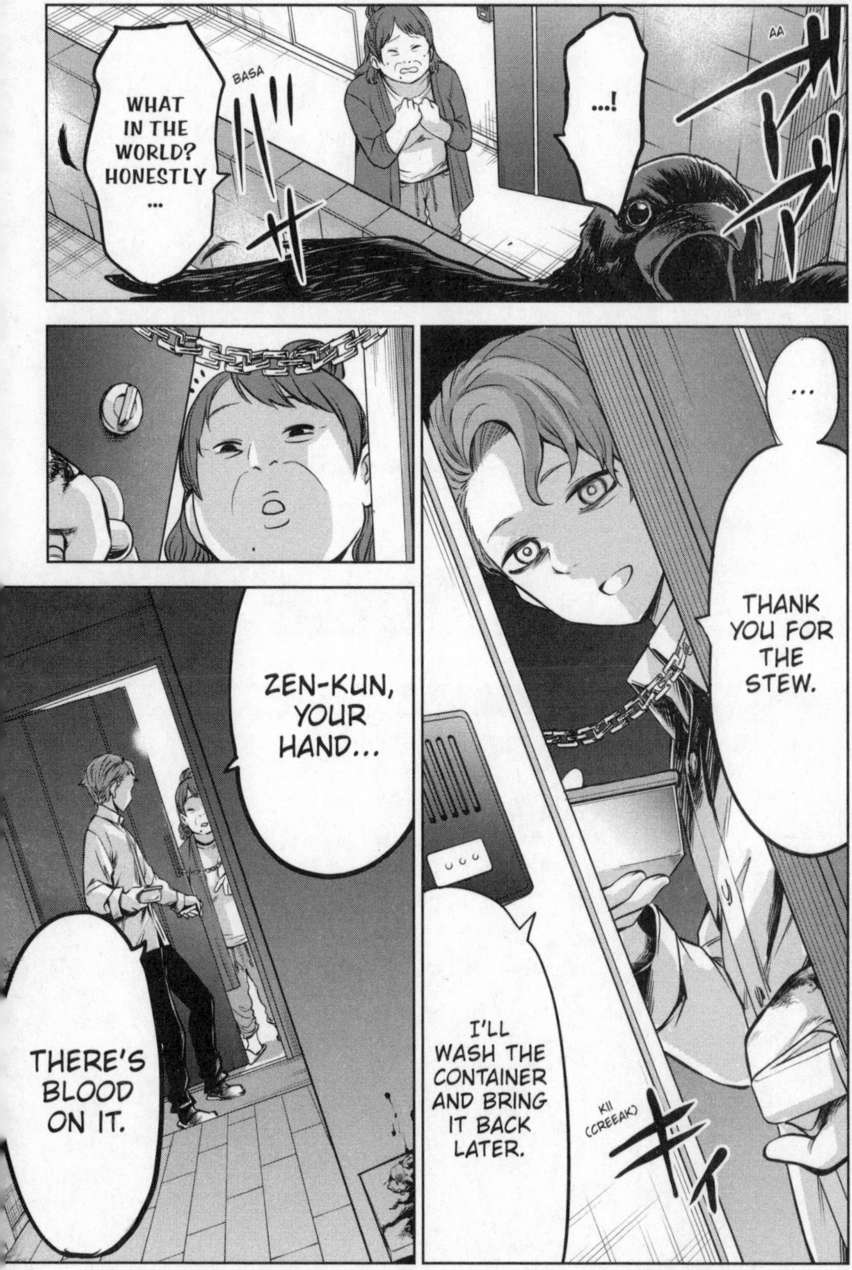
AA
...!
BASA
WHAT IN THE WORLD? HONESTLY ...
...
THANK YOU FOR THE STEW.
I'LL WASH THE CONTAINER AND BRING IT BACK LATER.
KII (CREEAK)
ZEN-KUN, YOUR HAND...
THERE'S BLOOD ON IT.

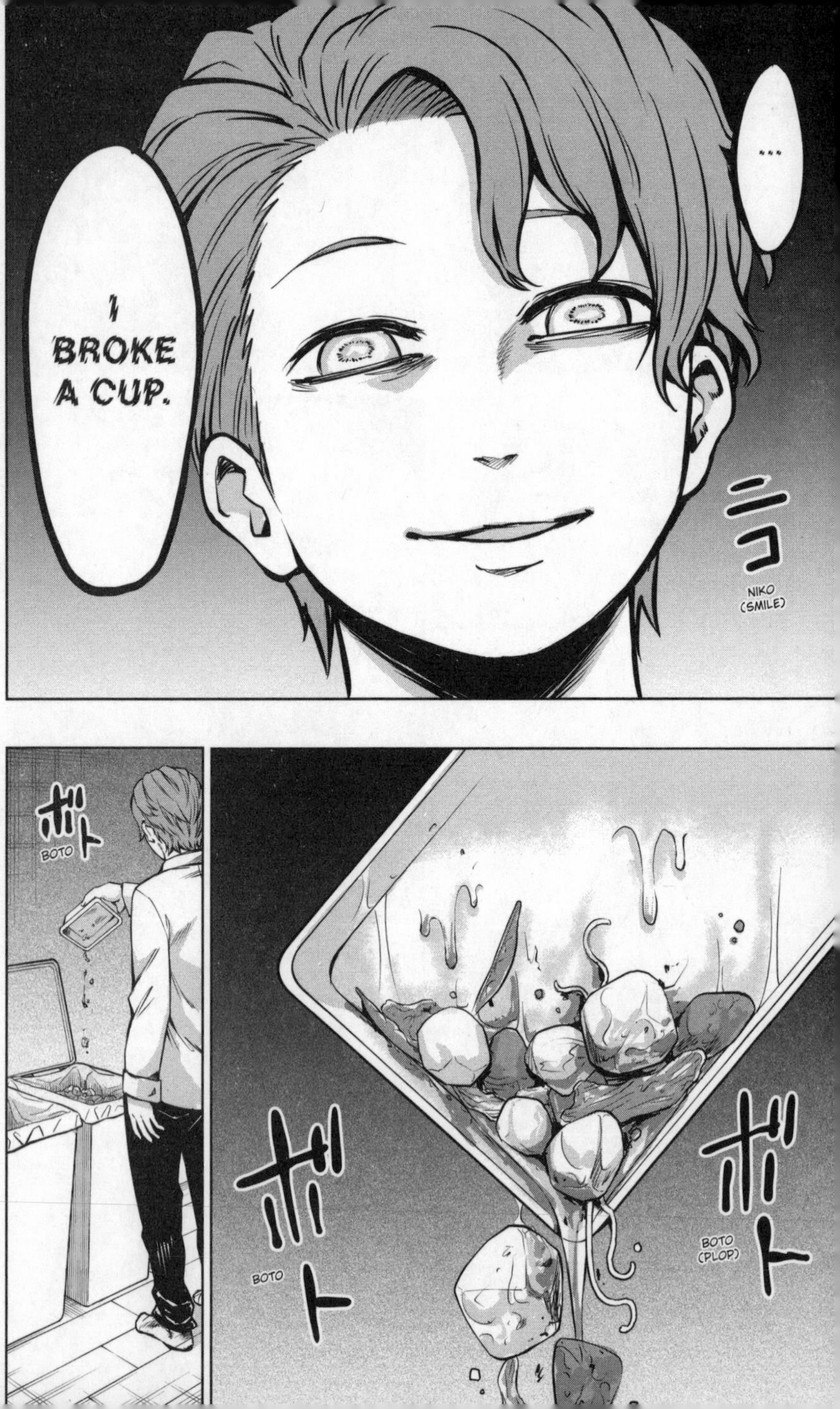
...
I BROKE A CUP.
ニコ
NIKO (SMILE)
ボト
BOTO (PLOP)
ボト
BOTO
ボト
BOTO

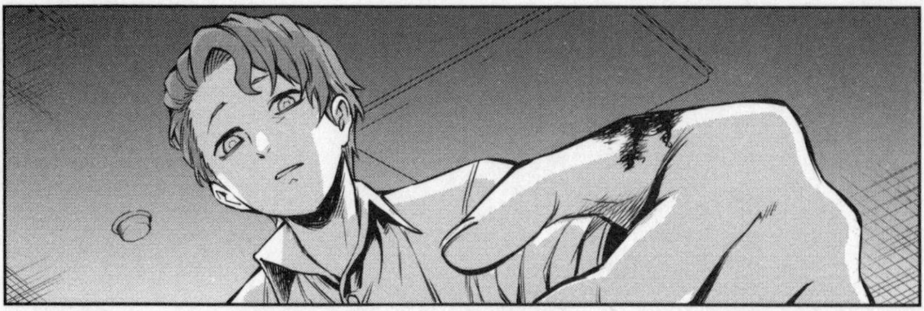

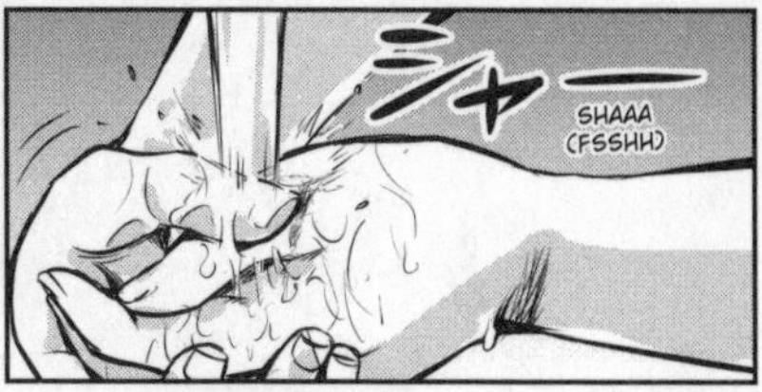
シャー
SHAAA
(FSSHH)

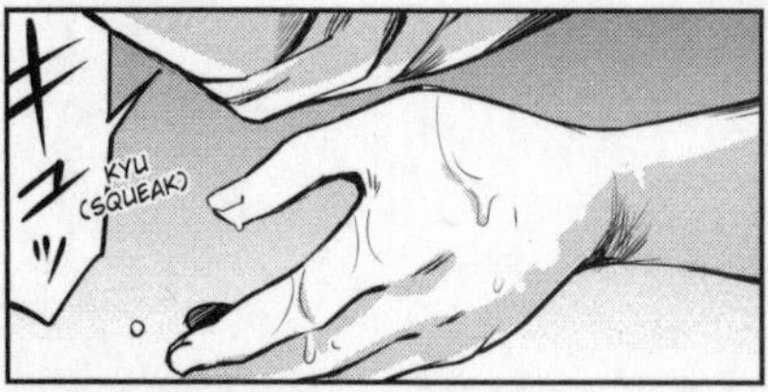
キュッ
KYU
(SQUEAK)

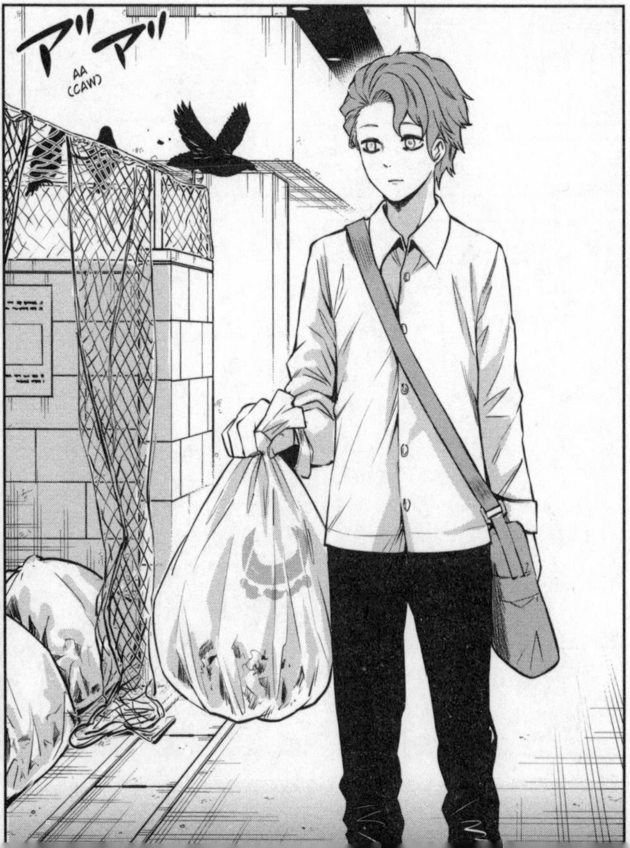
ア゛ア゛
AA
(CAW)

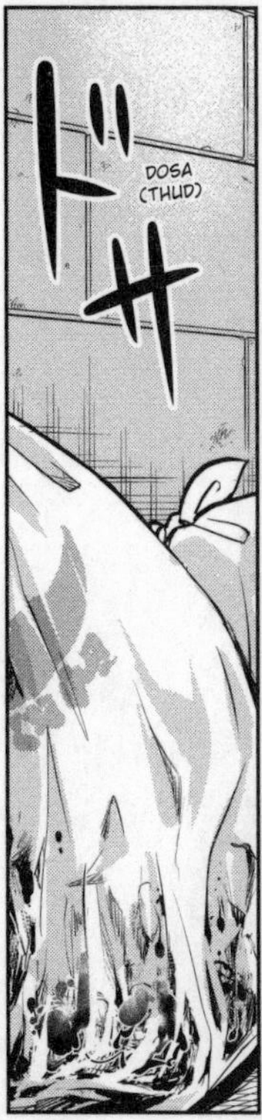
ドサ
DOSA
(THUD)

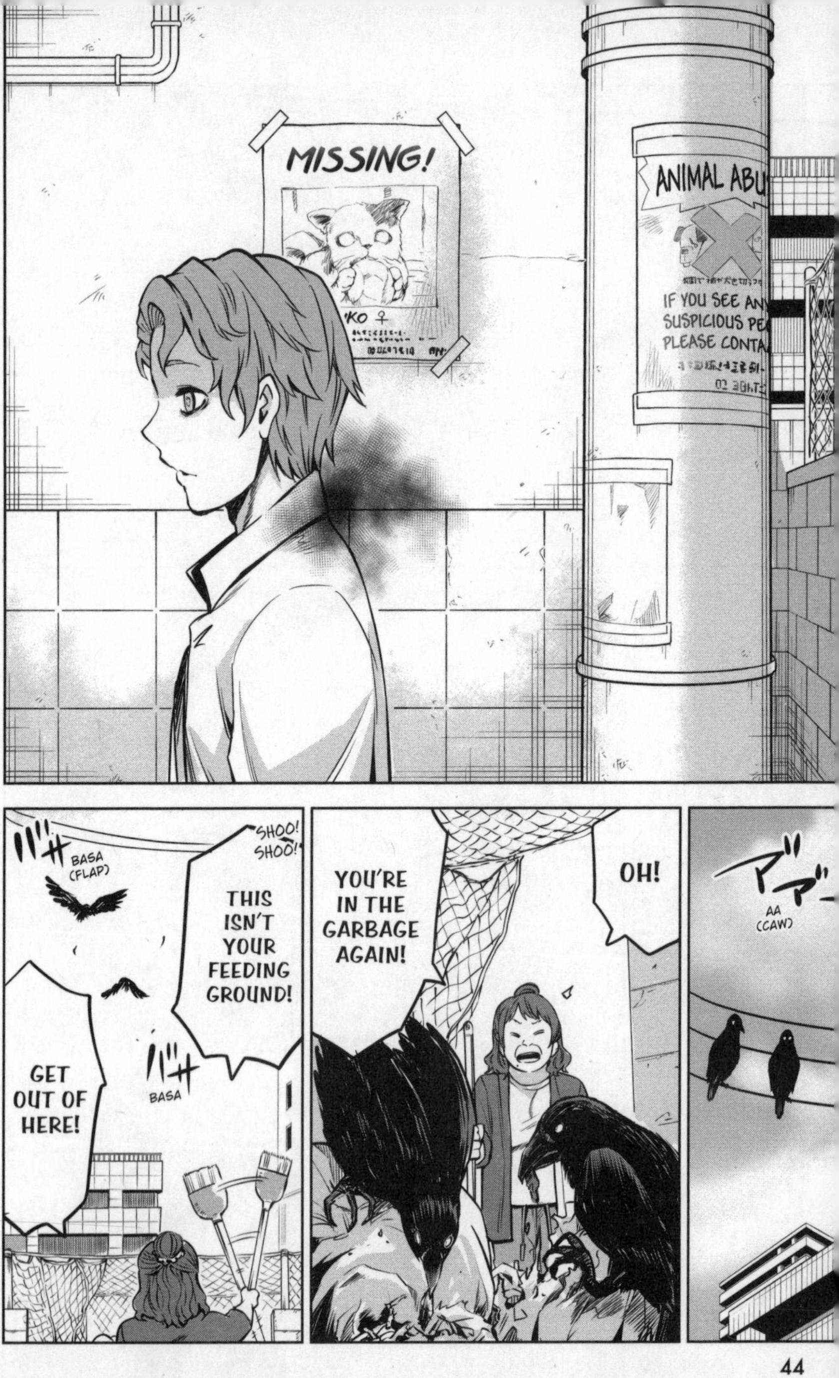
MISSING!
ANIMAL ABU
IF YOU SEE AN
SUSPICIOUS PE
PLEASE CONTA
アァ
AA (CAW)
OH!
YOU'RE IN THE GARBAGE AGAIN!
SHOO! SHOO!
THIS ISN'T YOUR FEEDING GROUND!
バサ
BASA (FLAP)
GET OUT OF HERE!
バサ
BASA

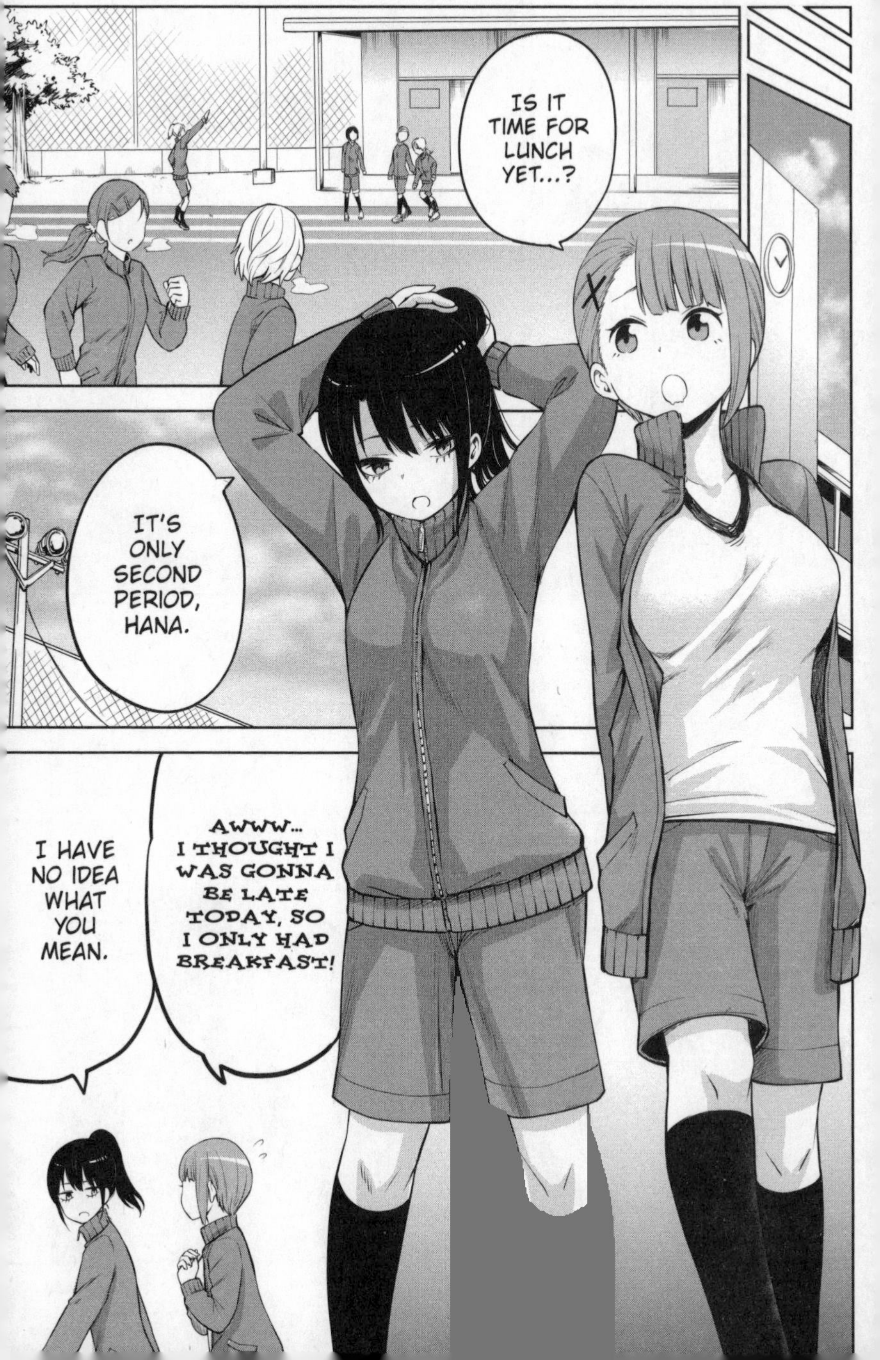
IS IT TIME FOR LUNCH YET...?
IT'S ONLY SECOND PERIOD, HANA.
AWWW... I THOUGHT I WAS GONNA BE LATE TODAY, SO I ONLY HAD BREAKFAST!
I HAVE NO IDEA WHAT YOU MEAN.

...

OHH?

HEAR ME OUT... LATELY...

AH!

YOU'RE MAKING FUN OF ME!

...I'VE BEEN SUPER HUNGRY...

SORRY, SORRY.

GEEZ... I'M REALLY WORRIED ABOUT THIS, YOU KNOW!

DON'T CALL ME A GLUTTON!

YOU'VE ALWAYS BEEN A GLUTTON, YOU KNOW.

...I LIKE THE FACT THAT YOU EAT A LOT.

BUT, YOU KNOW...

AT LEAST SAY I'M A BIG EATER.

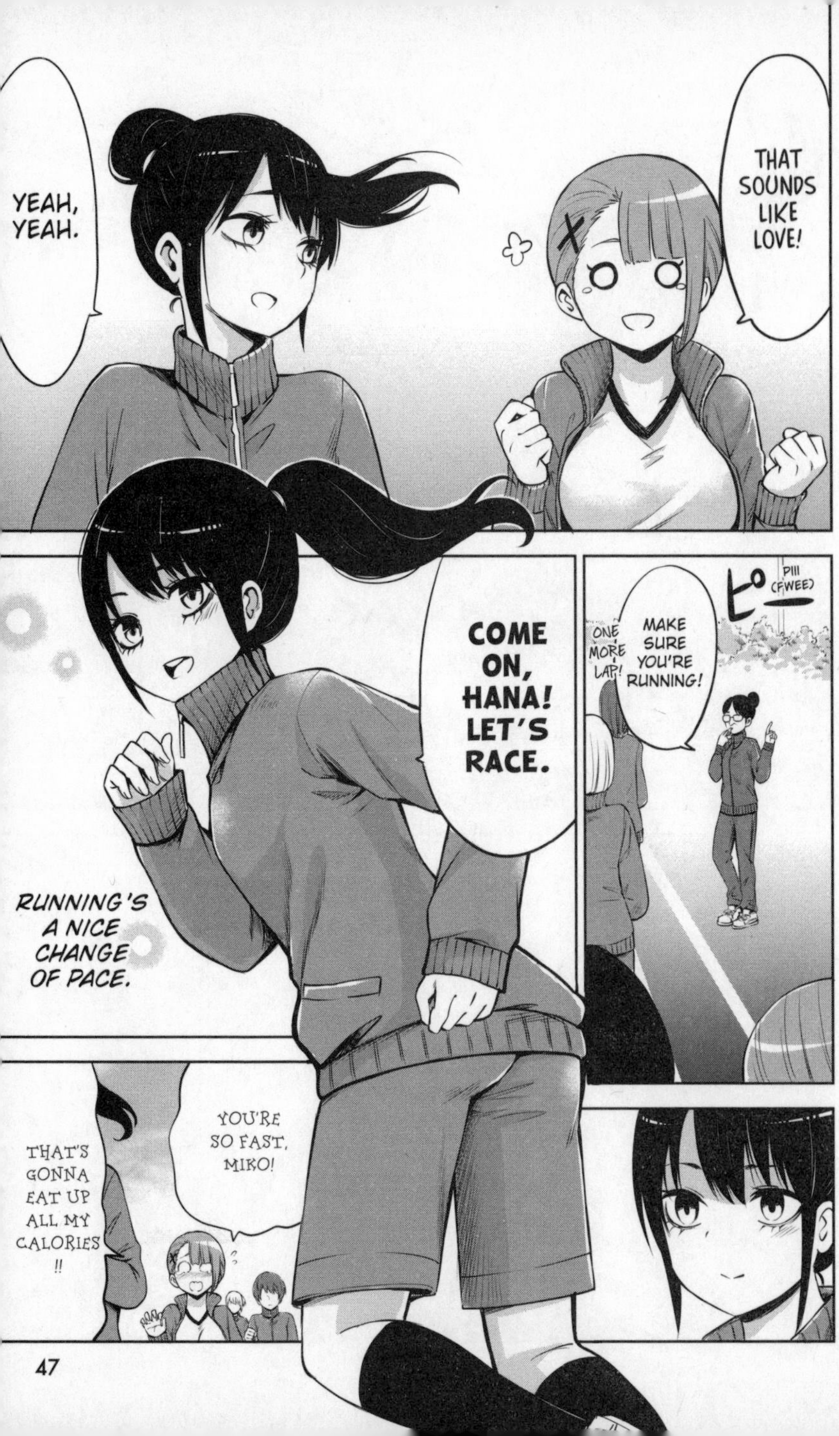
THAT SOUNDS LIKE LOVE!
YEAH, YEAH.
ピー PIII (FWEE)
MAKE SURE YOU'RE RUNNING!
ONE MORE LAP!
COME ON, HANA! LET'S RACE.
RUNNING'S A NICE CHANGE OF PACE.
YOU'RE SO FAST, MIKO!
THAT'S GONNA EAT UP ALL MY CALORIES!!

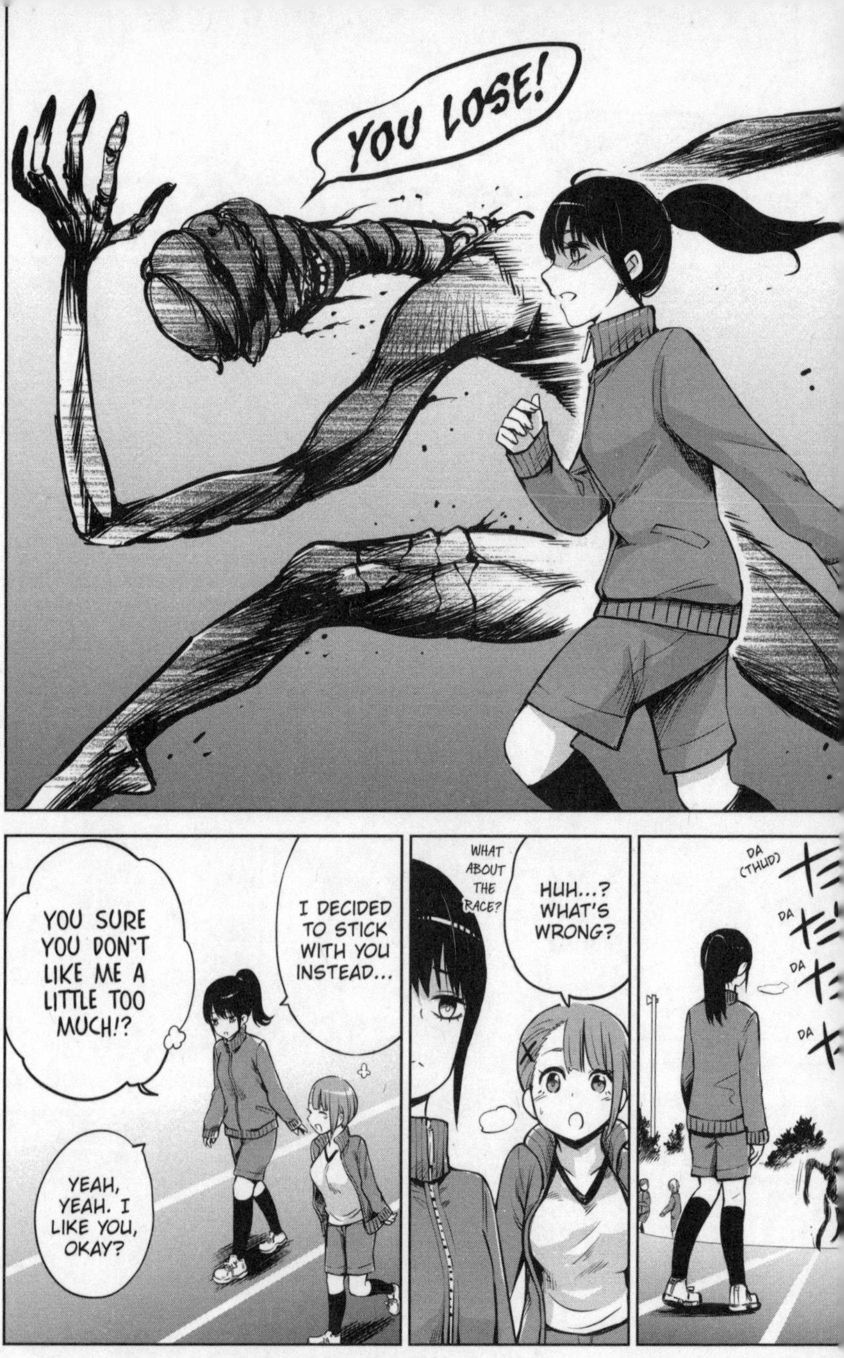
YOU LOSE!
DA (THUD)
DA
DA
DA
HUH...? WHAT'S WRONG?
WHAT ABOUT THE RACE?
I DECIDED TO STICK WITH YOU INSTEAD...
YOU SURE YOU DON'T LIKE ME A LITTLE TOO MUCH!?
YEAH, YEAH. I LIKE YOU, OKAY?

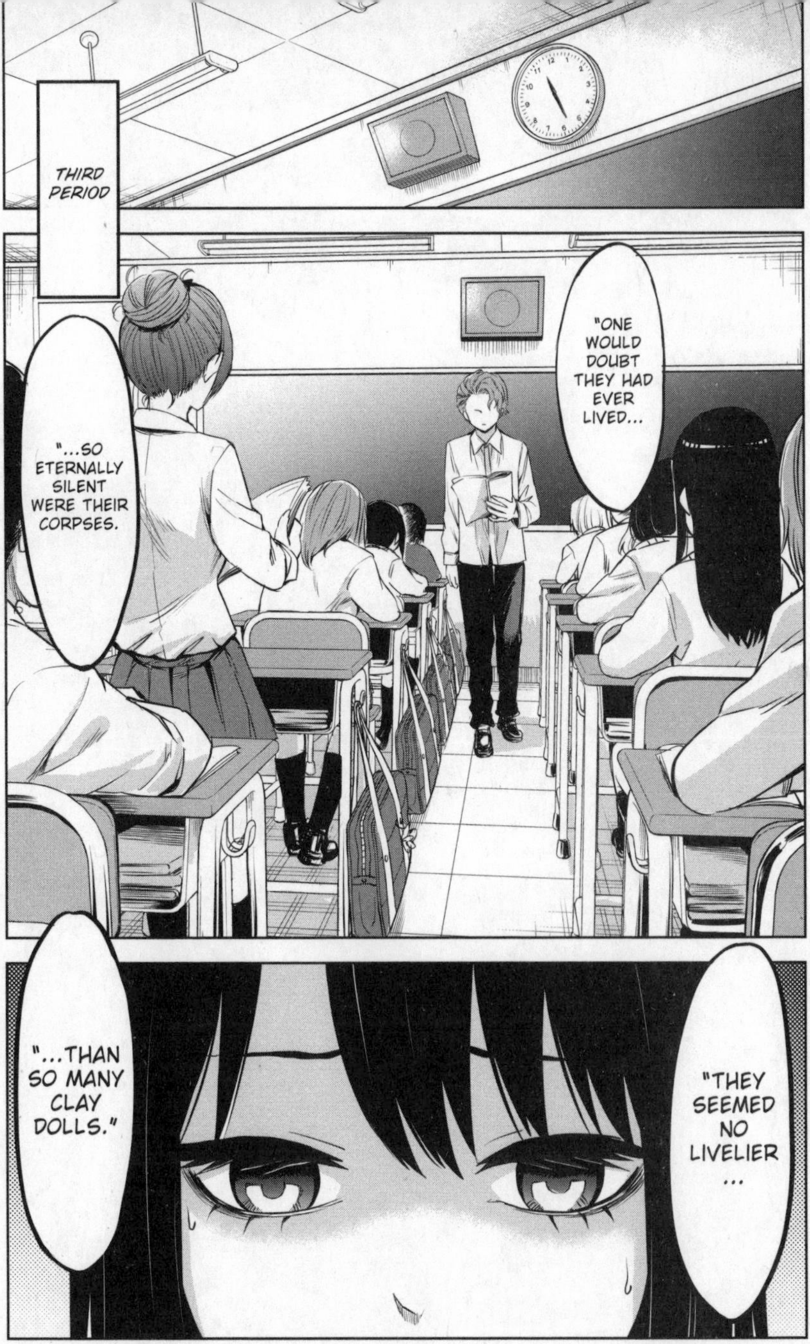
THIRD PERIOD
"ONE WOULD DOUBT THEY HAD EVER LIVED...
"...SO ETERNALLY SILENT WERE THEIR CORPSES.
"THEY SEEMED NO LIVELIER ...
"...THAN SO MANY CLAY DOLLS."

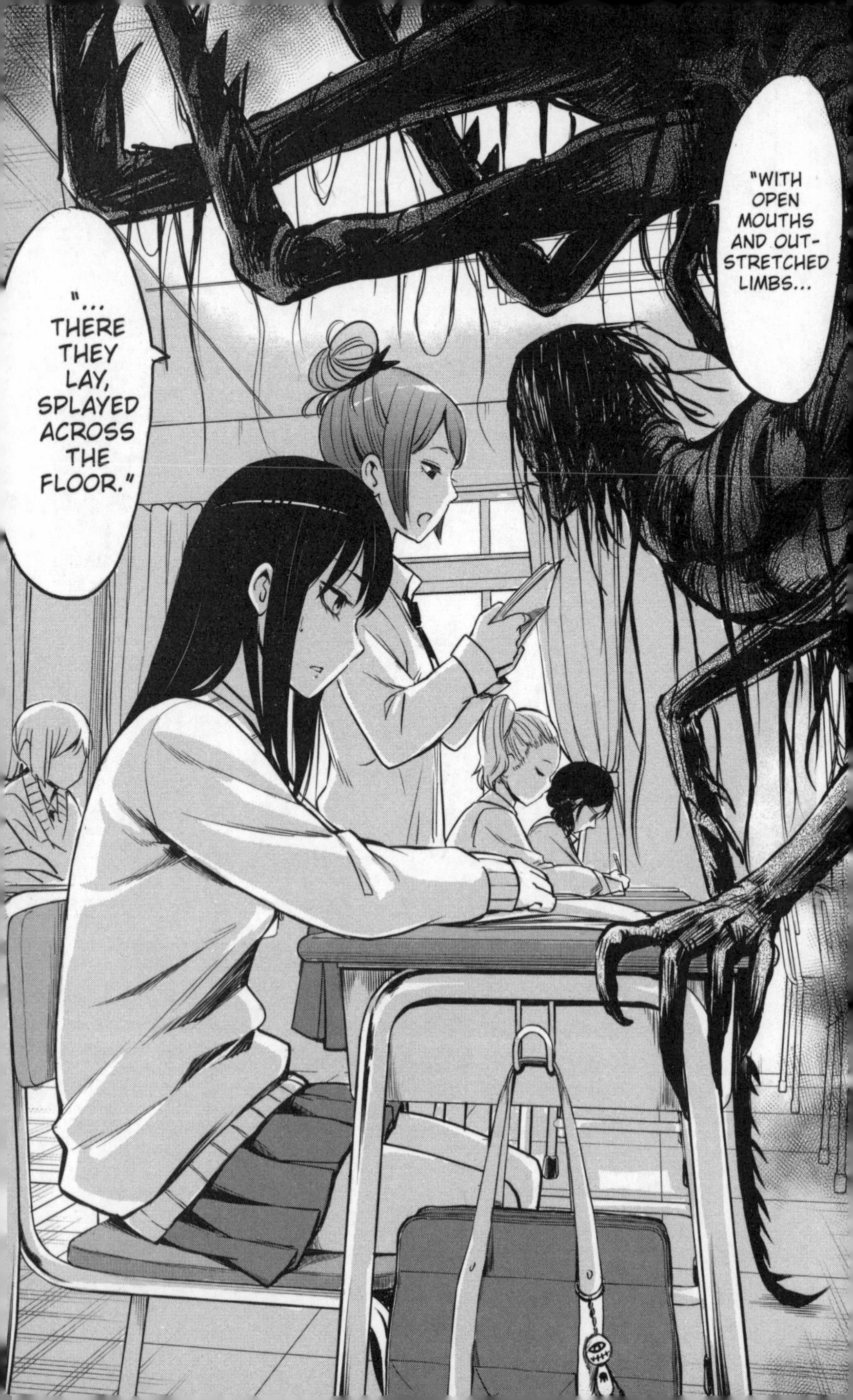
"WITH OPEN MOUTHS AND OUT-STRETCHED LIMBS...
"... THERE THEY LAY, SPLAYED ACROSS THE FLOOR."

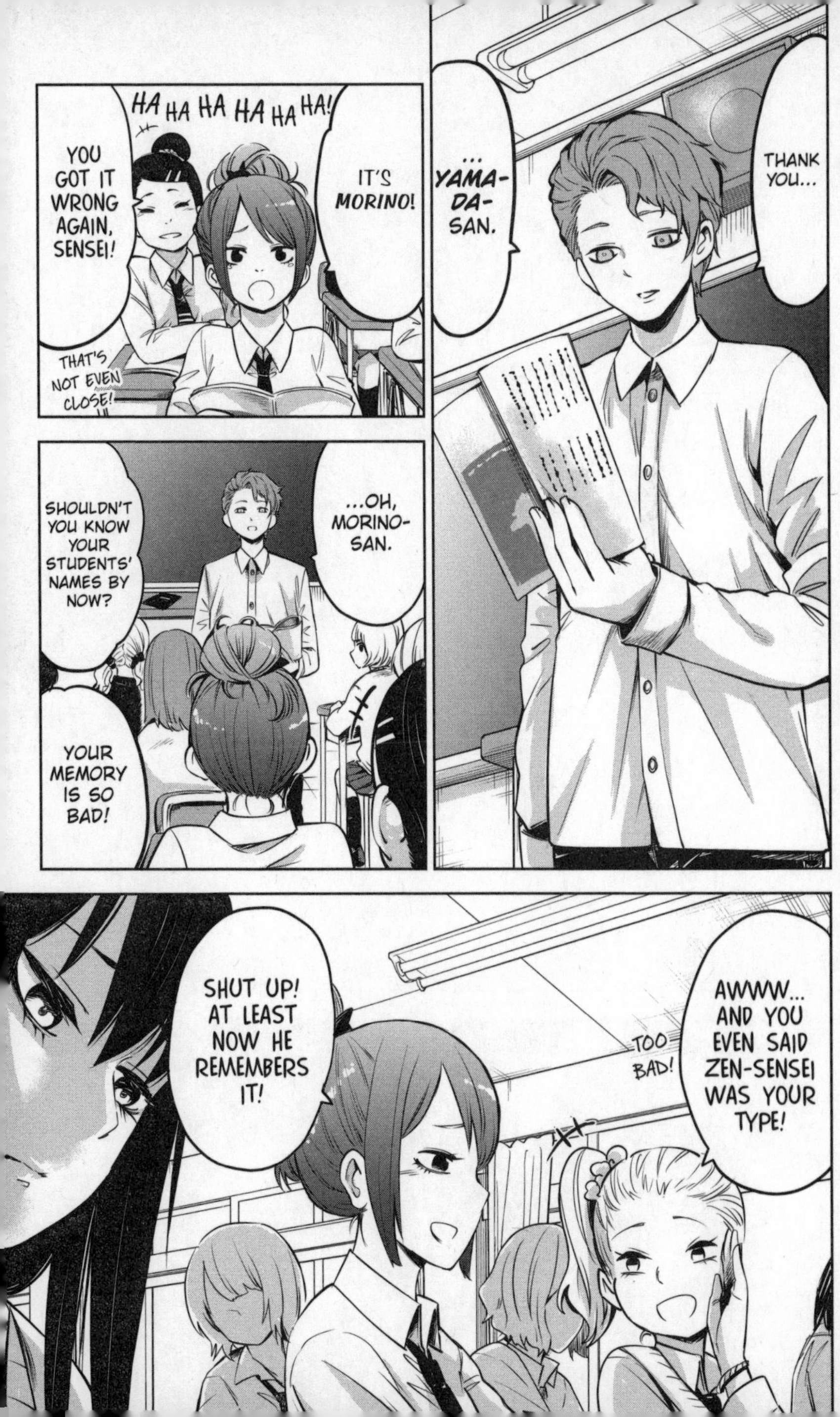
THANK YOU...
...YAMADA-SAN.
HA HA HA HA HA HA HA!
IT'S MORINO!
YOU GOT IT WRONG AGAIN, SENSEI!
THAT'S NOT EVEN CLOSE!
...OH, MORINO-SAN.
SHOULDN'T YOU KNOW YOUR STUDENTS' NAMES BY NOW?
YOUR MEMORY IS SO BAD!
AWWW... AND YOU EVEN SAID ZEN-SENSEI WAS YOUR TYPE!
TOO BAD!
SHUT UP! AT LEAST NOW HE REMEMBERS IT!

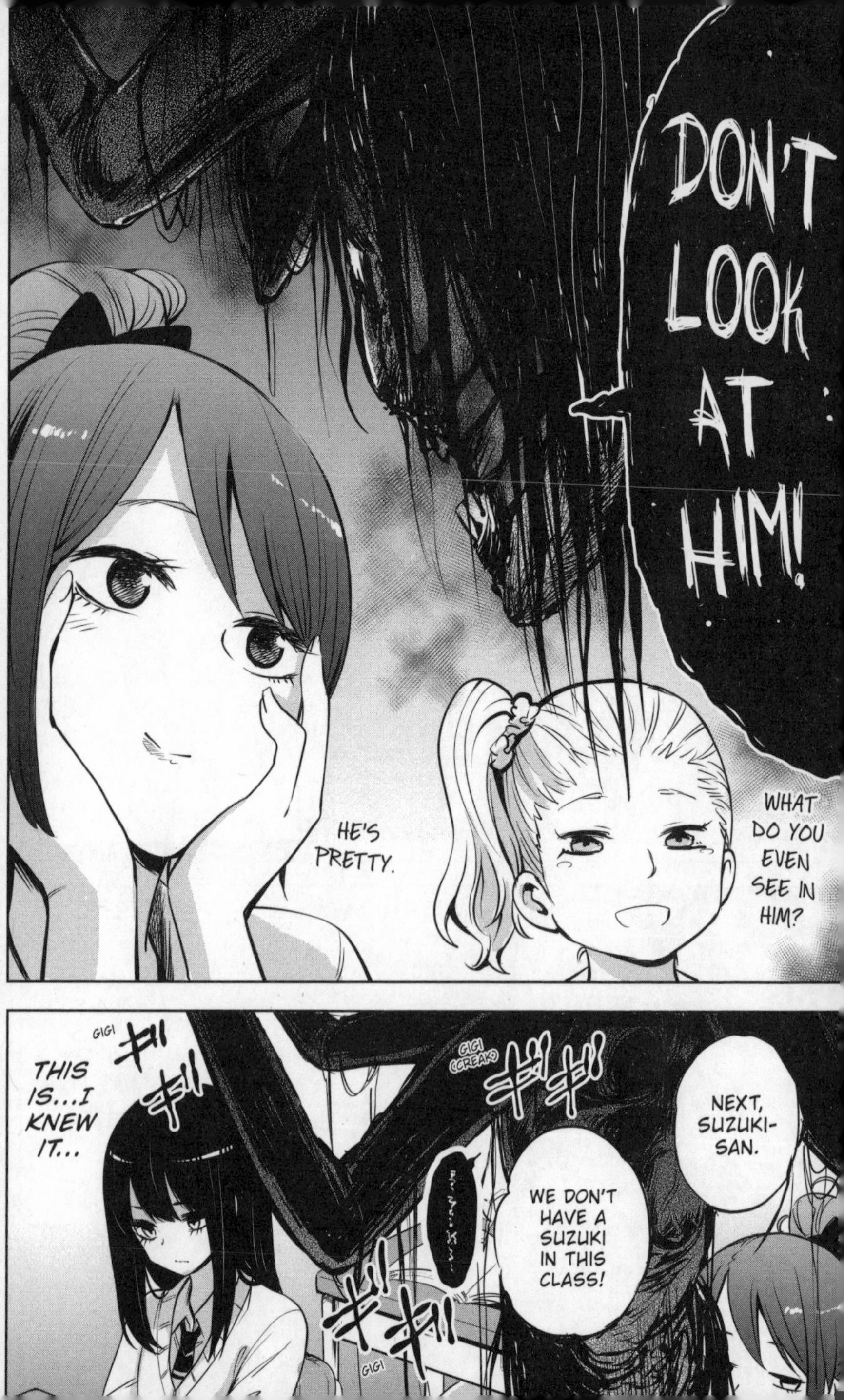
DON'T LOOK AT HIM!
WHAT DO YOU EVEN SEE IN HIM?
HE'S PRETTY.
NEXT, SUZUKI-SAN.
GIGI (CREAK)
WE DON'T HAVE A SUZUKI IN THIS CLASS!
GIGI
GIGI
THIS IS...I KNEW IT...

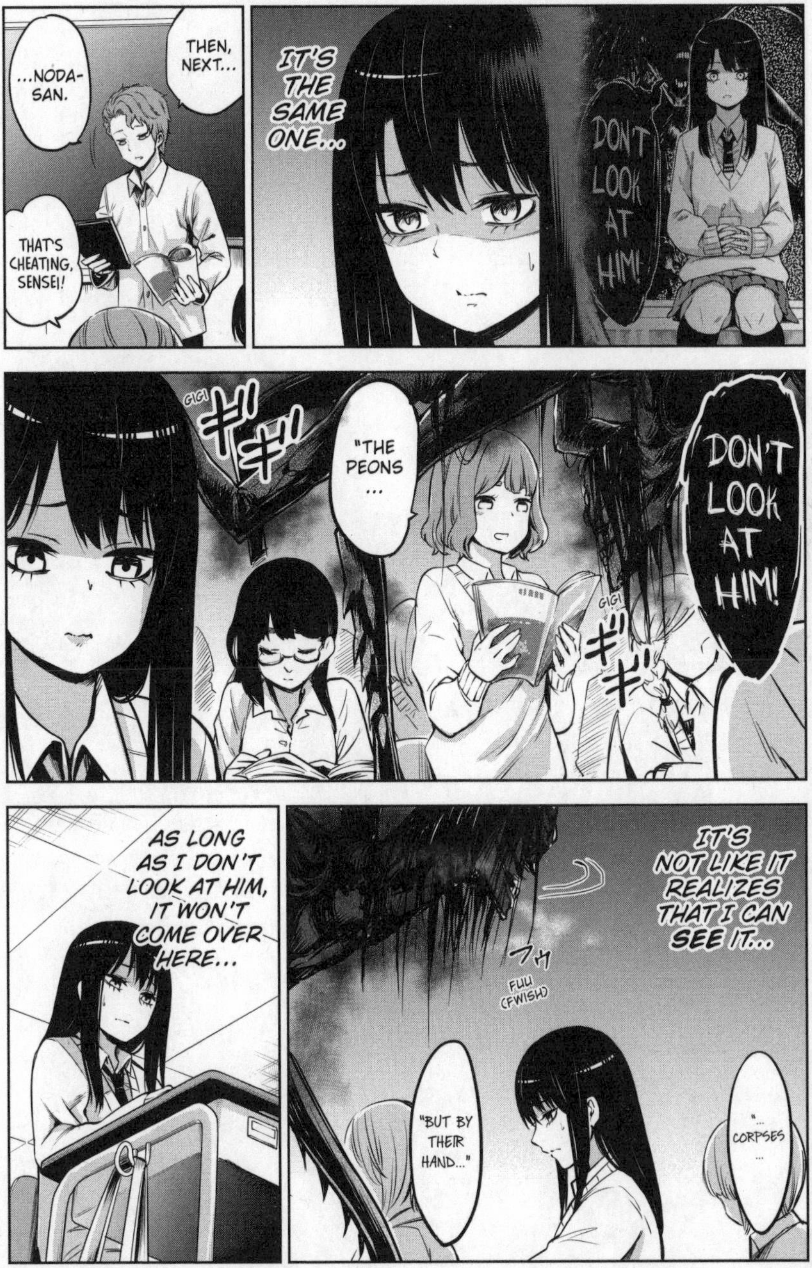
IT'S THE SAME ONE...
DON'T LOOK AT HIM!
THEN, NEXT...
...NODA-SAN.
THAT'S CHEATING, SENSEI!
DON'T LOOK AT HIM!
ギギ
GIGI
"THE PEONS...
ギギ
GIGI
IT'S NOT LIKE IT REALIZES THAT I CAN SEE IT...
フゥ
FUU (FWISH)
"...CORPSES...
"BUT BY THEIR HAND..."
AS LONG AS I DON'T LOOK AT HIM, IT WON'T COME OVER HERE...

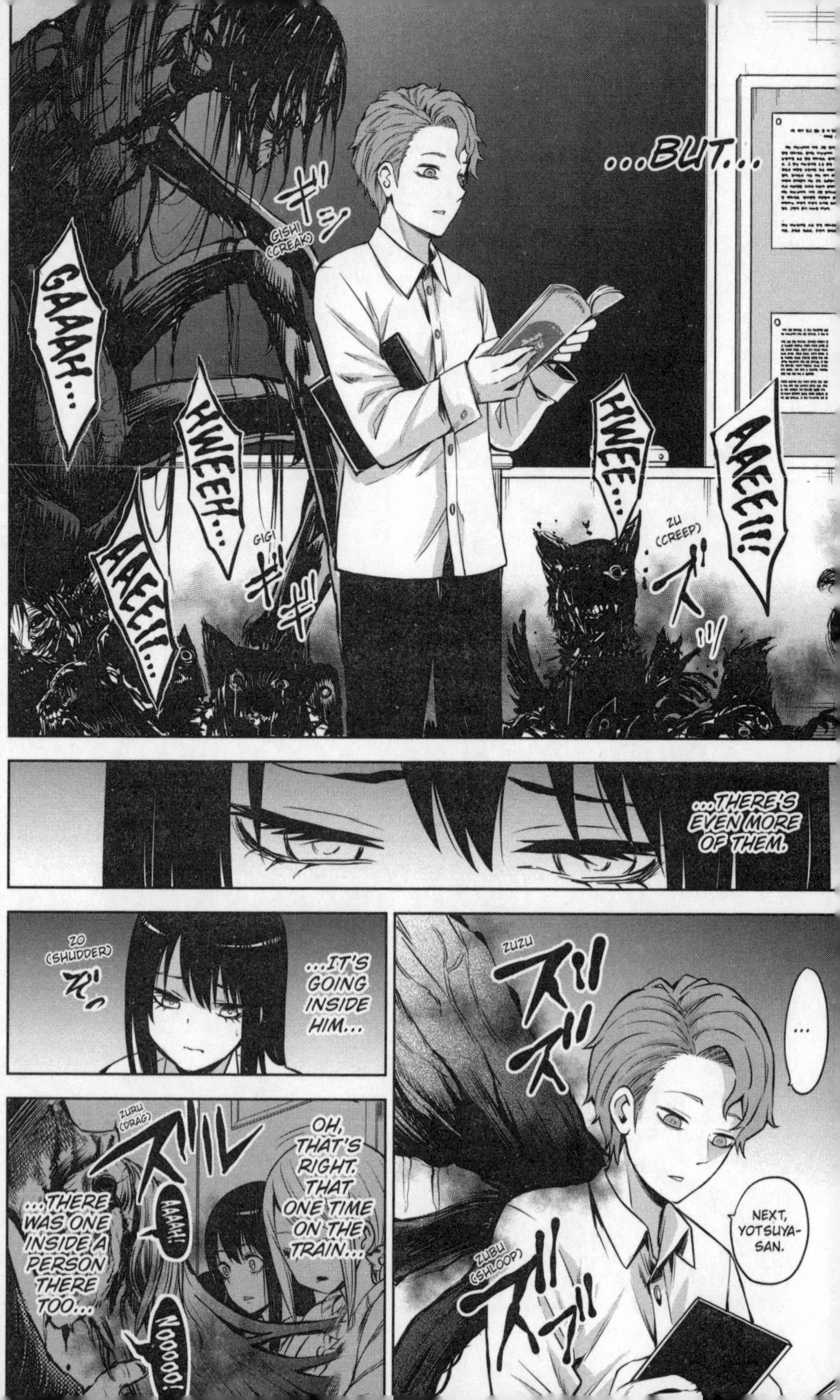

...BUT...
AAEE!!!
ZU (CREEP)
HWEE...
GISHI (CREAK)
GAAAH...
HWEEH...
GIGI
AAEE!!...
...THERE'S EVEN MORE OF THEM.
...
ZUZU
NEXT, YOTSUYA-SAN.
ZUBU (SHLOOP)
ZO (SHUDDER)
...IT'S GOING INSIDE HIM...
OH, THAT'S RIGHT. THAT ONE TIME ON THE TRAIN...
ZURU (DRAG)
AAAAH!
...THERE WAS ONE INSIDE A PERSON THERE TOO...
NOOOOO!

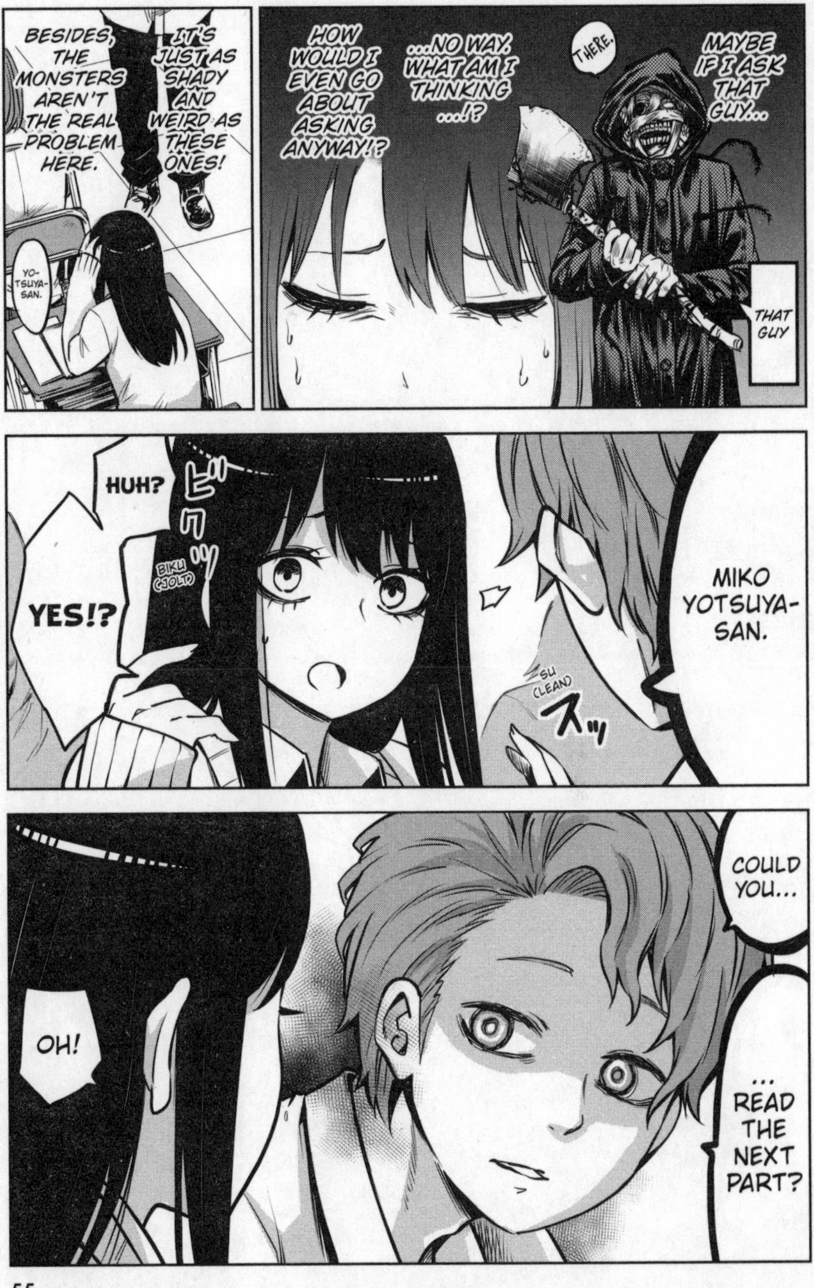
MAYBE IF I ASK THAT GUY...
THERE.
...NO WAY. WHAT AM I THINKING...!?
HOW WOULD I EVEN GO ABOUT ASKING ANYWAY!?
THAT GUY
IT'S JUST AS SHADY AND WEIRD AS THESE ONES!
BESIDES, THE MONSTERS AREN'T THE REAL PROBLEM HERE.
YO-TSUYA-SAN.
MIKO YOTSUYA-SAN.
SU (LEAN)
スッ
ビクッ
BIKU (JOLT)
HUH?
YES!?
COULD YOU...
...READ THE NEXT PART?
OH!

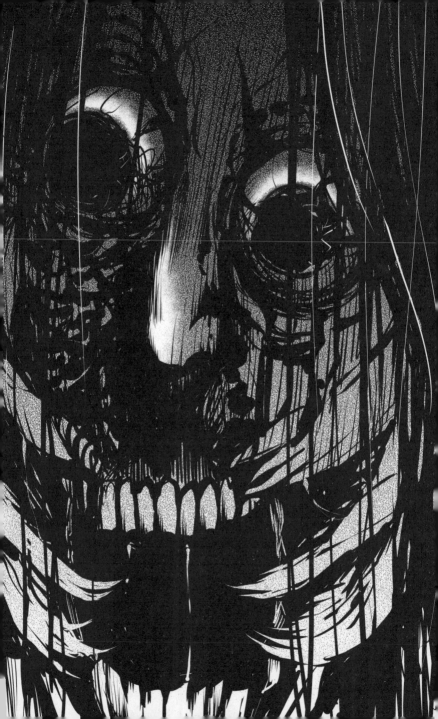

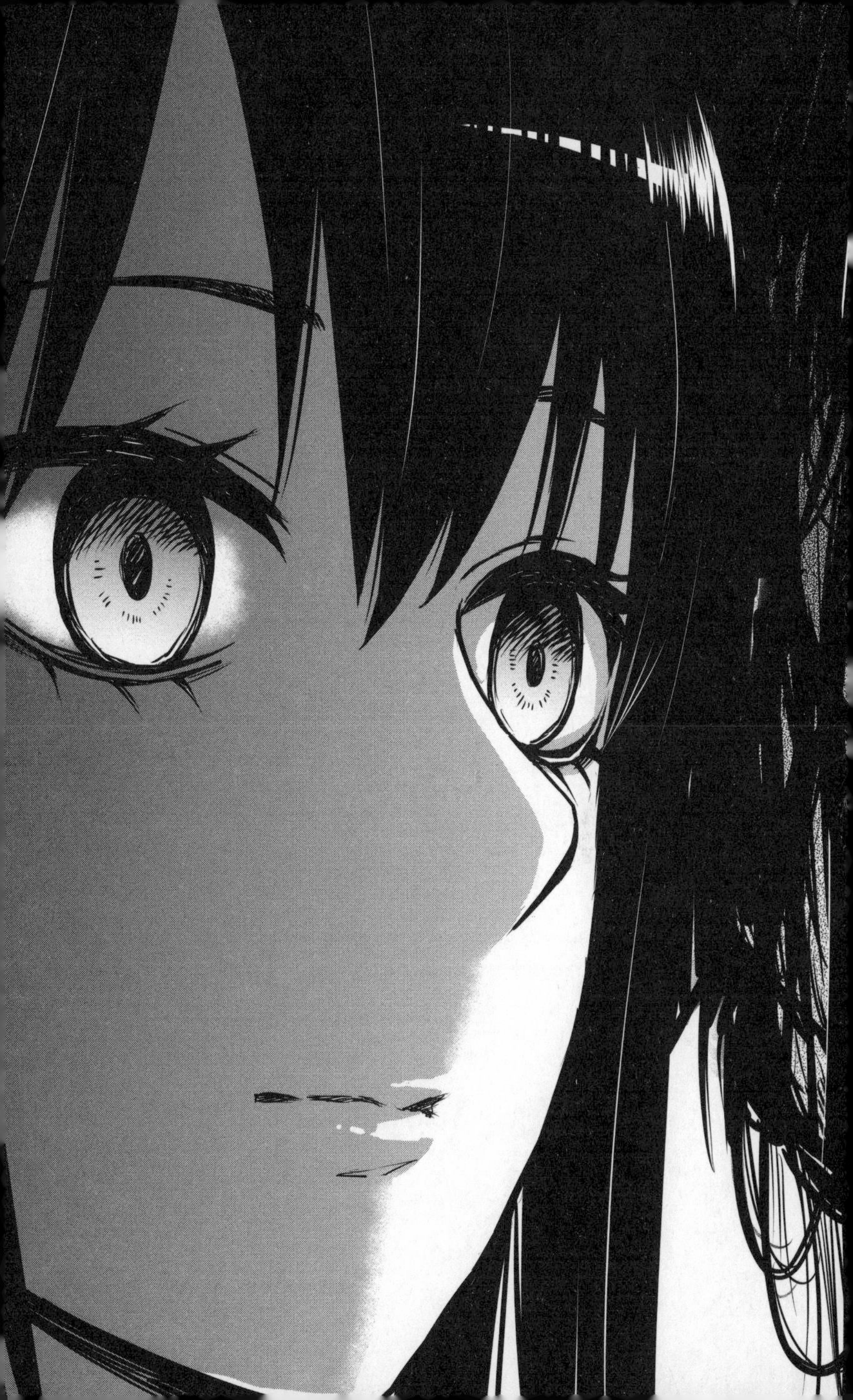

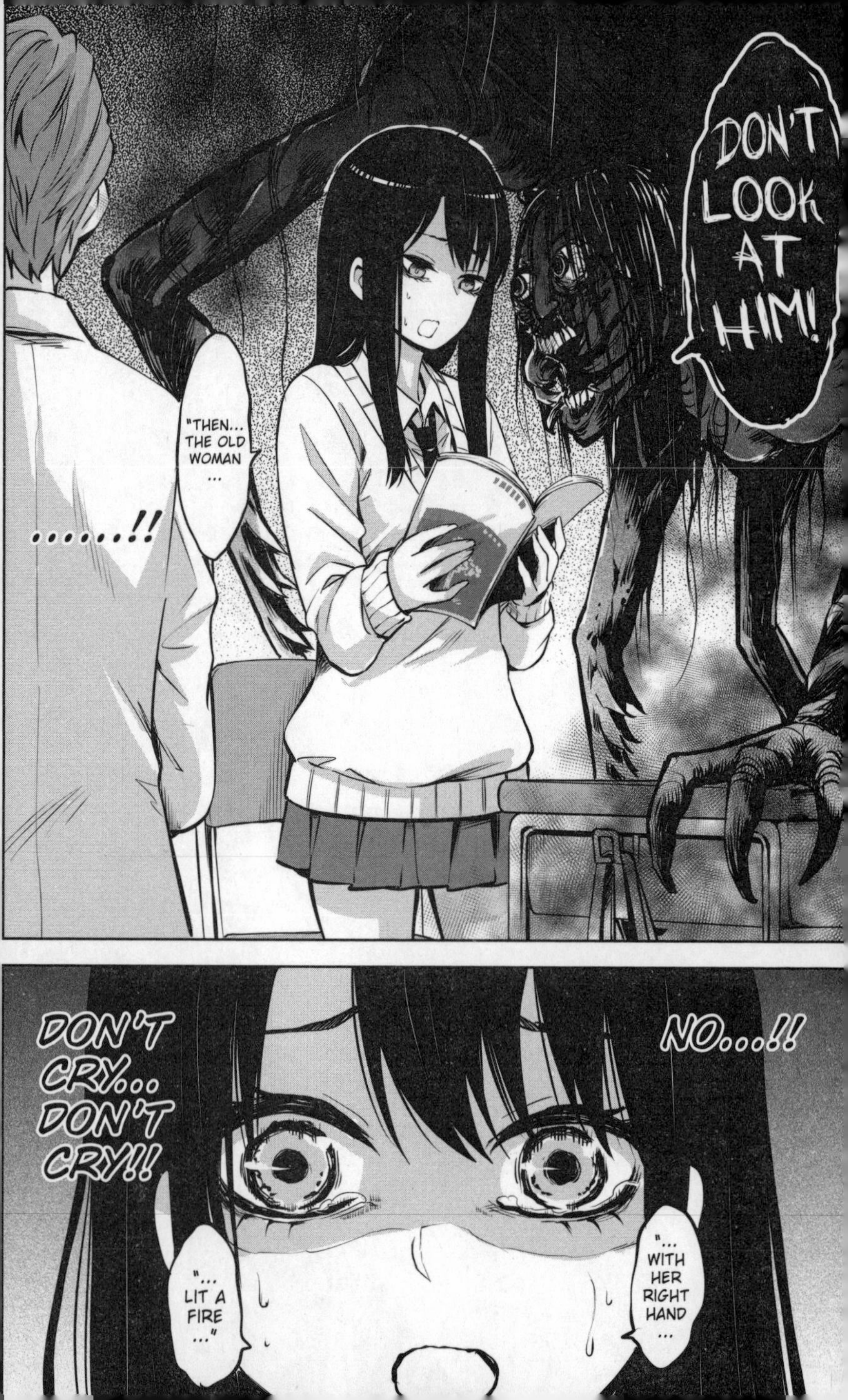
DON'T LOOK AT HIM!
"THEN... THE OLD WOMAN ...
......!!
NO...!!
DON'T CRY... DON'T CRY!!
"... WITH HER RIGHT HAND ...
"... LIT A FIRE ..."

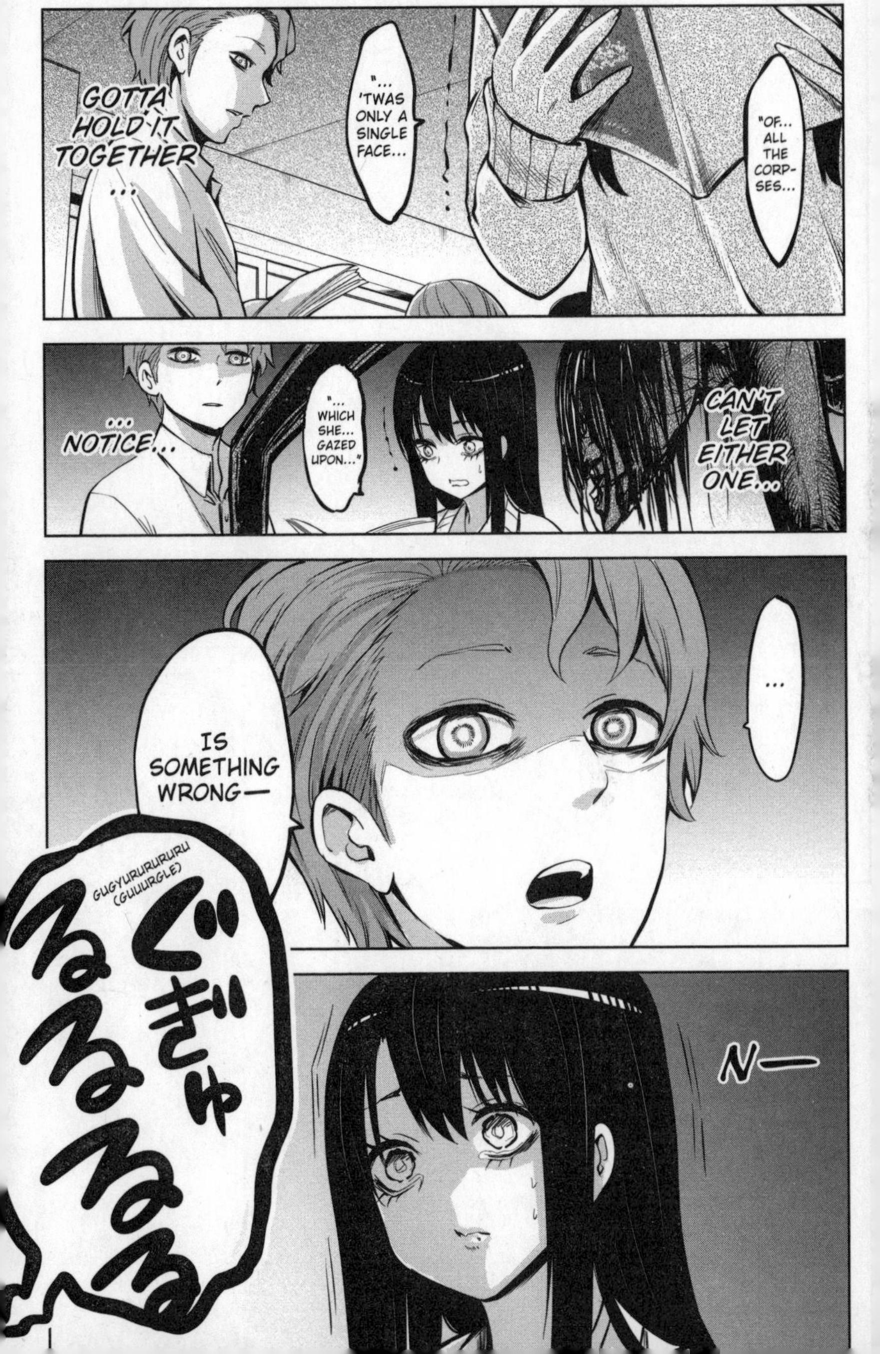
"OF... ALL THE CORPSES...
"...'TWAS ONLY A SINGLE FACE...
GOTTA HOLD IT TOGETHER
...
CAN'T LET EITHER ONE...
"...WHICH SHE... GAZED UPON..."
...NOTICE...
...
IS SOMETHING WRONG—
N—
ぐぎゅるるるる
GUGYURURURURU (GUUURGLE)

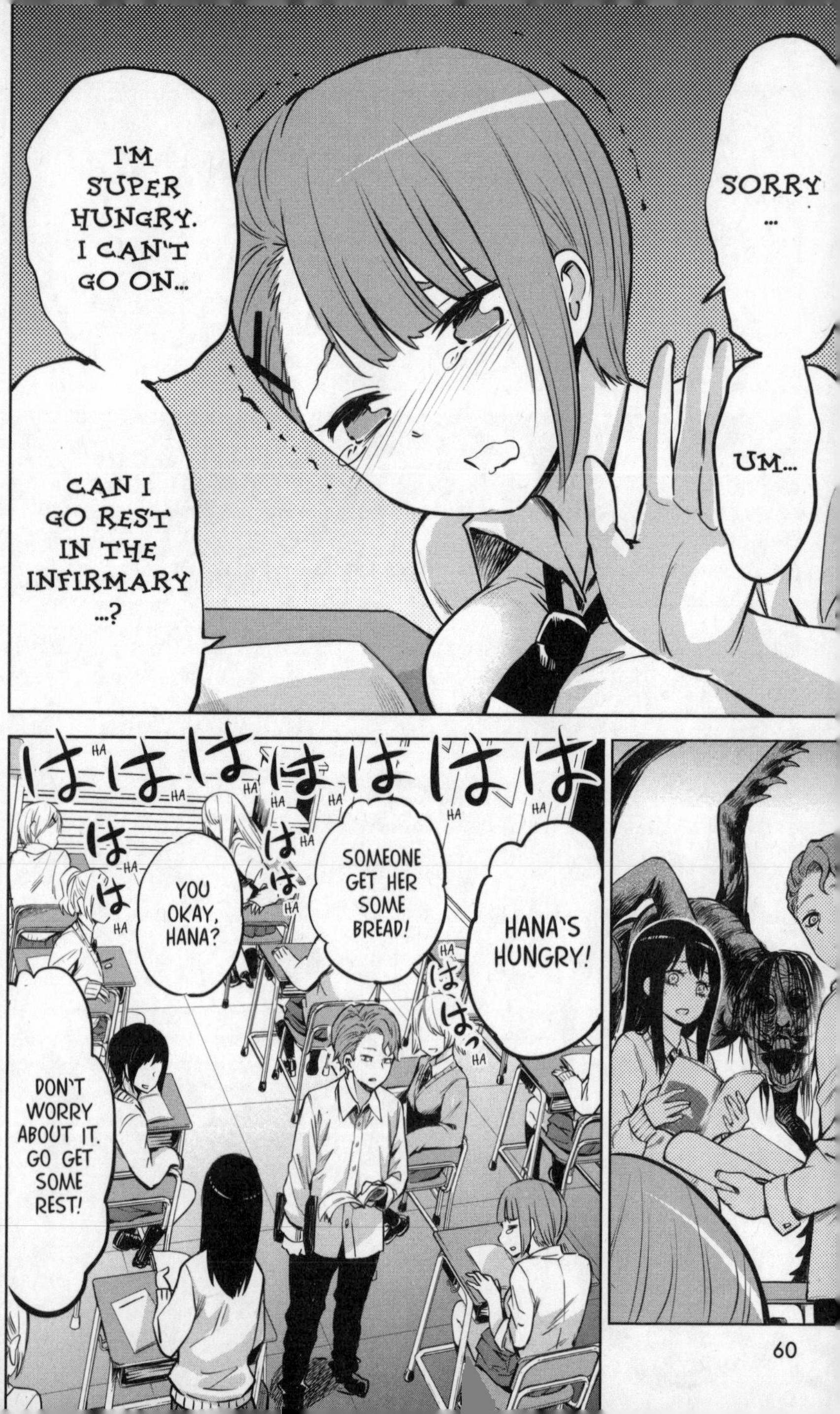
SORRY...
UM...
I'M SUPER HUNGRY. I CAN'T GO ON...
CAN I GO REST IN THE INFIRMARY...?
ははははははははは
HA HA HA HA HA HA HA HA HA HA
HANA'S HUNGRY!
ははっ
SOMEONE GET HER SOME BREAD!
YOU OKAY, HANA?
DON'T WORRY ABOUT IT. GO GET SOME REST!

GATA
(CLATTER)

ガタ

GET HER
SOMETHING
TO EAT!

GO
FOR
IT!

GOOD
ONE,
MIKO!

I'LL
...

...TAKE
HER
THERE
...!

NGH
...

SORRY...
MIKO...

I JUST
GOT
SUPER
HUNGRY
AFTER
THIRD
PERIOD
STARTED
...

I
REALLY
DON'T
GET IT...

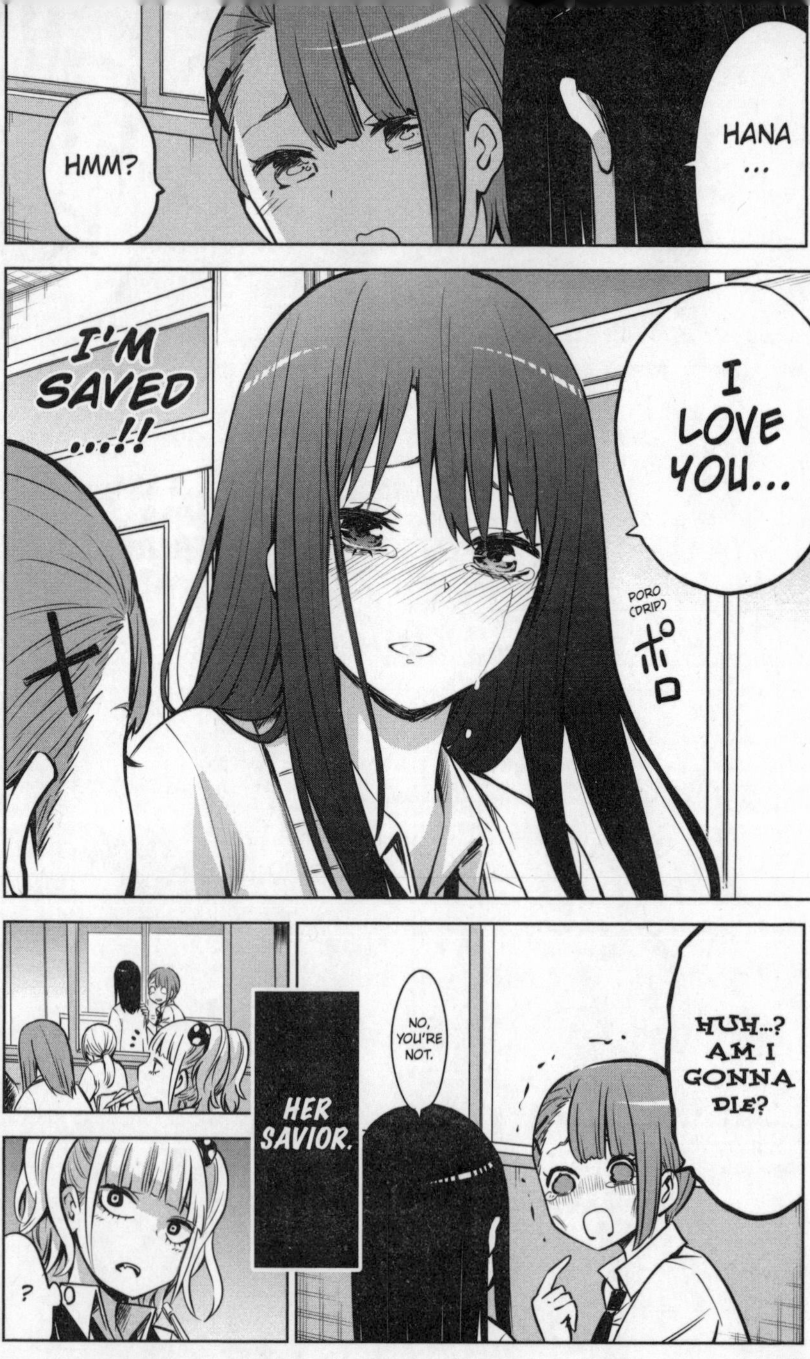
HANA ...
HMM?
I LOVE YOU...
PORO (DRIP)
ポロ
I'M SAVED ...!!
HUH...? AM I GONNA DIE?
NO, YOU'RE NOT.
HER SAVIOR.
?

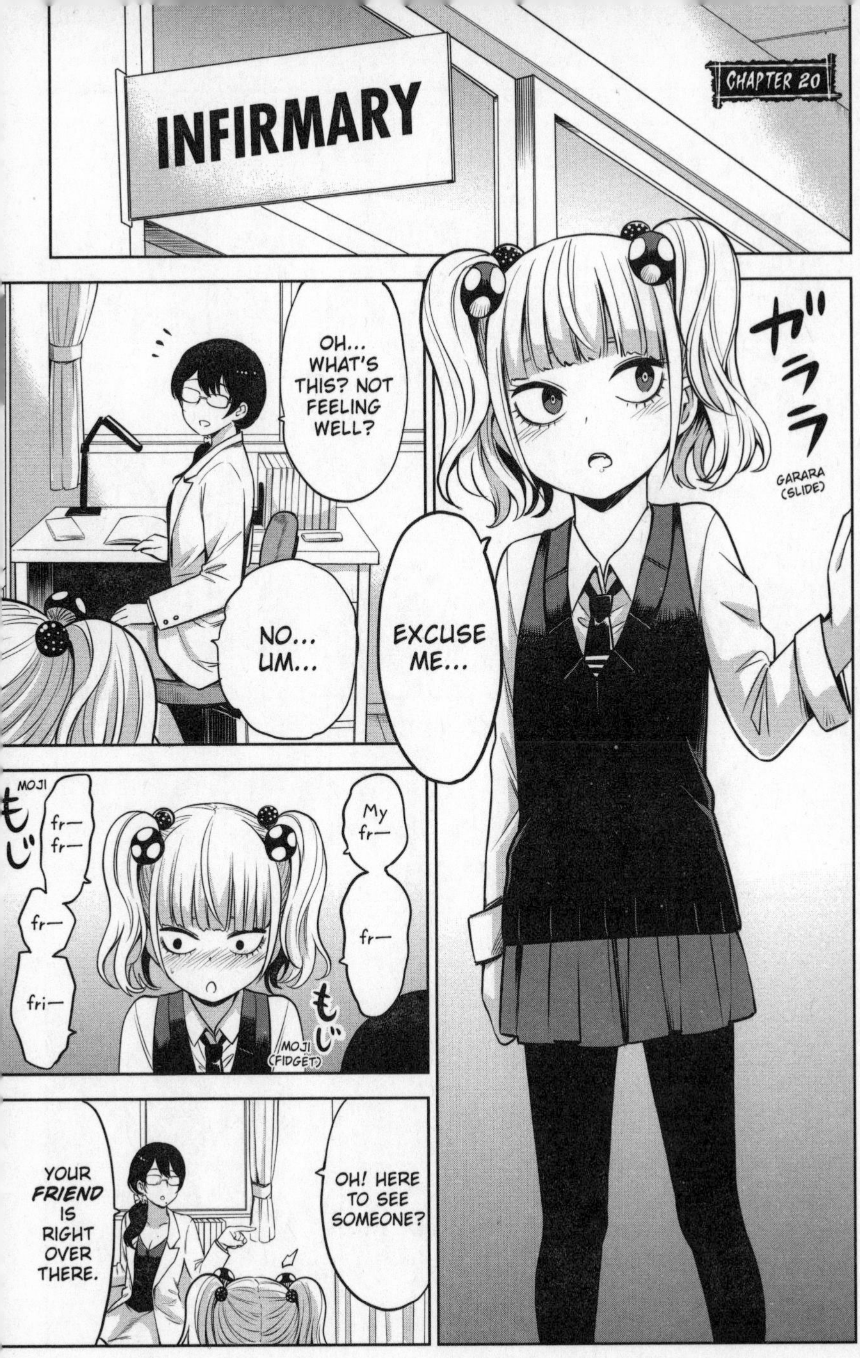
CHAPTER 20
INFIRMARY
ガララ
GARARA (SLIDE)
EXCUSE ME...
OH... WHAT'S THIS? NOT FEELING WELL?
NO... UM...
My fr—
fr—
もじ
MOJI (FIDGET)
fr— fr—
fr—
fri—
もじ
MOJI
OH! HERE TO SEE SOMEONE?
YOUR *FRIEND* IS RIGHT OVER THERE.

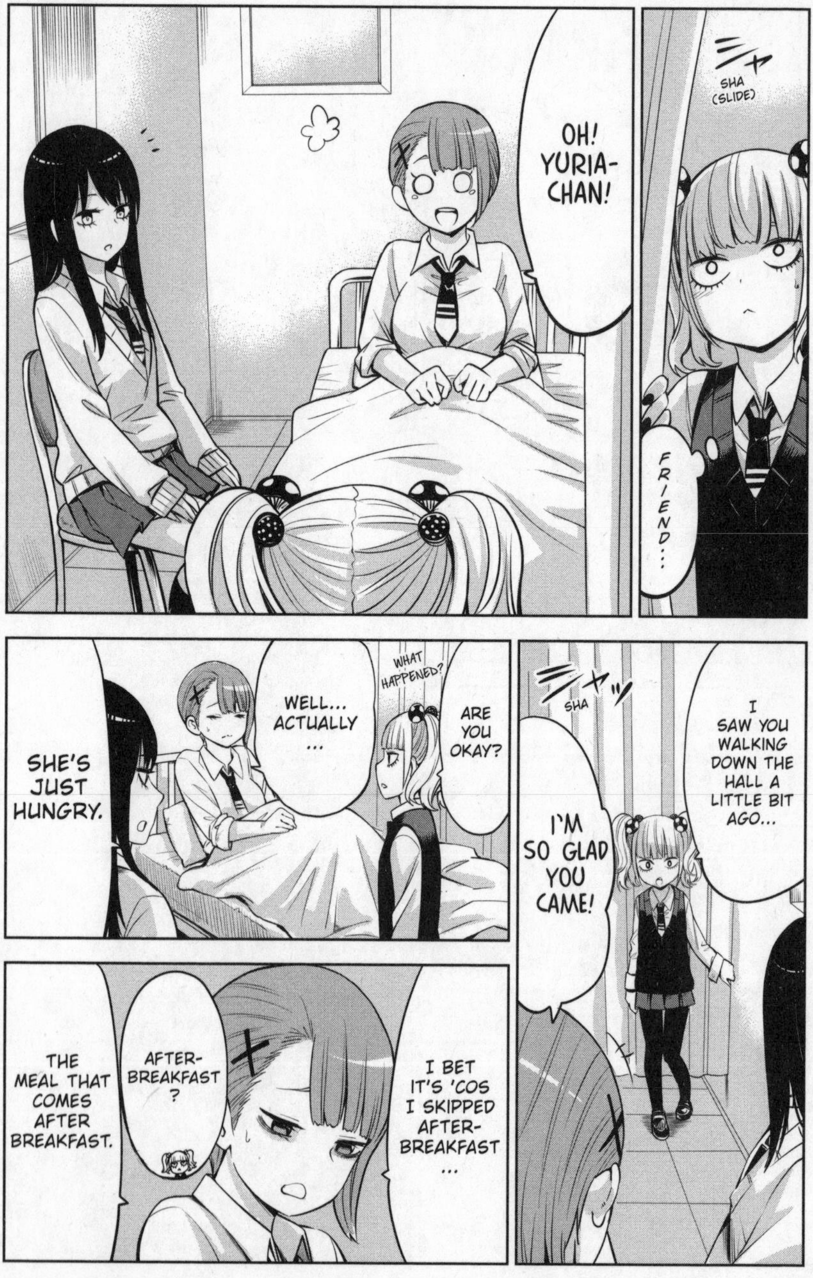
シャ
SHA (SLIDE)
FRIEND...
OH! YURIA-CHAN!
I SAW YOU WALKING DOWN THE HALL A LITTLE BIT AGO...
シャッ
SHA
I'M SO GLAD YOU CAME!
ARE YOU OKAY?
WHAT HAPPENED?
WELL... ACTUALLY...
SHE'S JUST HUNGRY.
I BET IT'S 'COS I SKIPPED AFTER-BREAKFAST...
AFTER-BREAKFAST?
THE MEAL THAT COMES AFTER BREAKFAST.

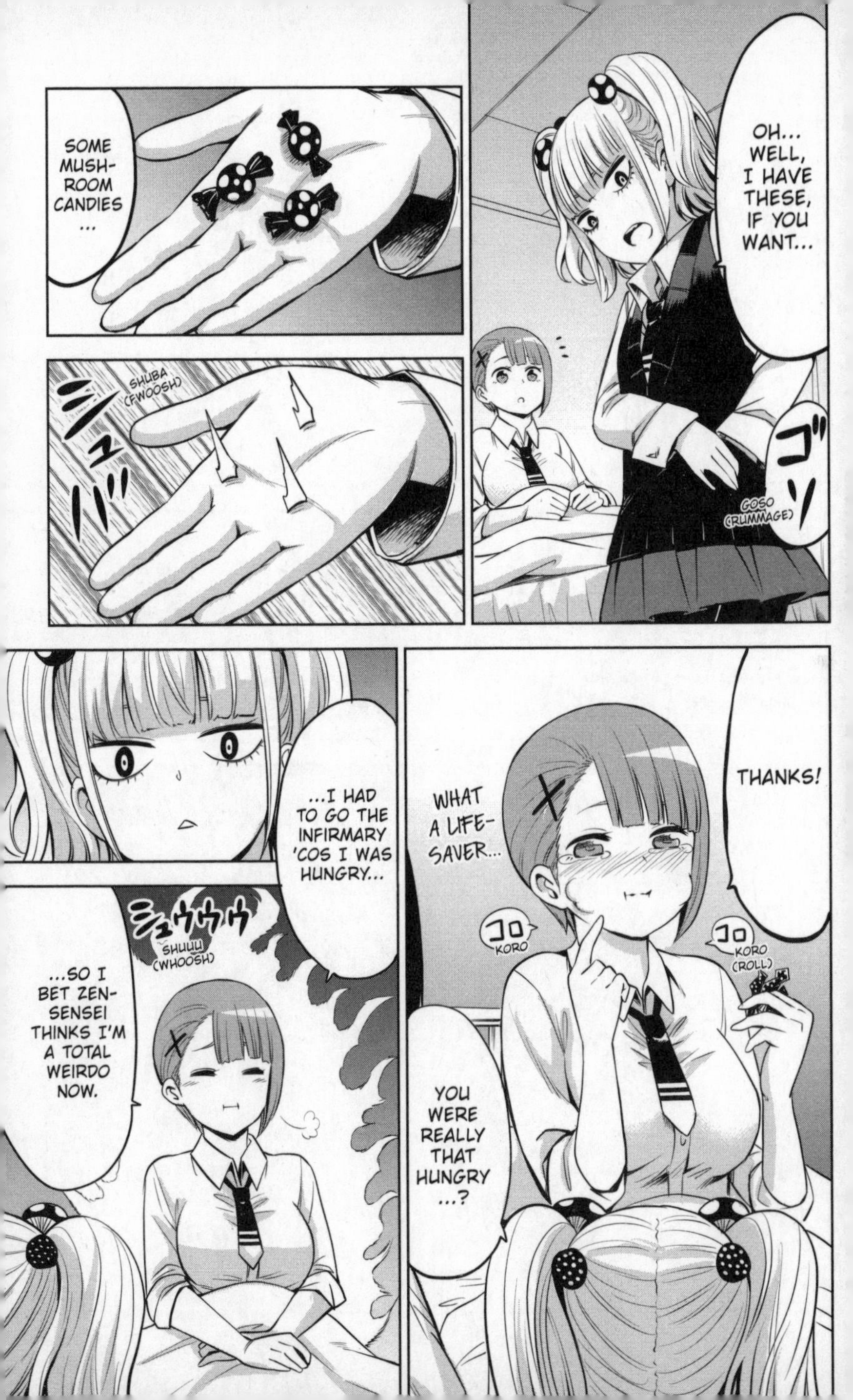
OH... WELL, I HAVE THESE, IF YOU WANT...
ゴソ
GOSO (RUMMAGE)
SOME MUSH-ROOM CANDIES ...
シュバッ
SHUBA (FWOOSH)
THANKS!
WHAT A LIFE-SAVER...
コロ
KORO
コロ
KORO (ROLL)
YOU WERE REALLY THAT HUNGRY ...?
...I HAD TO GO THE INFIRMARY 'COS I WAS HUNGRY...
シュウウウ
SHUUU (WHOOSH)
...SO I BET ZEN-SENSEI THINKS I'M A TOTAL WEIRDO NOW.

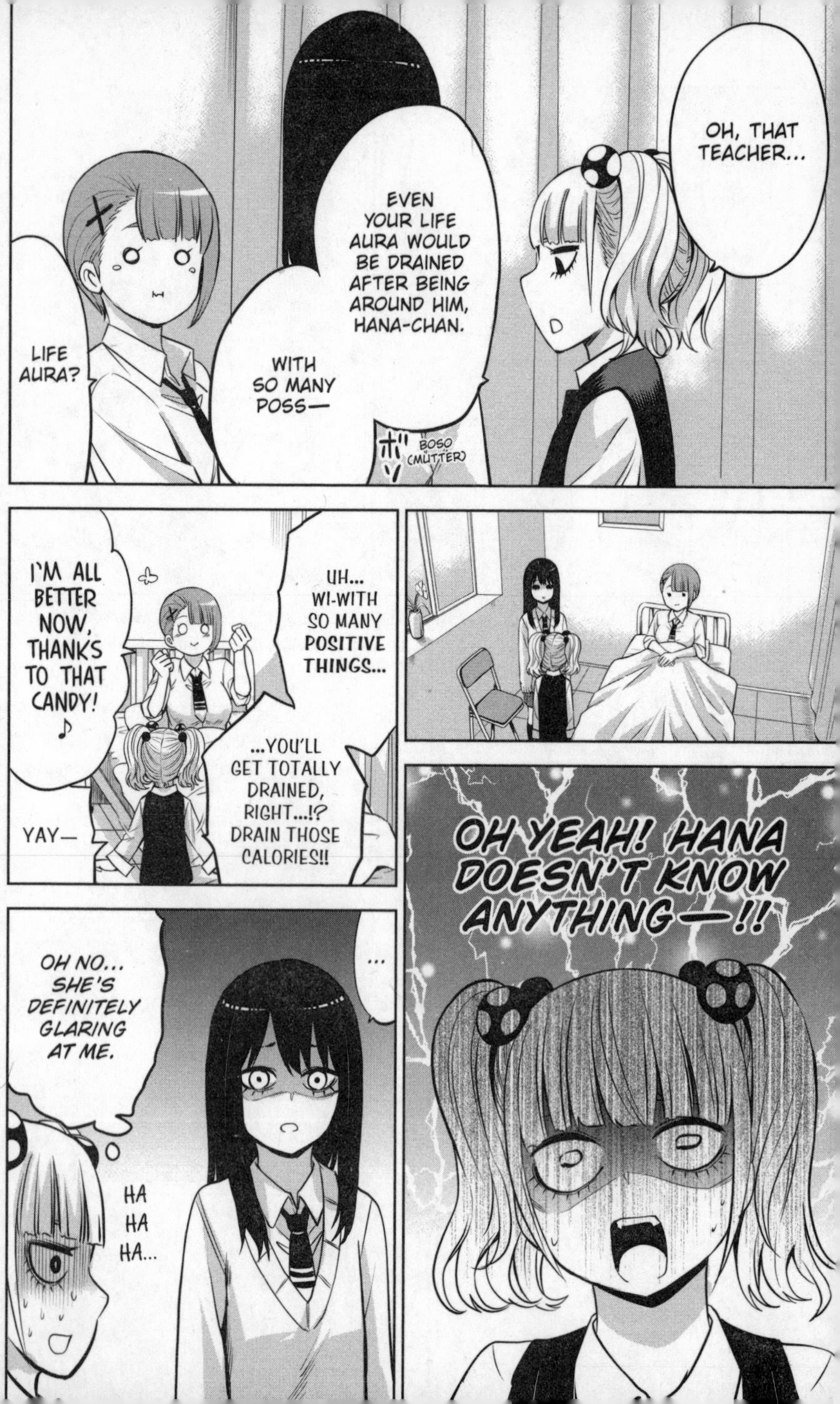
OH, THAT TEACHER...
EVEN YOUR LIFE AURA WOULD BE DRAINED AFTER BEING AROUND HIM, HANA-CHAN.
WITH SO MANY POSS—
BOSO (MUTTER)
LIFE AURA?
UH... WI-WITH SO MANY POSITIVE THINGS...
I'M ALL BETTER NOW, THANKS TO THAT CANDY! ♪
...YOU'LL GET TOTALLY DRAINED, RIGHT...!? DRAIN THOSE CALORIES!!
YAY—
OH YEAH! HANA DOESN'T KNOW ANYTHING—!!
...
OH NO... SHE'S DEFINITELY GLARING AT ME.
HA HA HA...

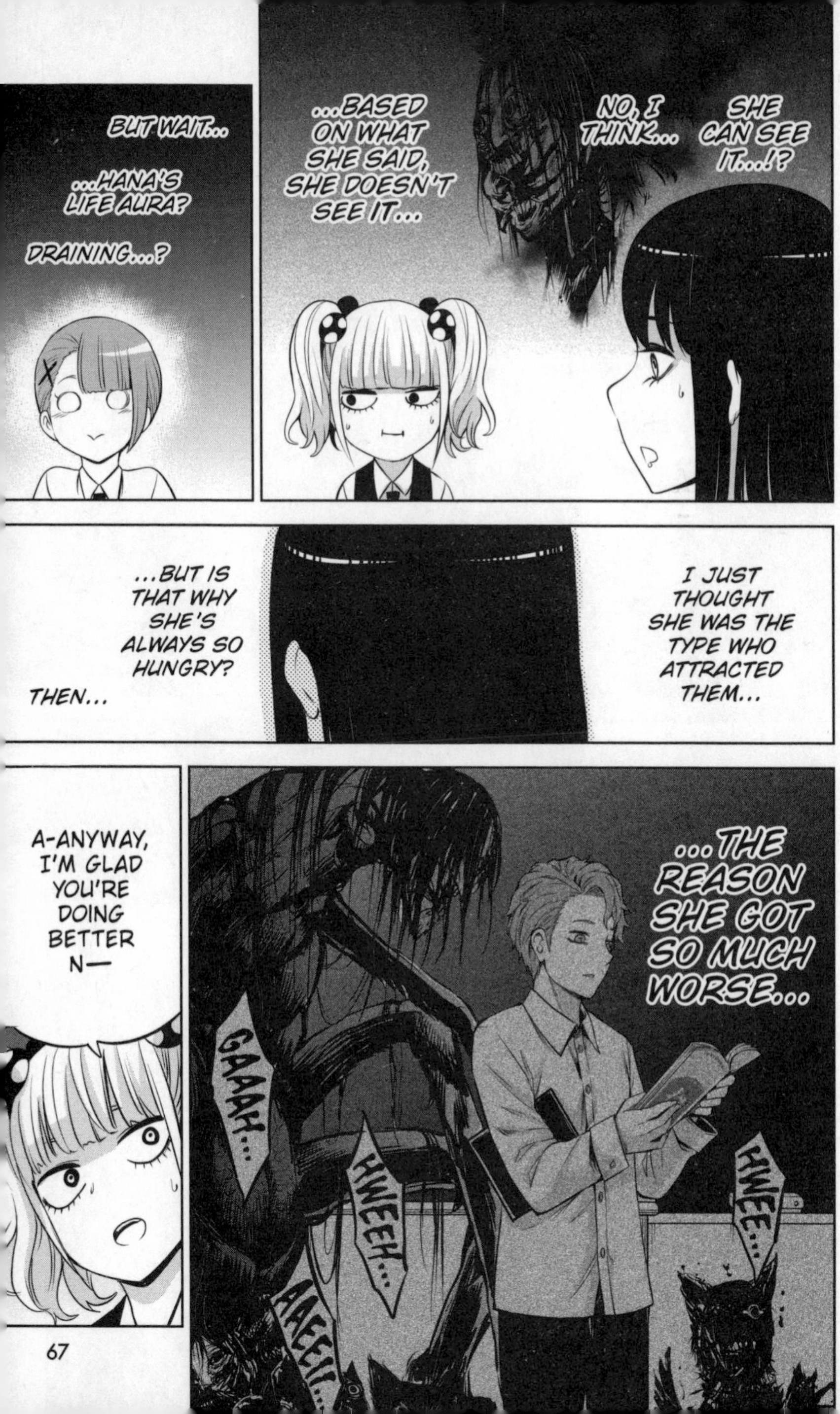
SHE CAN SEE IT...!?
NO, I THINK...
...BASED ON WHAT SHE SAID, SHE DOESN'T SEE IT...
BUT WAIT...
...HANA'S LIFE AURA?
DRAINING...?
I JUST THOUGHT SHE WAS THE TYPE WHO ATTRACTED THEM...
...BUT IS THAT WHY SHE'S ALWAYS SO HUNGRY?
THEN...
...THE REASON SHE GOT SO MUCH WORSE...
HWEE...
GAAAAH...
HWEEEH...
AAEEII...
A-ANYWAY, I'M GLAD YOU'RE DOING BETTER N—

OH,
SORRY.

HUH?

YOUR
FACE IS
KINDA
SCARY,
MIKO.

*PURU
(TREMBLE)*

PURU

DID SHE
SNAP!?

BUT I
COVERED
IT UP...!!

SHE MIGHT
TELL ME
SOMETHING
NEW...

*BOSO
(WHISPER)*

CAN I
SPEAK
WITH
YOU,
YURIA-
CHAN?

OH!

SHUBA (FWSH!)

SORRY...! WE HAVE TO CHANGE ROOMS FOR NEXT PERIOD...!!

BADGER!

BADGER!

GI (SQUEEZE)

S E R P E N T D R O P !!

NEXT TIME I'LL KILL YOU.

HERE YOU GO!

YAAAY !!

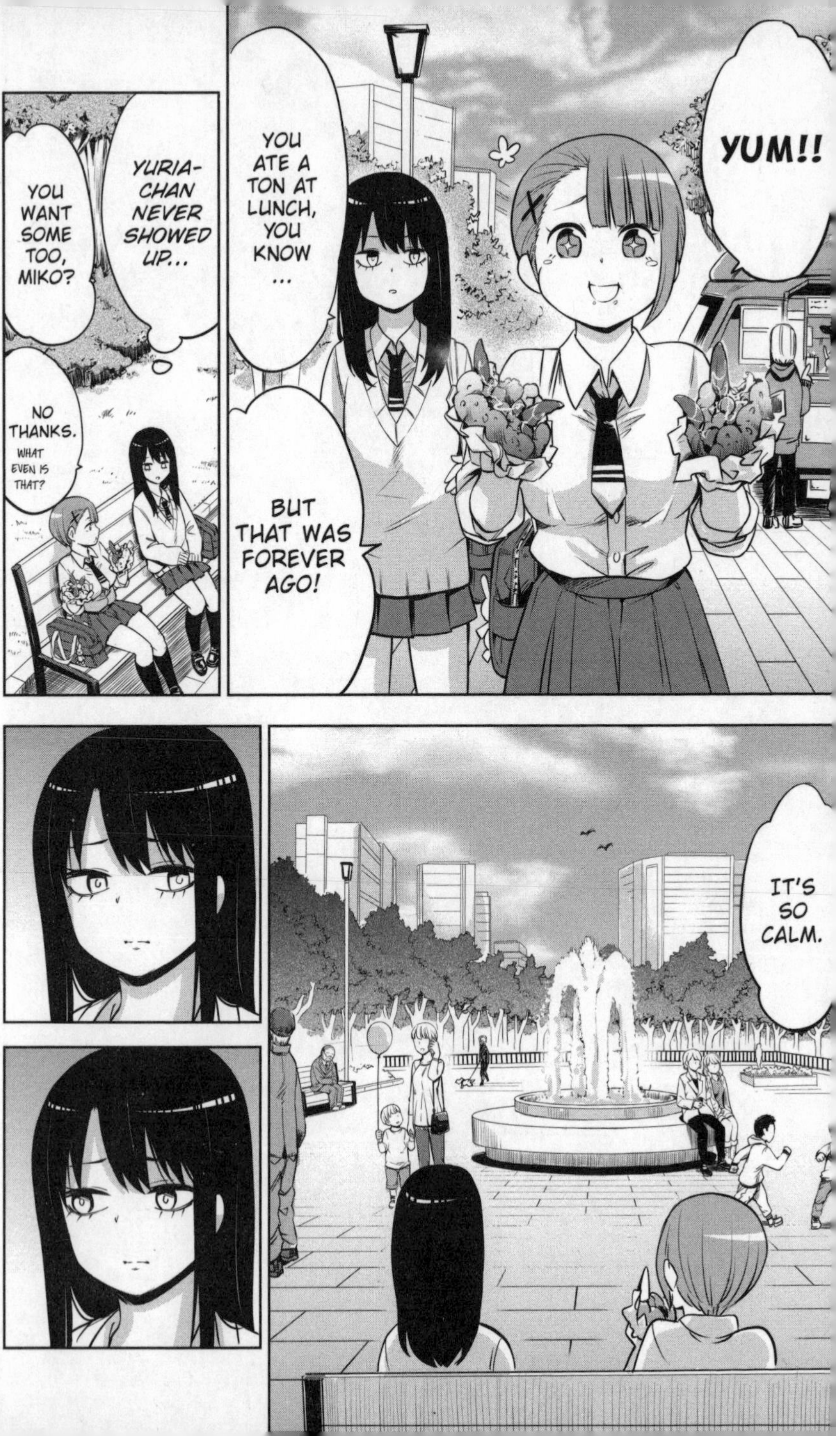
YUM!!
YOU ATE A TON AT LUNCH, YOU KNOW...
BUT THAT WAS FOREVER AGO!
YURIA-CHAN NEVER SHOWED UP...
YOU WANT SOME TOO, MIKO?
NO THANKS.
WHAT EVEN IS THAT?
IT'S SO CALM.

THAT ONE'S GONNA GO INSIDE THAT PERSON.

ズズ
ZUZU (CREEP)

...THEY REALLY ARE ALL OVER...

NOW THAT I'M PAYING ATTENTION...

ZABAA (RUSTLE)

I CAN'T SEE STUFF LIKE LIFE AURAS...

GARI (SMAK)

MOSHA

MOSHA (CRUNCH)

BOKI (CRACK)

BORI (MUNCH)

SHAKI (CHEW)

SAKU (CHOMP)

SO PEACE-FUL...

BYE BYE!

I REALLY SHOULDN'T LOOK...

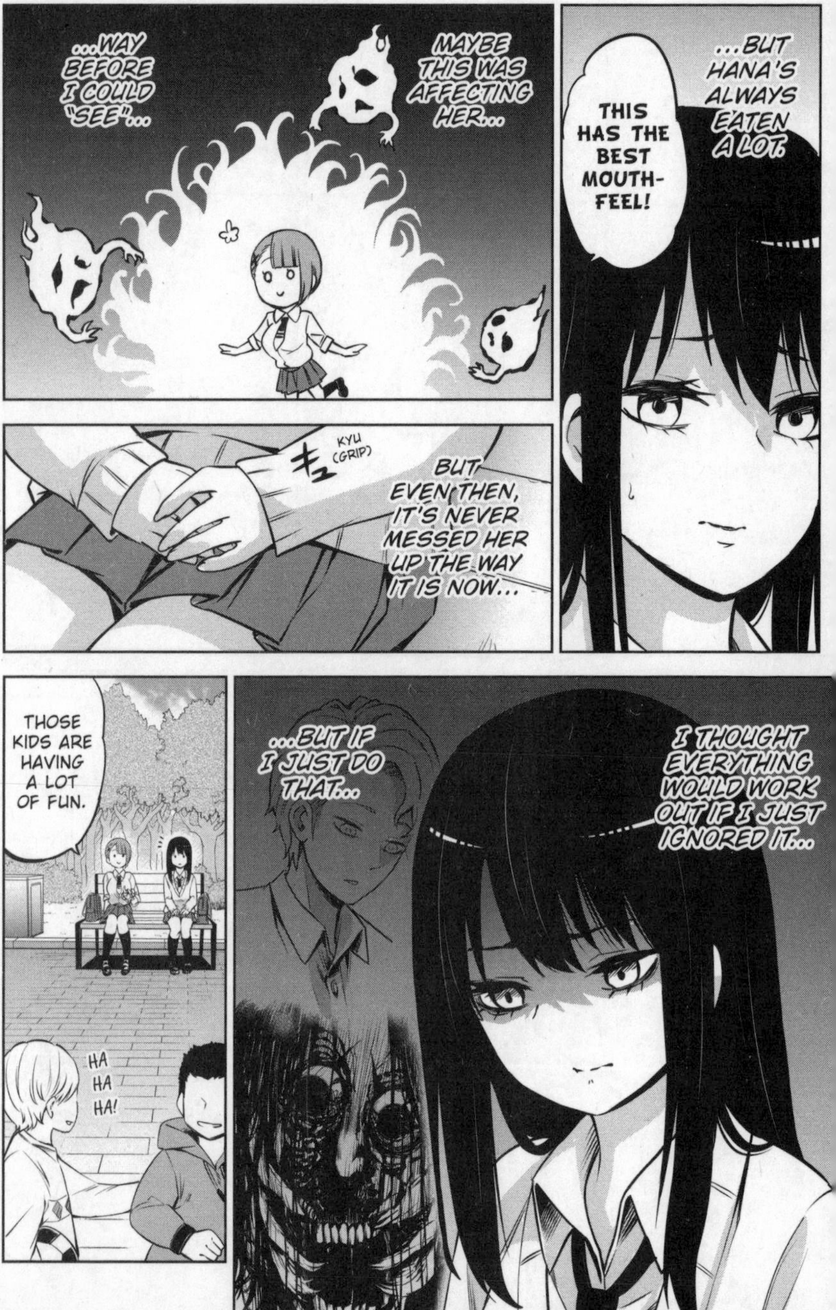
...BUT HANA'S ALWAYS EATEN A LOT.
THIS HAS THE BEST MOUTH-FEEL!
MAYBE THIS WAS AFFECTING HER...
...WAY BEFORE I COULD "SEE"...
KYU (GRIP)
BUT EVEN THEN, IT'S NEVER MESSED HER UP THE WAY IT IS NOW...
I THOUGHT EVERYTHING WOULD WORK OUT IF I JUST IGNORED IT...
...BUT IF I JUST DO THAT...
THOSE KIDS ARE HAVING A LOT OF FUN.
HA HA HA!

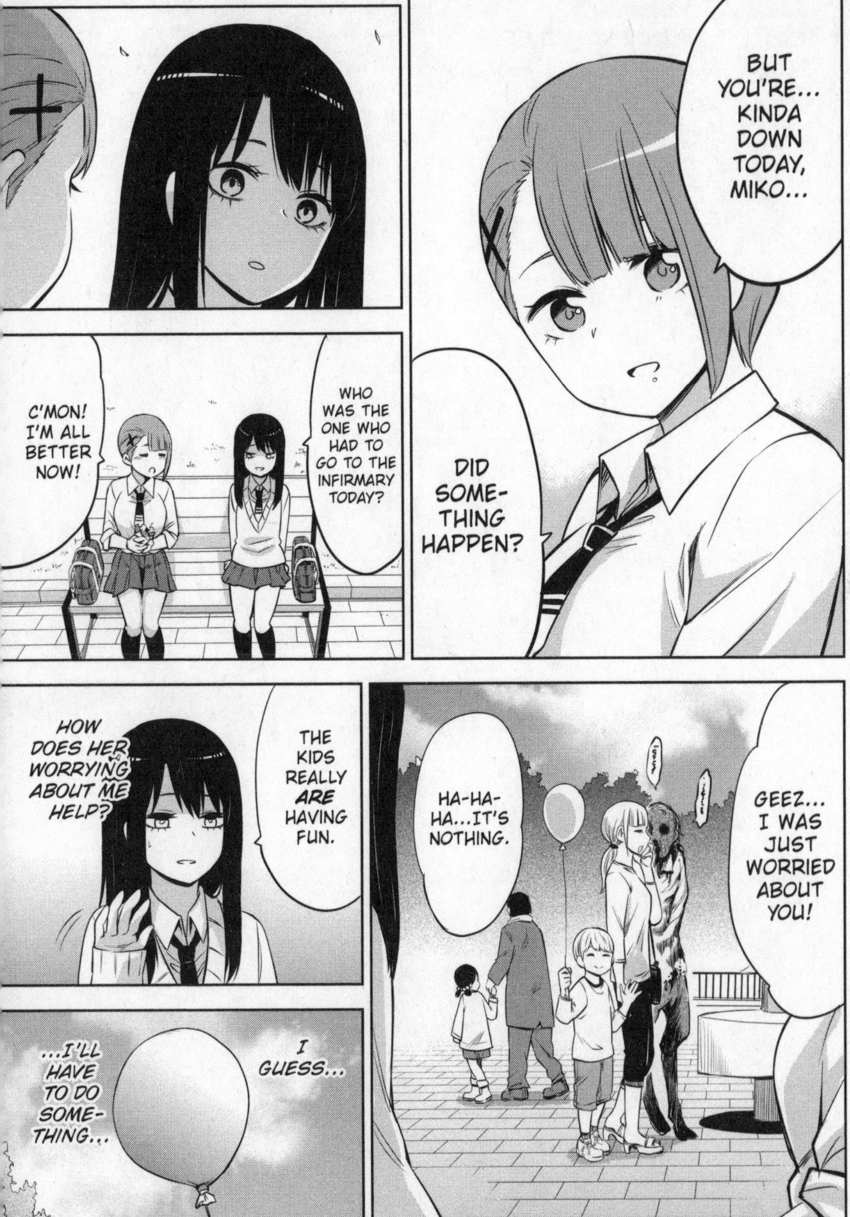
BUT YOU'RE... KINDA DOWN TODAY, MIKO...
DID SOMETHING HAPPEN?
WHO WAS THE ONE WHO HAD TO GO TO THE INFIRMARY TODAY?
C'MON! I'M ALL BETTER NOW!
GEEZ... I WAS JUST WORRIED ABOUT YOU!
HA-HA-HA...IT'S NOTHING.
THE KIDS REALLY ARE HAVING FUN.
HOW DOES HER WORRYING ABOUT ME HELP?
I GUESS...
...I'LL HAVE TO DO SOMETHING...

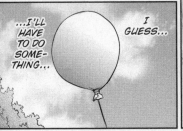

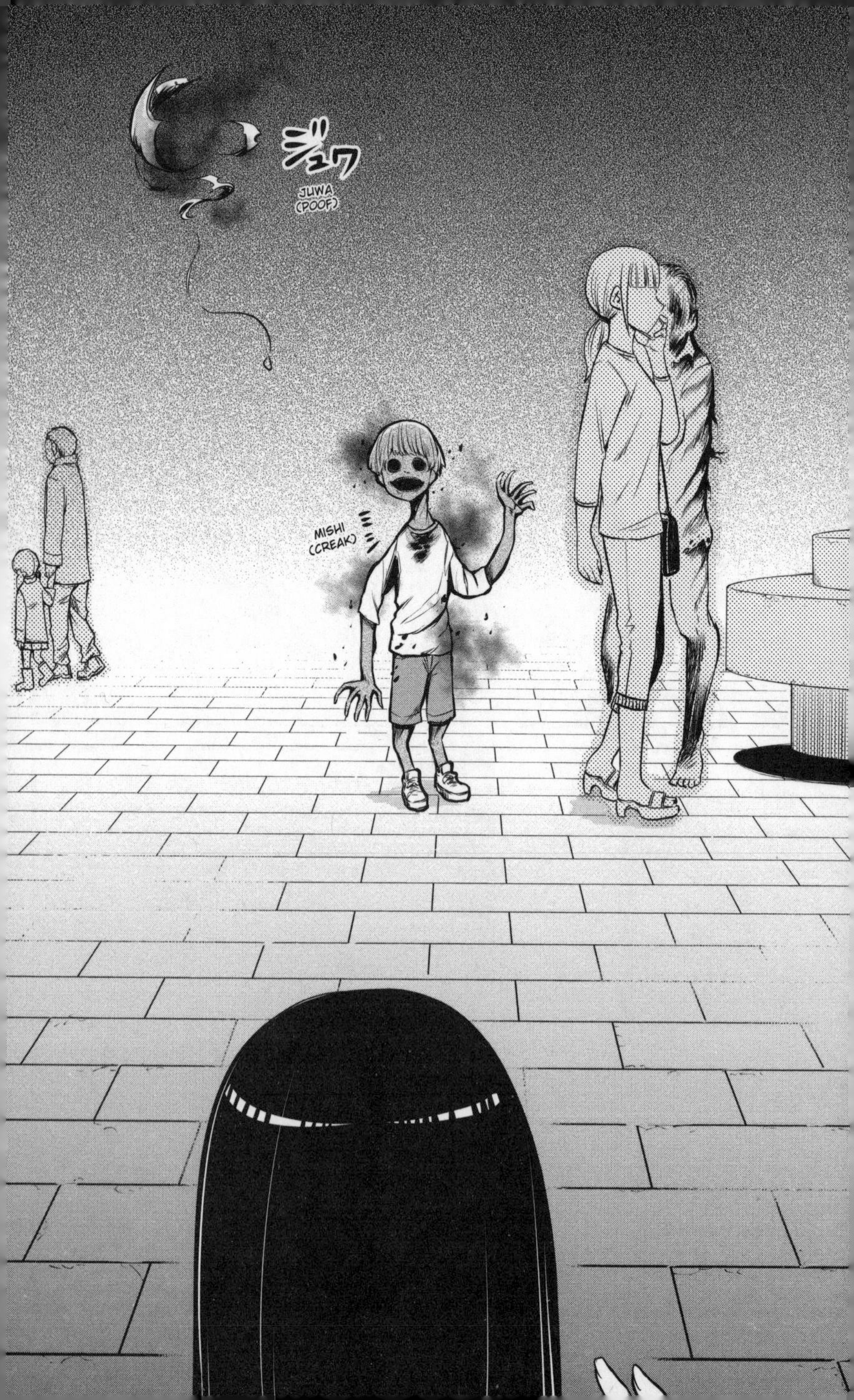
ジュワ
JUWA (POOF)
MISHI (CREAK)

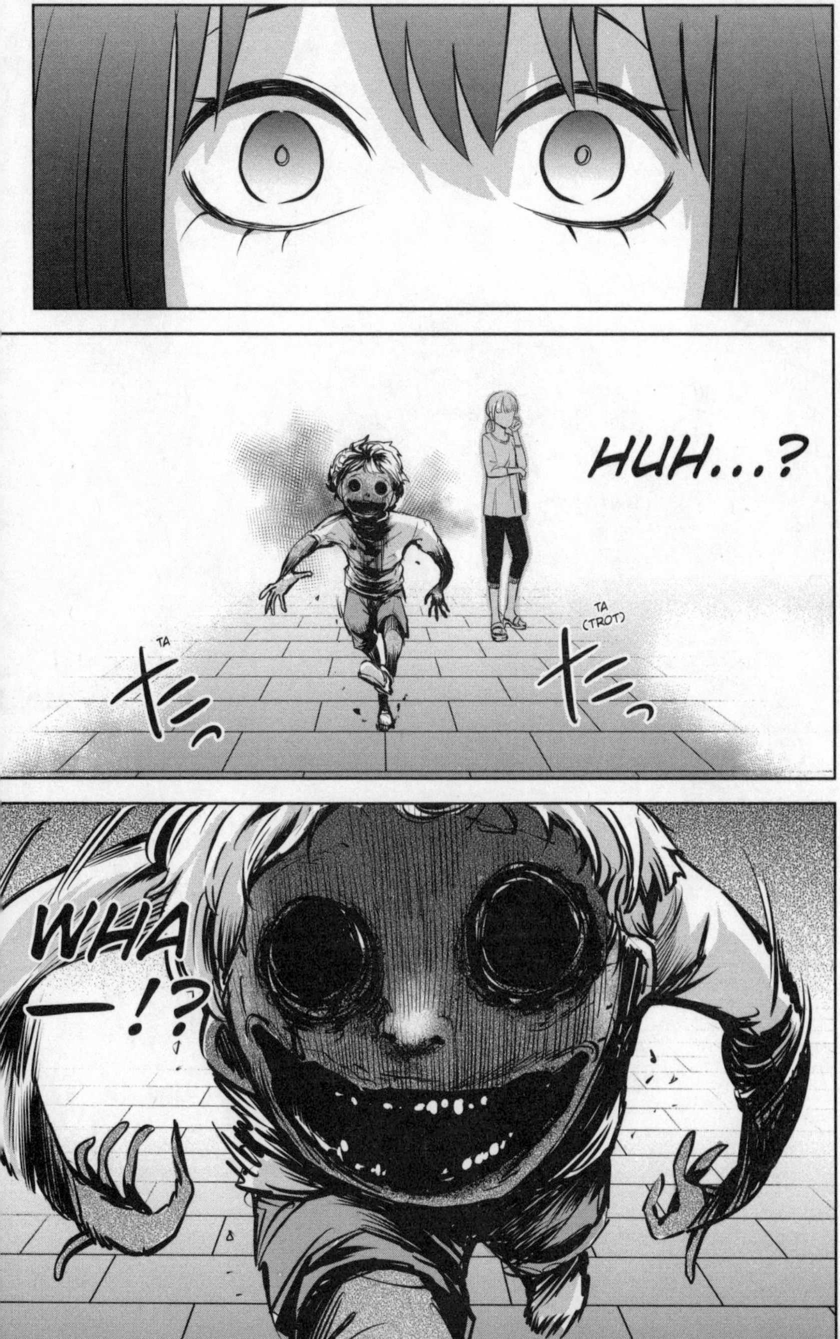
HUH...?
TA
(TROT)
TA
WHA—!?

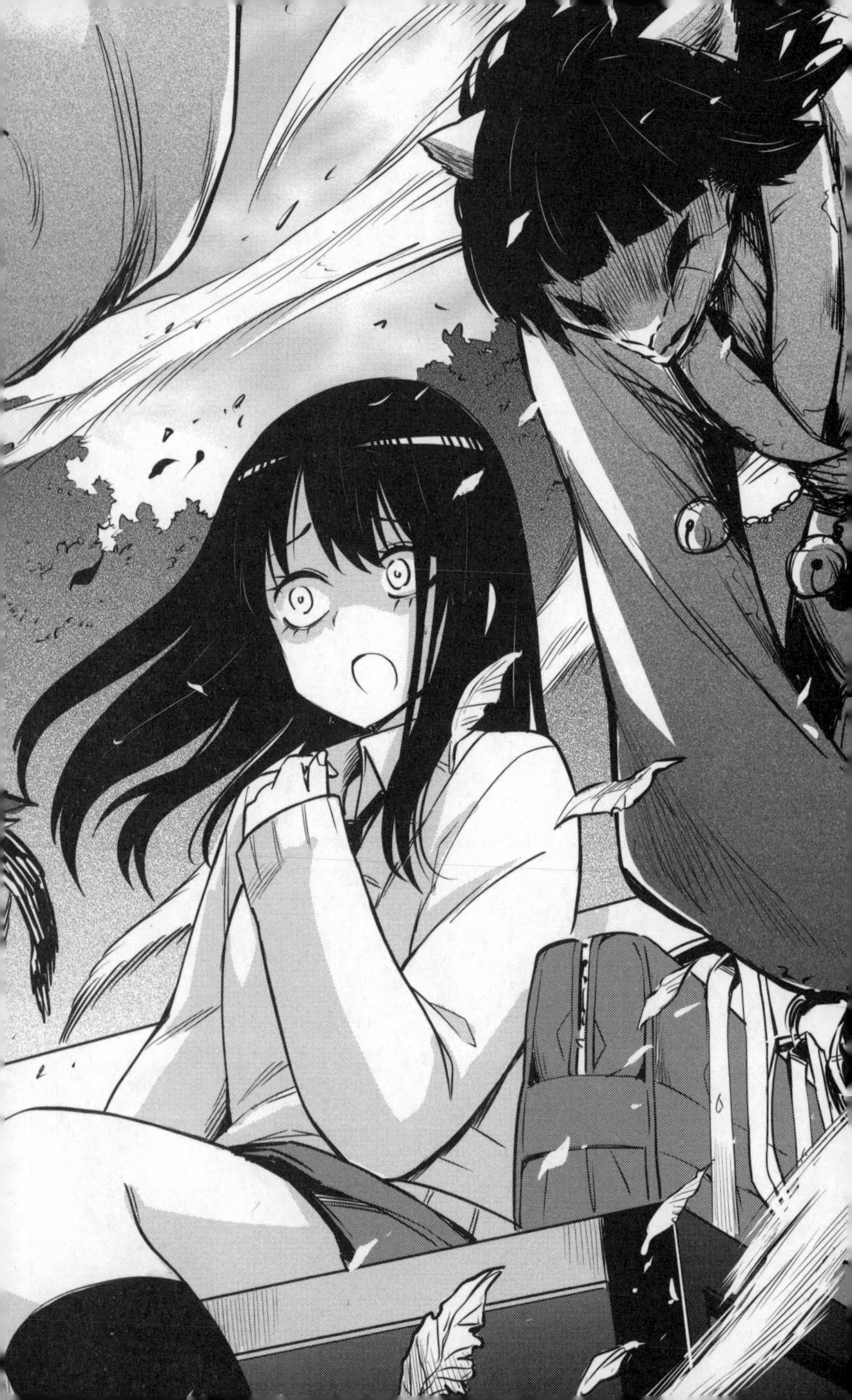

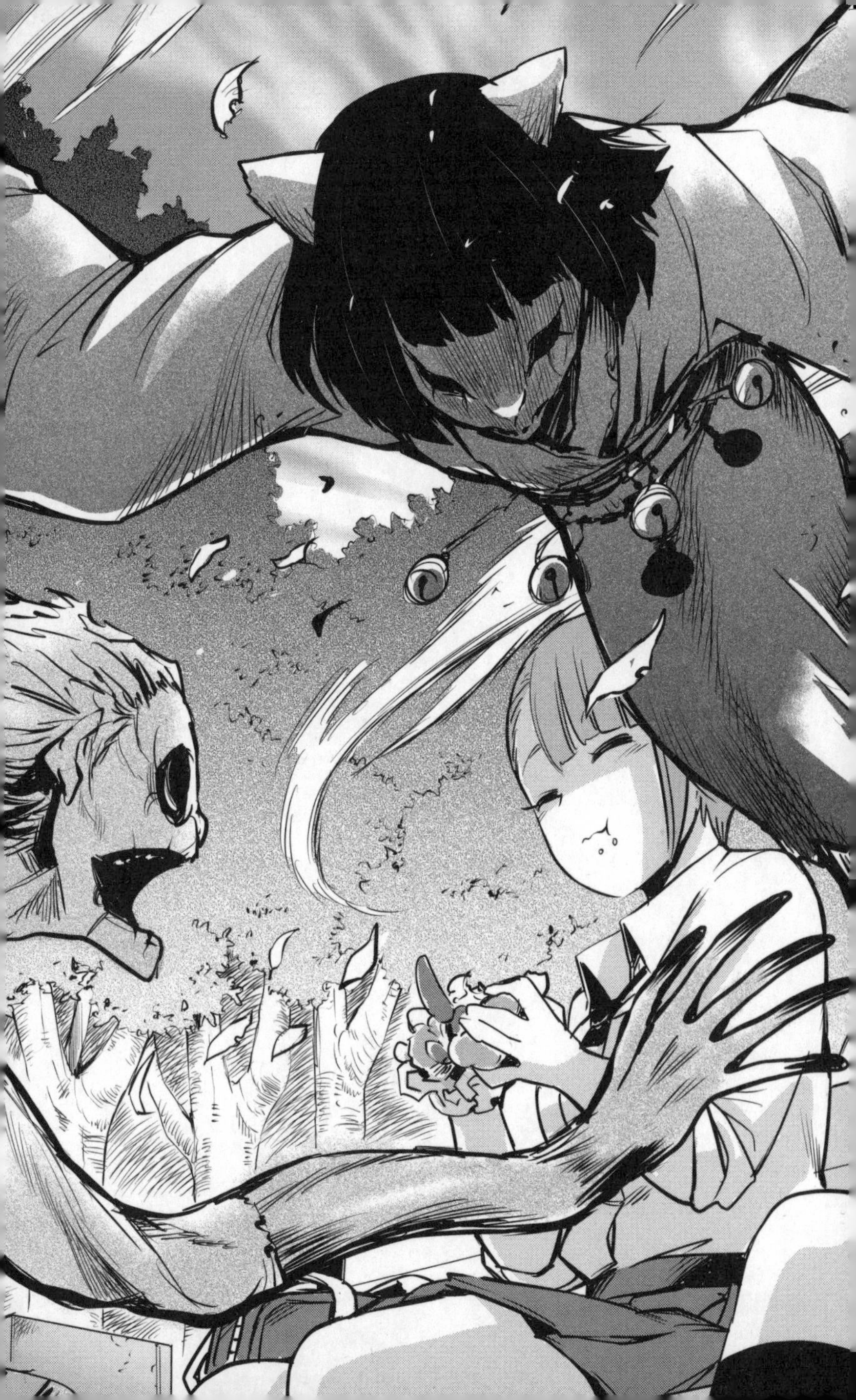

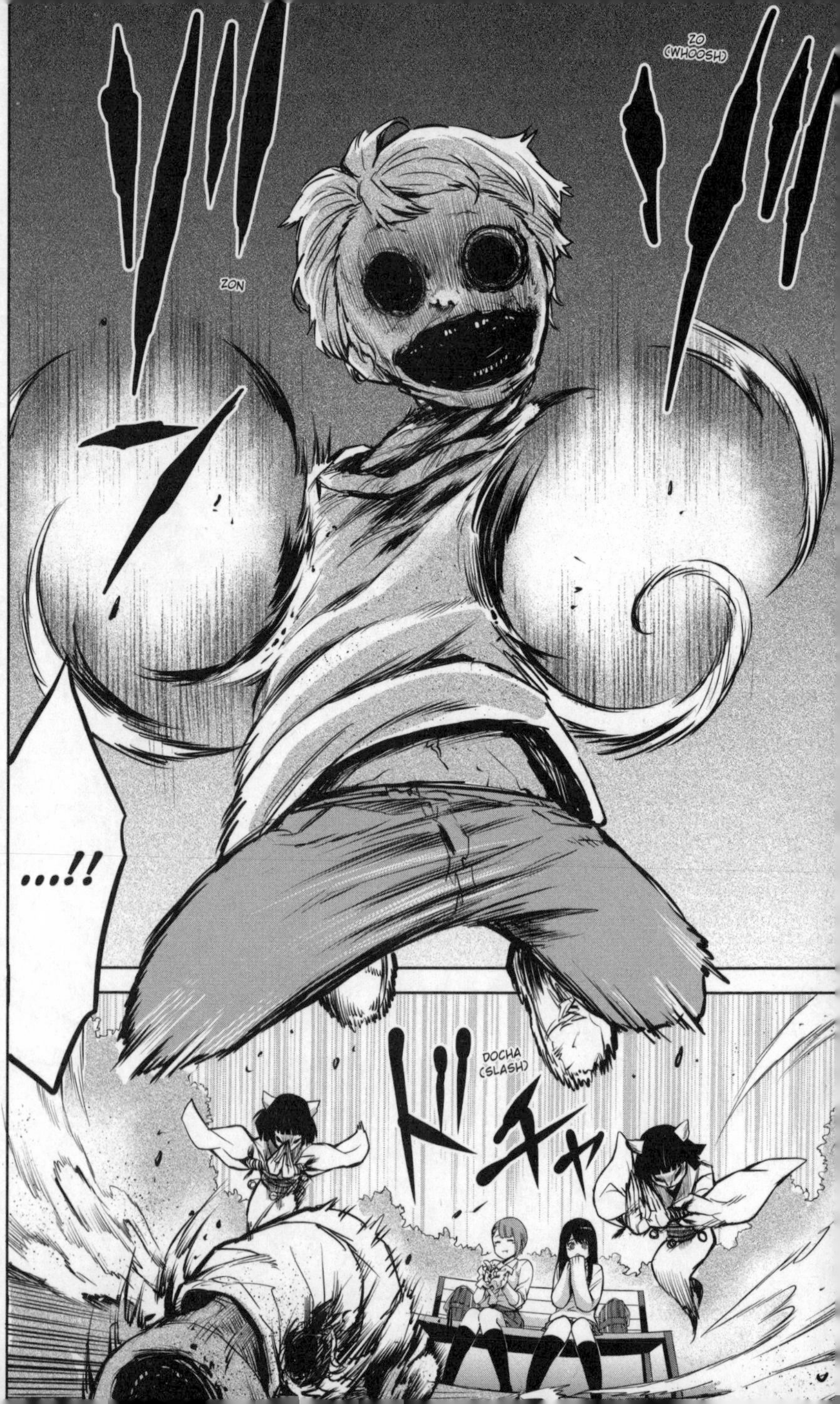
ZO
(WHOOSH)
ZON
...!!
DOCHA
(SLASH)

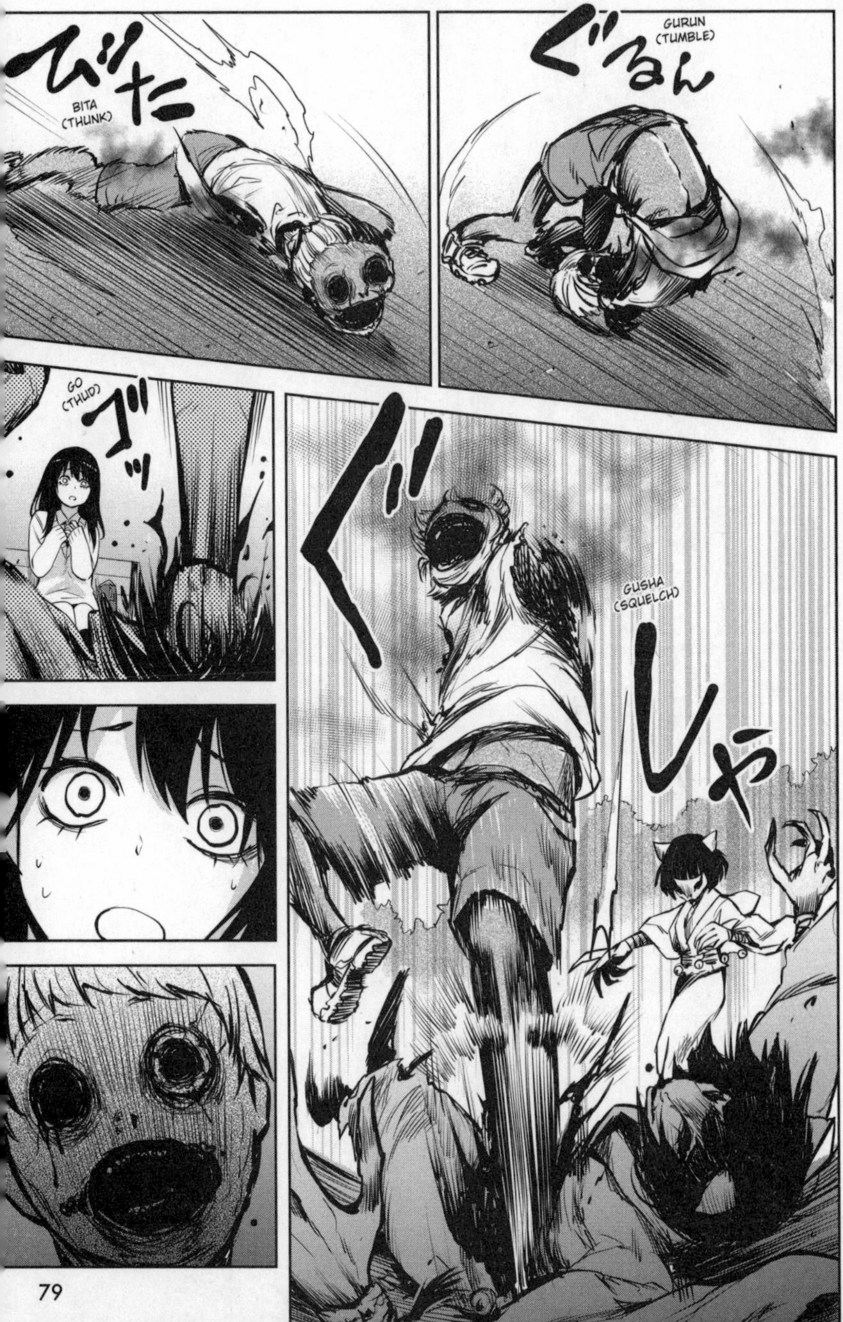
GURUN (TUMBLE)
ぐるん
びたっ
BITA (THUNK)
ぐしゃ
GUSHA (SQUELCH)
GO (THUD)
ゴッ

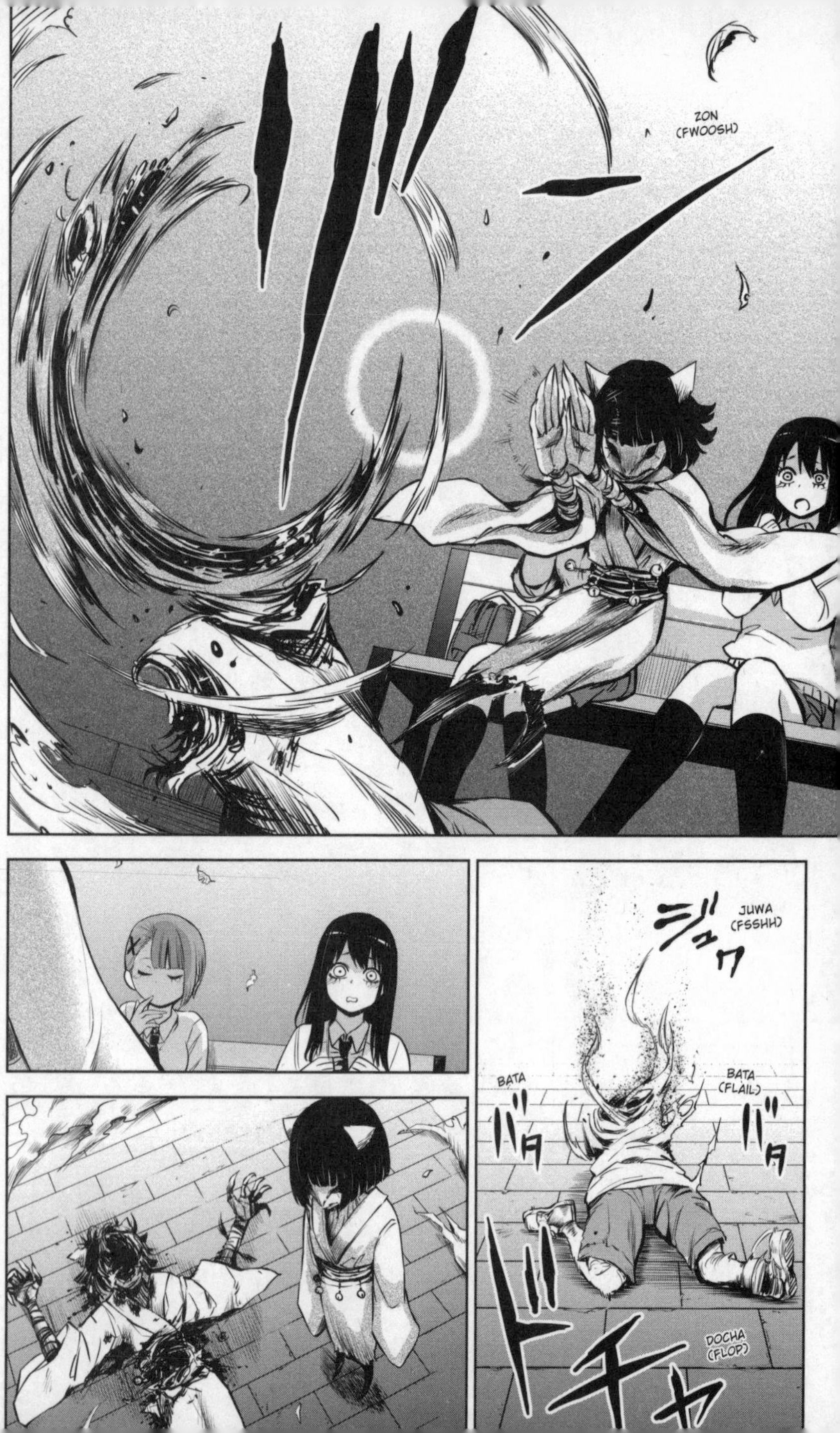

ZON
(FWOOSH)
ジュワ
JUWA
(FSSHH)
BATA
(FLAIL)
バタ
BATA
バタ
DOCHA
(FLOP)
ドチャ

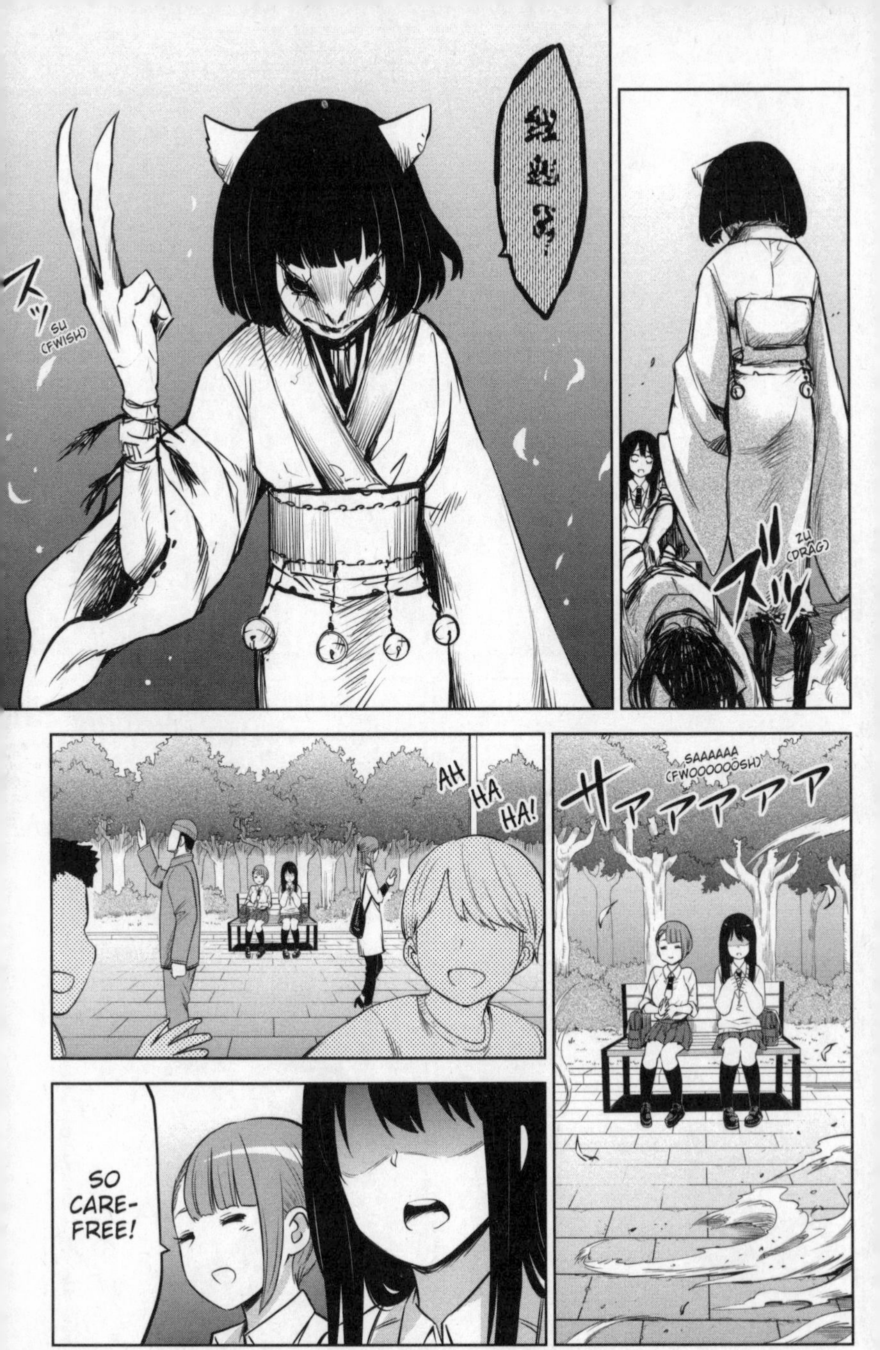
ズッ
ZU
(DRAG)
スッ
SU
(FWISH)
サァァァァァ
SAAAAAA
(FWOOOOOOSH)
AH HA HA!
SO CARE-FREE!

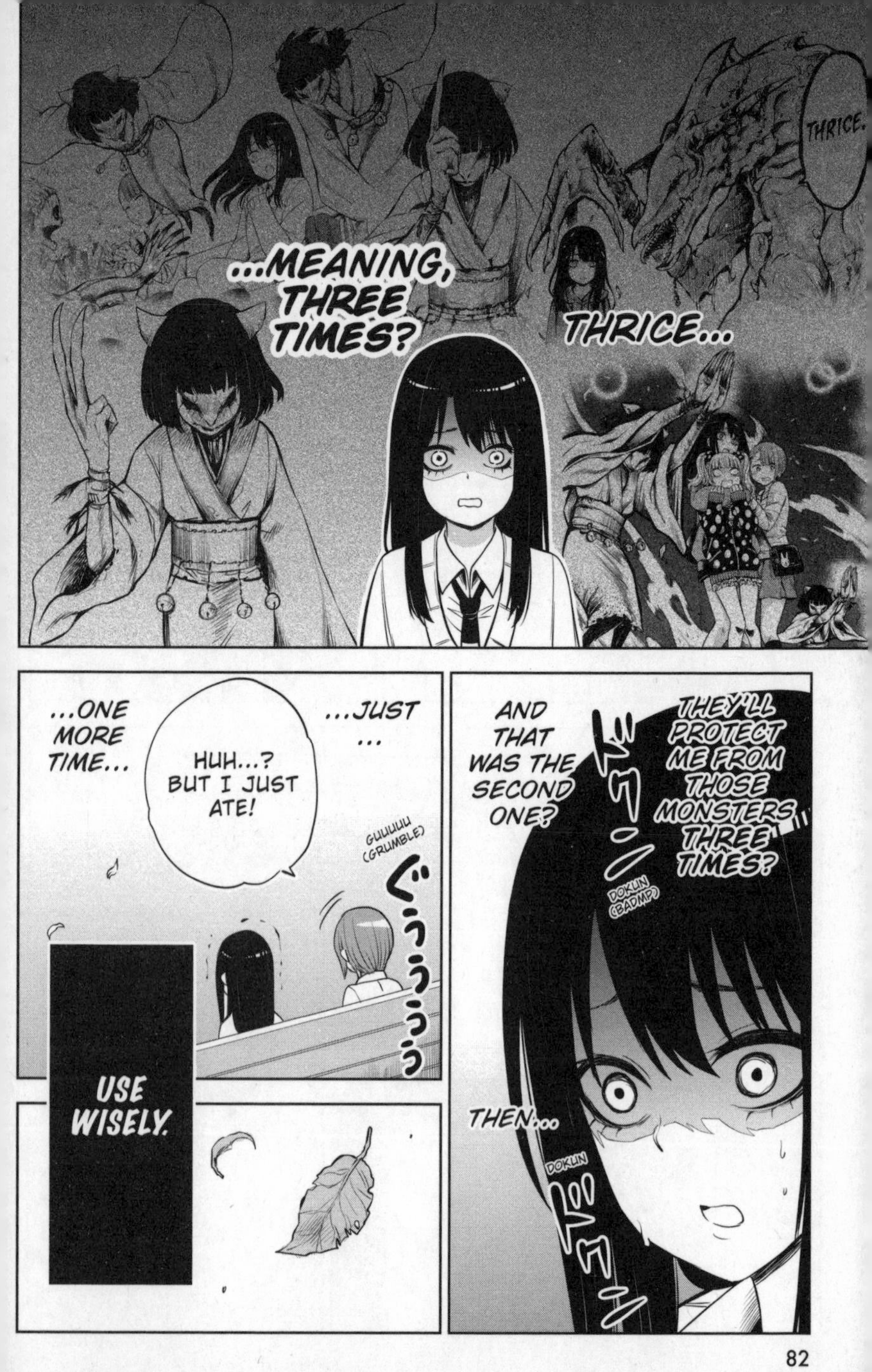
THRICE.
THRICE...
...MEANING, THREE TIMES?
THEY'LL PROTECT ME FROM THOSE MONSTERS THREE TIMES?
DOKUN (BADMP)
AND THAT WAS THE SECOND ONE?
THEN...
DOKUN
...JUST ...
GUUUUU (GRUMBLE)
HUH...? BUT I JUST ATE!
...ONE MORE TIME...
USE WISELY.

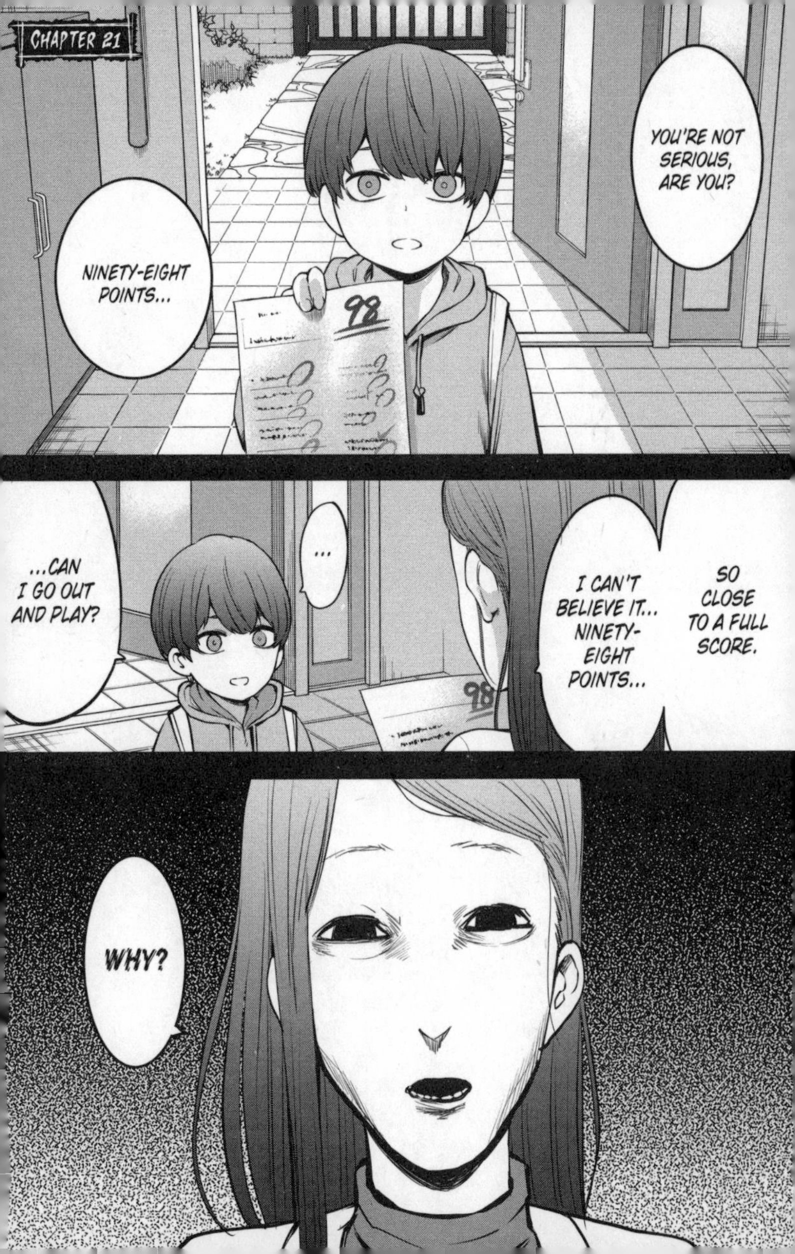
CHAPTER 21
YOU'RE NOT SERIOUS, ARE YOU?
NINETY-EIGHT POINTS...
SO CLOSE TO A FULL SCORE.
I CAN'T BELIEVE IT... NINETY-EIGHT POINTS...
...
...CAN I GO OUT AND PLAY?
WHY?

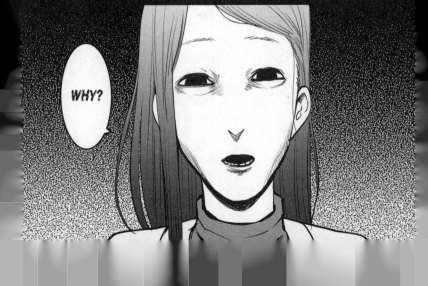

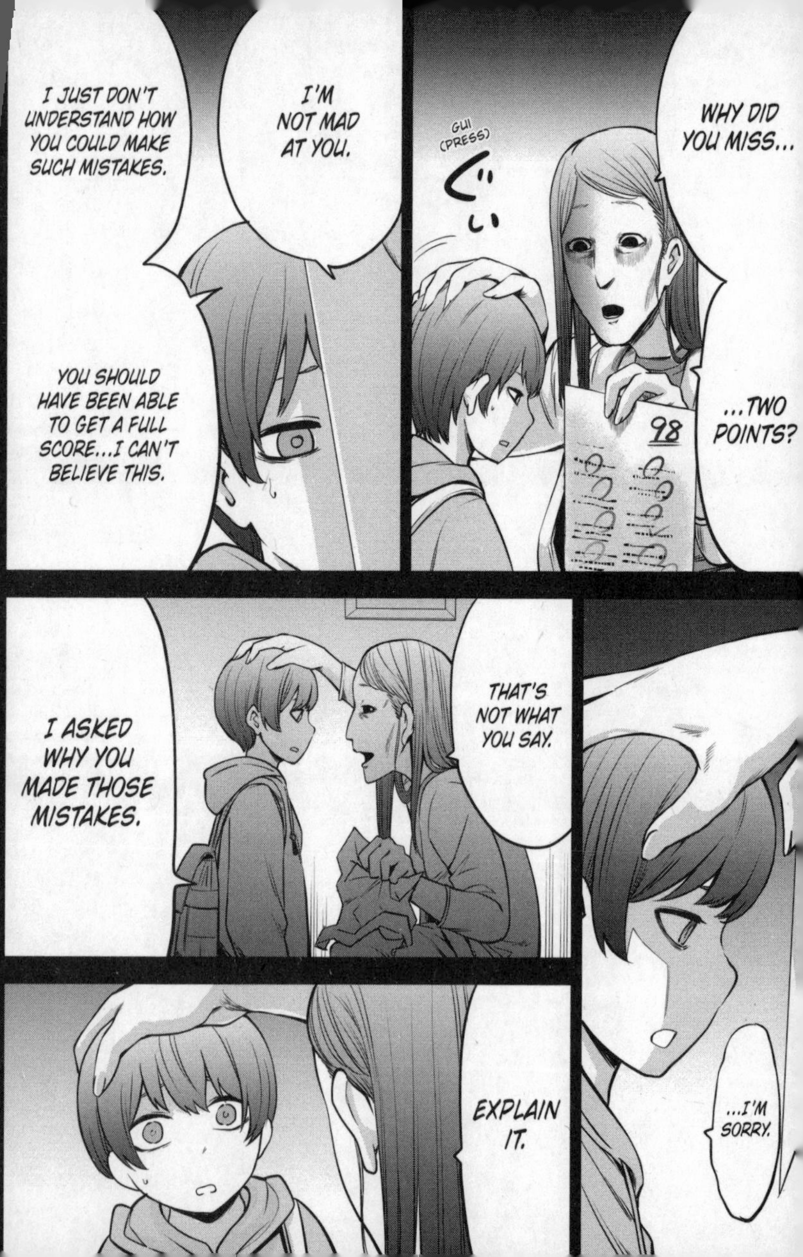
WHY DID YOU MISS...
GUI (PRESS)
ぐい
...TWO POINTS?
98
I'M NOT MAD AT YOU.
I JUST DON'T UNDERSTAND HOW YOU COULD MAKE SUCH MISTAKES.
YOU SHOULD HAVE BEEN ABLE TO GET A FULL SCORE...I CAN'T BELIEVE THIS.
...I'M SORRY.
THAT'S NOT WHAT YOU SAY.
I ASKED WHY YOU MADE THOSE MISTAKES.
EXPLAIN IT.

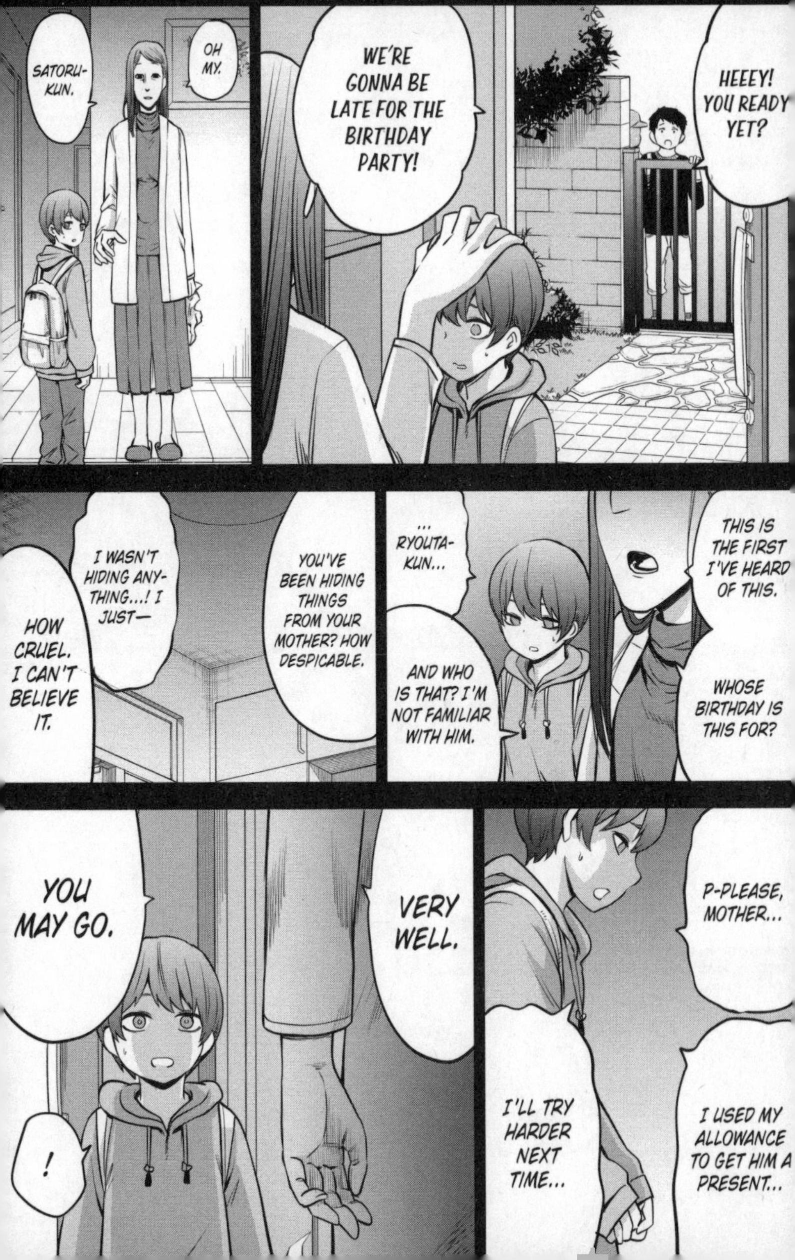
HEEEY! YOU READY YET?
WE'RE GONNA BE LATE FOR THE BIRTHDAY PARTY!
OH MY.
SATORU-KUN.
THIS IS THE FIRST I'VE HEARD OF THIS.
WHOSE BIRTHDAY IS THIS FOR?
... RYOUTA-KUN...
AND WHO IS THAT? I'M NOT FAMILIAR WITH HIM.
YOU'VE BEEN HIDING THINGS FROM YOUR MOTHER? HOW DESPICABLE.
I WASN'T HIDING ANY-THING...! I JUST—
HOW CRUEL. I CAN'T BELIEVE IT.
P-PLEASE, MOTHER...
I USED MY ALLOWANCE TO GET HIM A PRESENT...
I'LL TRY HARDER NEXT TIME...
VERY WELL.
YOU MAY GO.
!

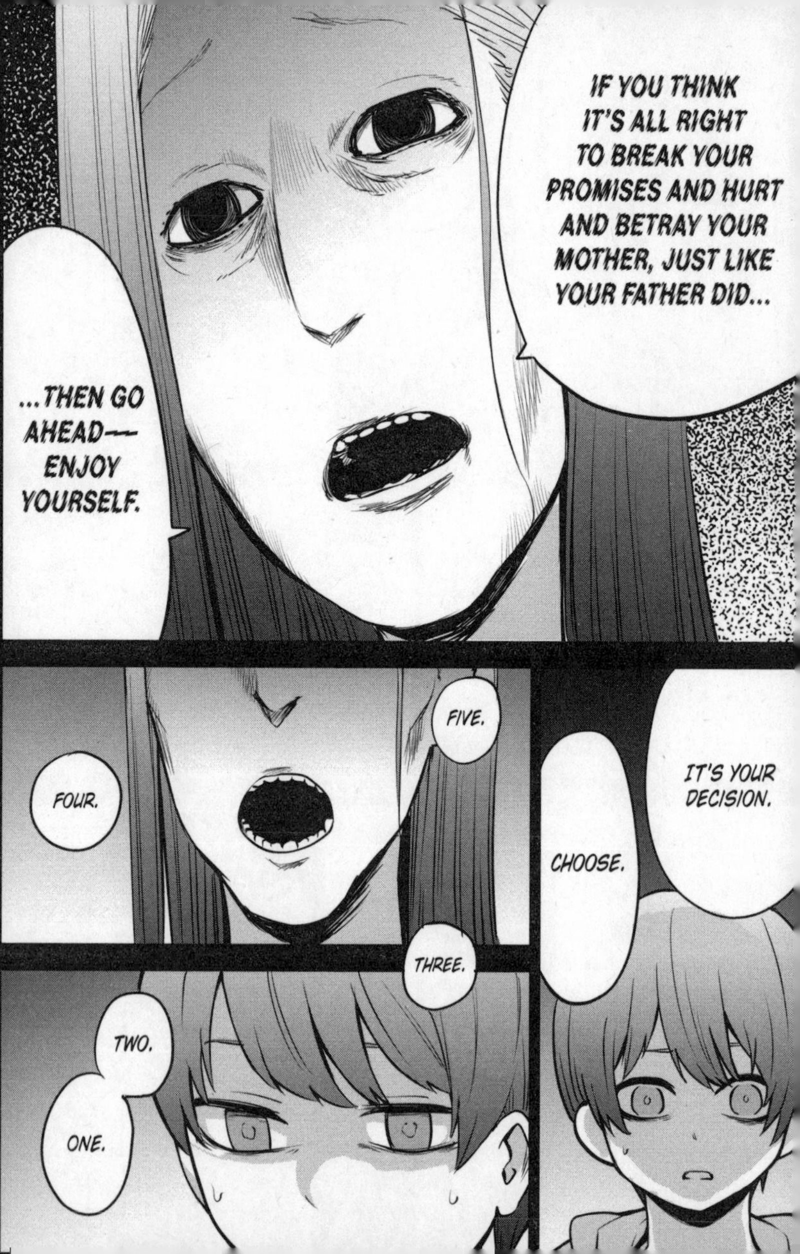
IF YOU THINK IT'S ALL RIGHT TO BREAK YOUR PROMISES AND HURT AND BETRAY YOUR MOTHER, JUST LIKE YOUR FATHER DID...
...THEN GO AHEAD—ENJOY YOURSELF.
IT'S YOUR DECISION.
CHOOSE.
FIVE.
FOUR.
THREE.
TWO.
ONE.

...I CAN'T GO TODAY.

SORRY...

GACHAN (SLAM)

YOU'RE NOT ALLOWED TO PLAY...

...WITH THOSE BOYS ANYMORE.

...ZEN.

YOU MADE THE RIGHT CHOICE...

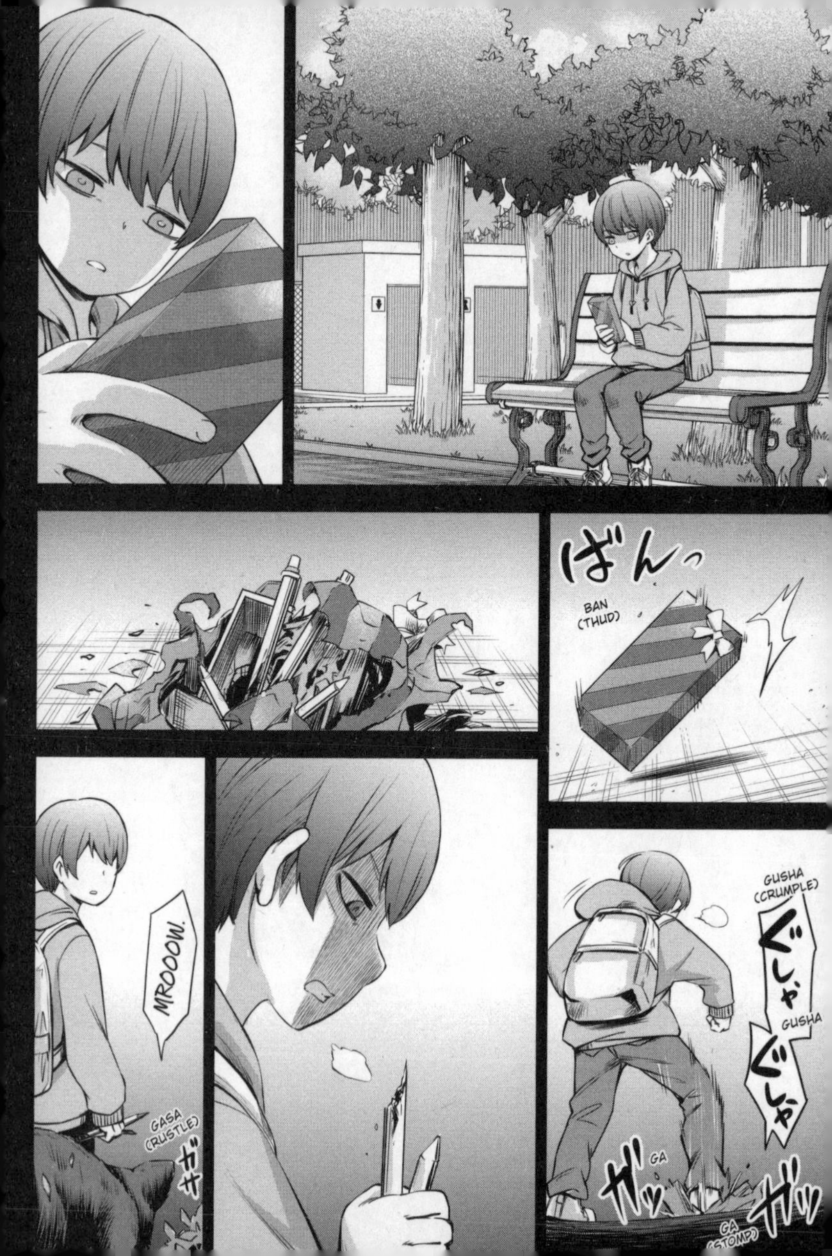

ばんっ
BAN (THUD)
GUSHA (CRUMPLE)
ぐしゃ
GUSHA
ぐしゃ
GA
ガッ
GA (STOMP)
ガッ
MROOOW.
GASA (RUSTLE)
ガサ

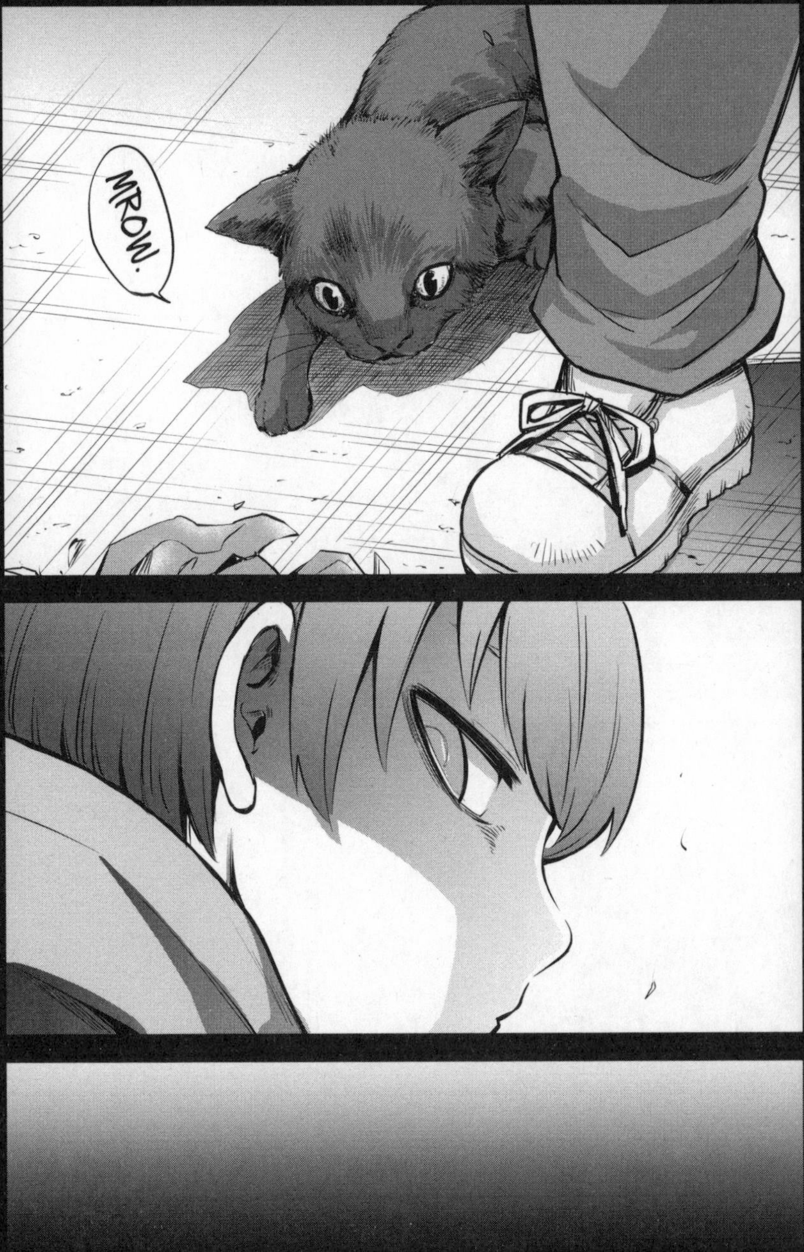
MROW.

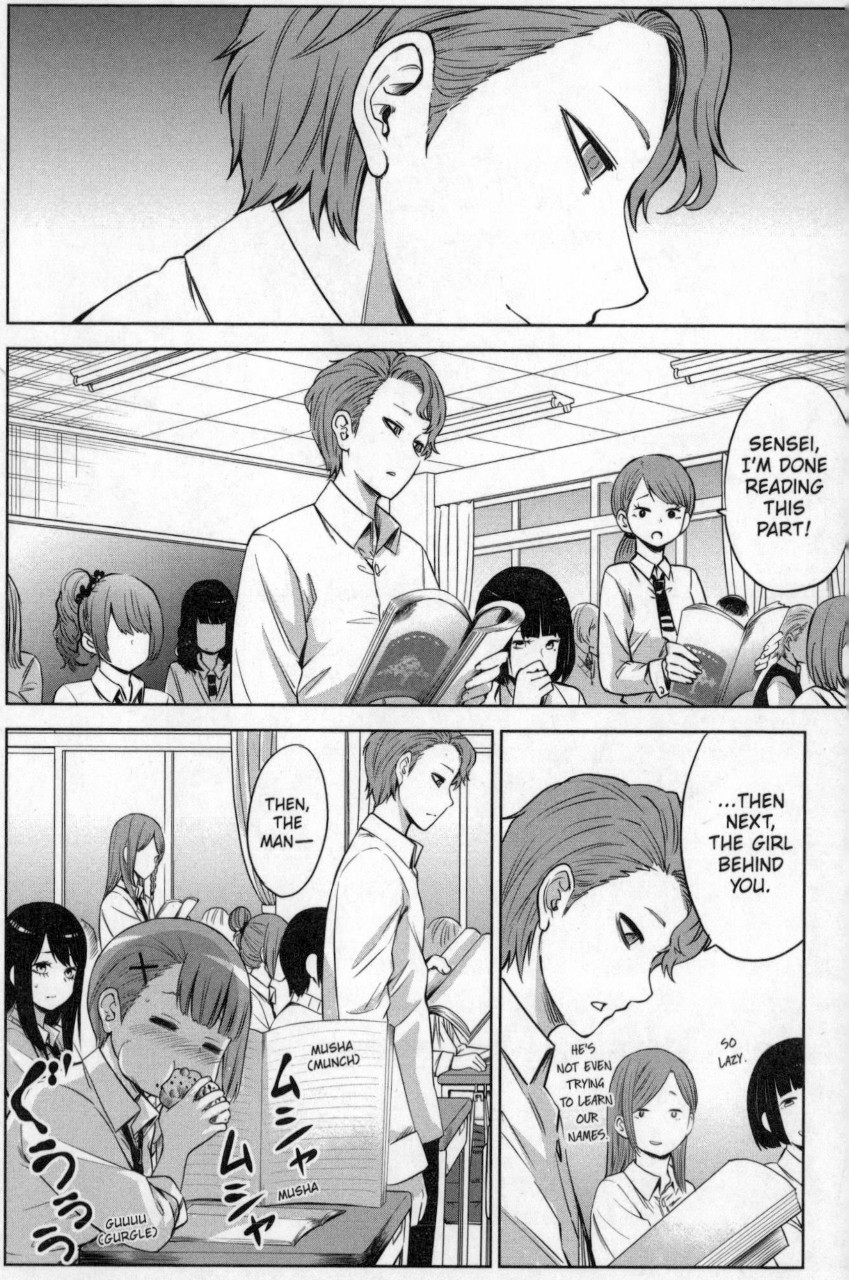

SENSEI, I'M DONE READING THIS PART!
...THEN NEXT, THE GIRL BEHIND YOU.
SO LAZY.
HE'S NOT EVEN TRYING TO LEARN OUR NAMES.
THEN, THE MAN—
ムシャ
MUSHA (MUNCH)
ムシャ
MUSHA
ぐううう
GUUUU (GURGLE)

SURE, A BOY-FRIEND.

HUH...? A BOY-FRIEND?

SORRY, HANA... I HAVE PLANS TODAY.

GOOD-BYE, SENSEI!

SU— (F.WISH)

スッ

HE MUST BE SHAKING UP THE WORKPLACE.

DON'T YOU THINK HE LEAVES SUPER EARLY?

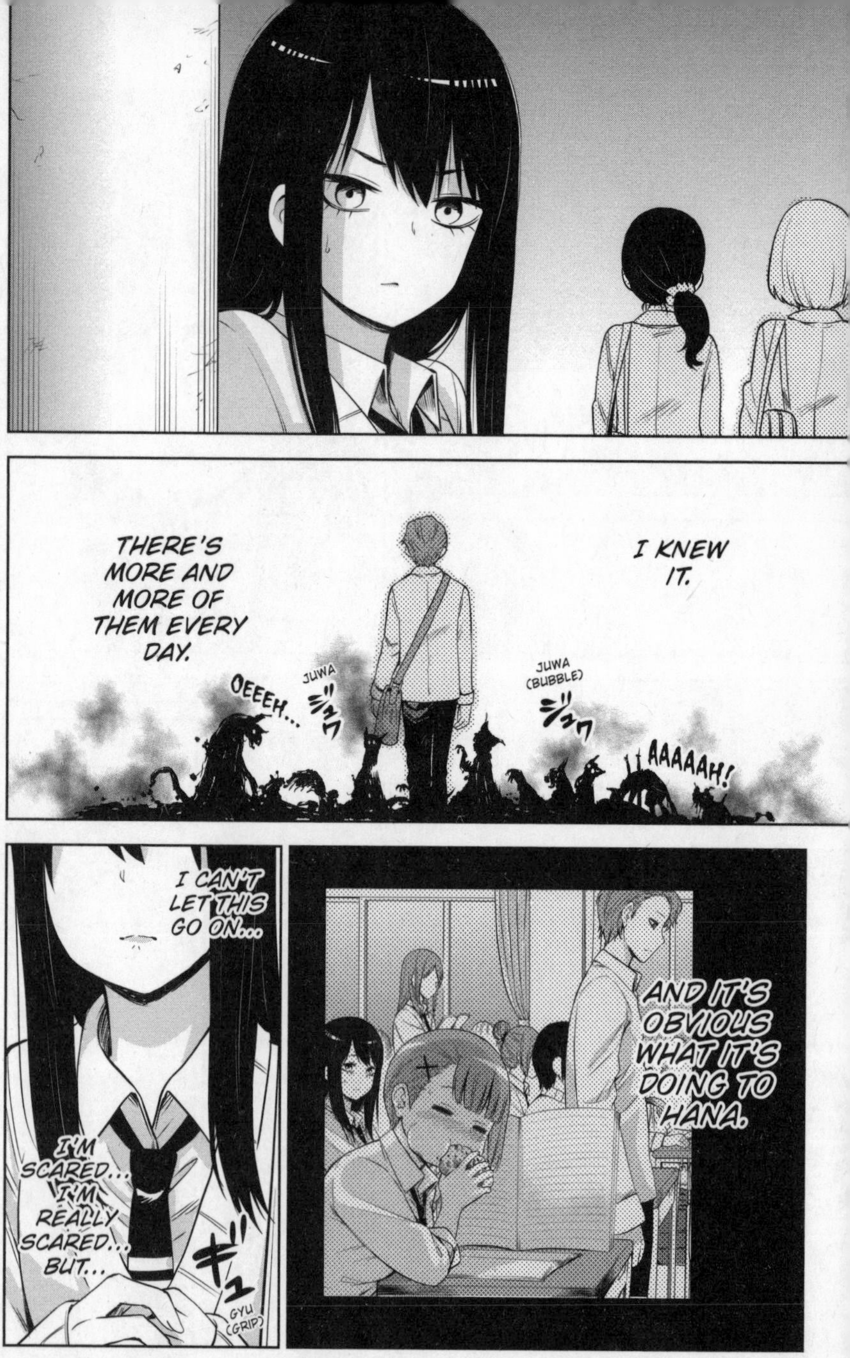
I KNEW IT.
THERE'S MORE AND MORE OF THEM EVERY DAY.
AAAAAH!
ジュワ
JUWA (BUBBLE)
ジュワ
JUWA
OEEEH...
AND IT'S OBVIOUS WHAT IT'S DOING TO HANA.
I CAN'T LET THIS GO ON...
I'M SCARED... I'M REALLY SCARED... BUT...
ギュ
GYU (GRIP)

...I DON'T WANT HANA...

...TO SUFFER.

GU (CLENCH)

GYORO (GLARE)

GYORO (GLARE)

...IT WILL NOTICE ME!!

IF I LOOK AT HIM...

GOKU (GULP)

ZUZU (CREEP)

ZU

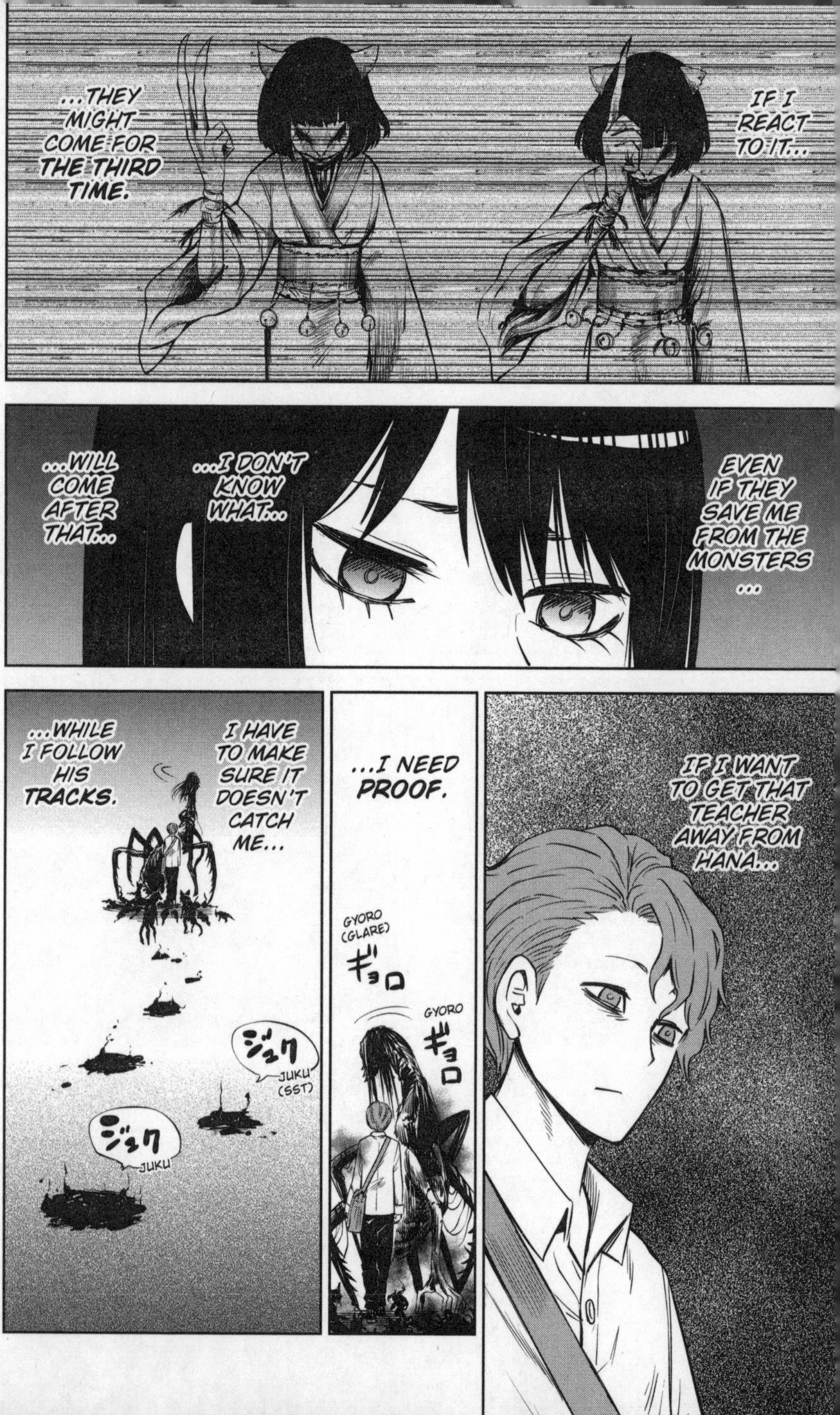
IF I REACT TO IT...
...THEY MIGHT COME FOR THE THIRD TIME.
EVEN IF THEY SAVE ME FROM THE MONSTERS...
...I DON'T KNOW WHAT...
...WILL COME AFTER THAT...
IF I WANT TO GET THAT TEACHER AWAY FROM HANA...
...I NEED PROOF.
ギョロ
GYORO (GLARE)
ギョロ
GYORO
I HAVE TO MAKE SURE IT DOESN'T CATCH ME...
...WHILE I FOLLOW HIS TRACKS.
ジュク
JUKU (SST)
ジュク
JUKU

IF I DO THAT, HE WON'T BE ABLE TO COME TO SCHOOL ANYMORE.

IF IT LOOKS LIKE HE'S GOING TO DO ANYTHING BAD, I'LL REPORT HIM...

...SO I HAVE TO DO IT...

...BUT ONLY I CAN DO THIS...

I DON'T HAVE ANY SPECIAL POWERS— I JUST SEE THINGS...

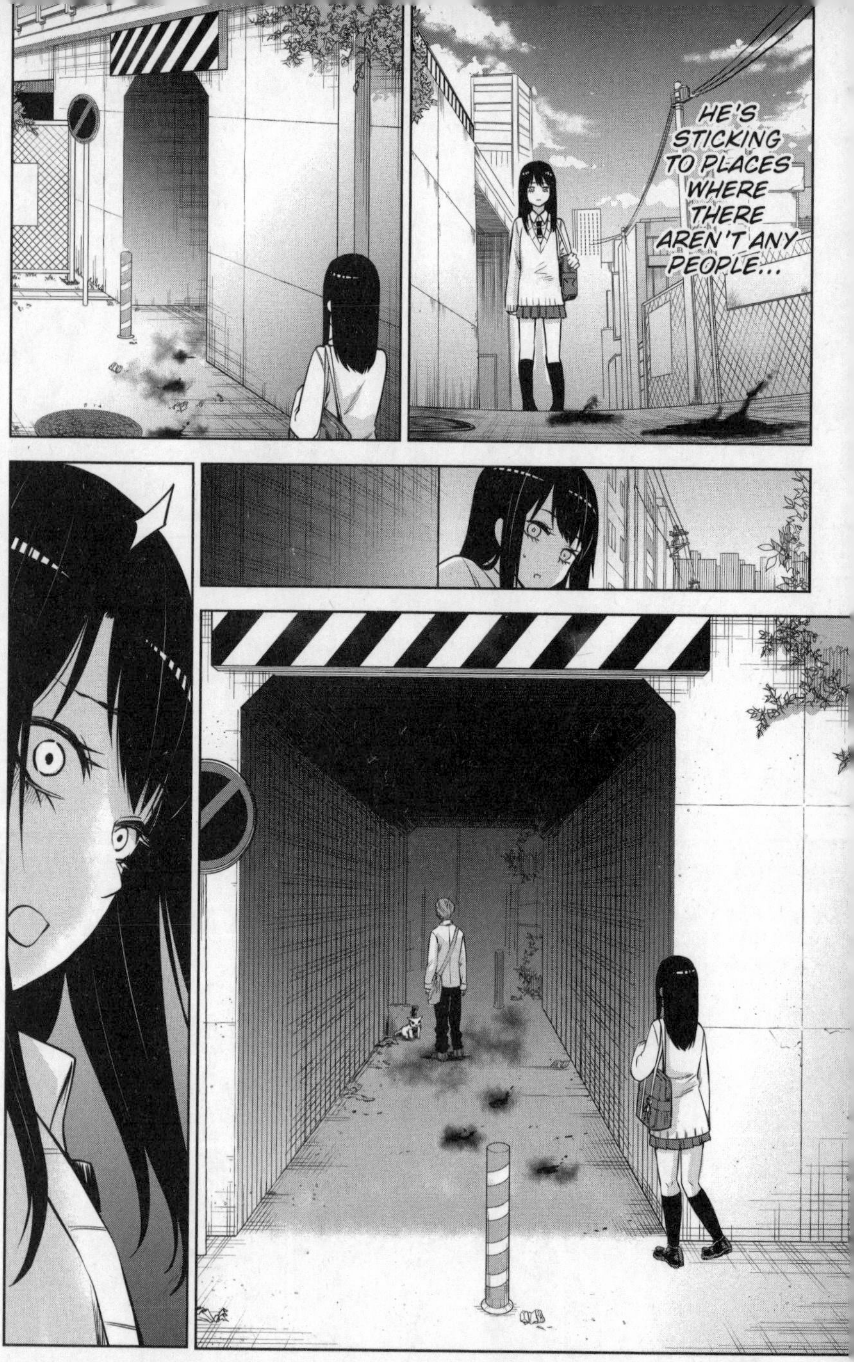
HE'S STICKING TO PLACES WHERE THERE AREN'T ANY PEOPLE...

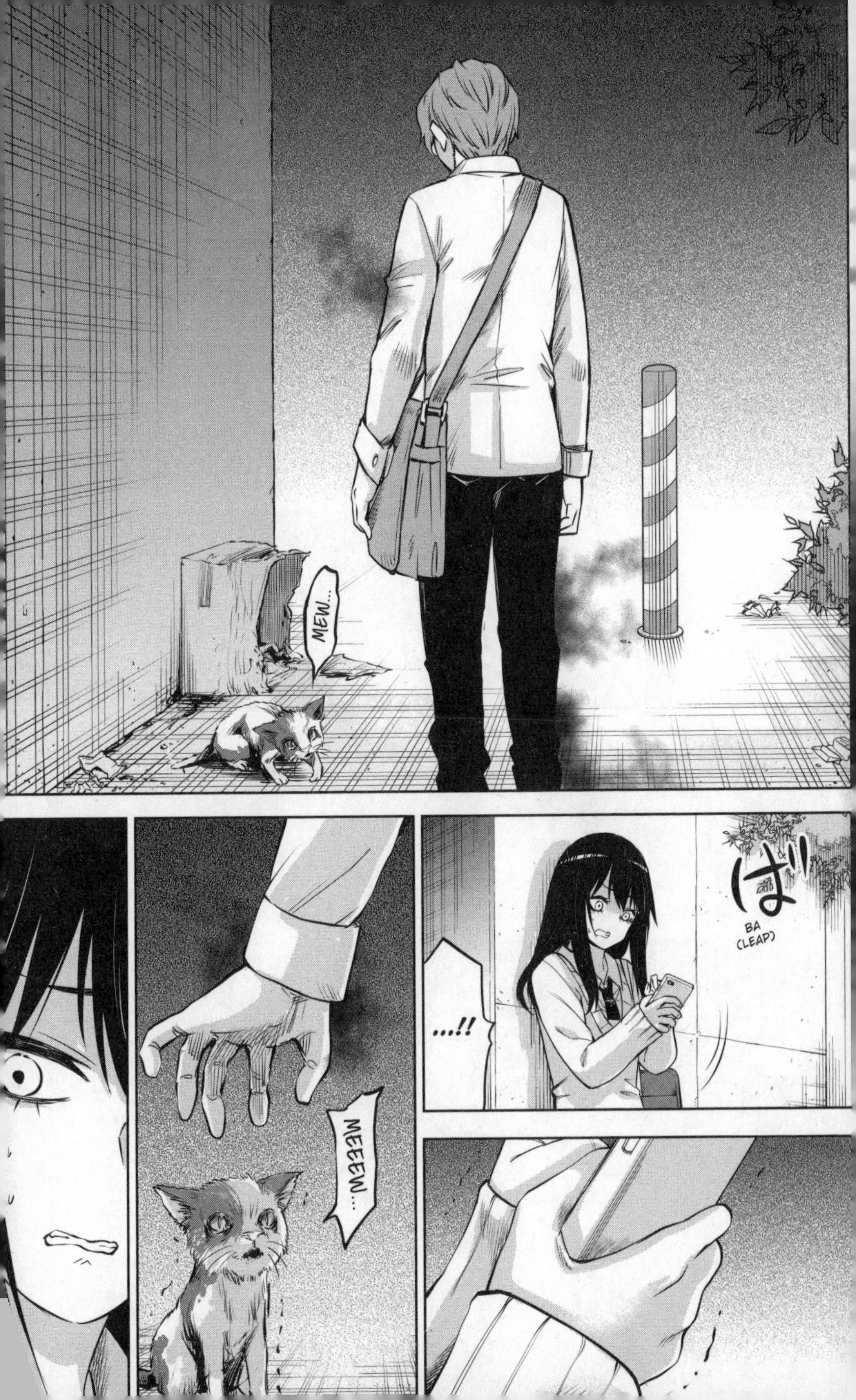
MEW...
ば
BA (LEAP)
...!!
MEEEW...

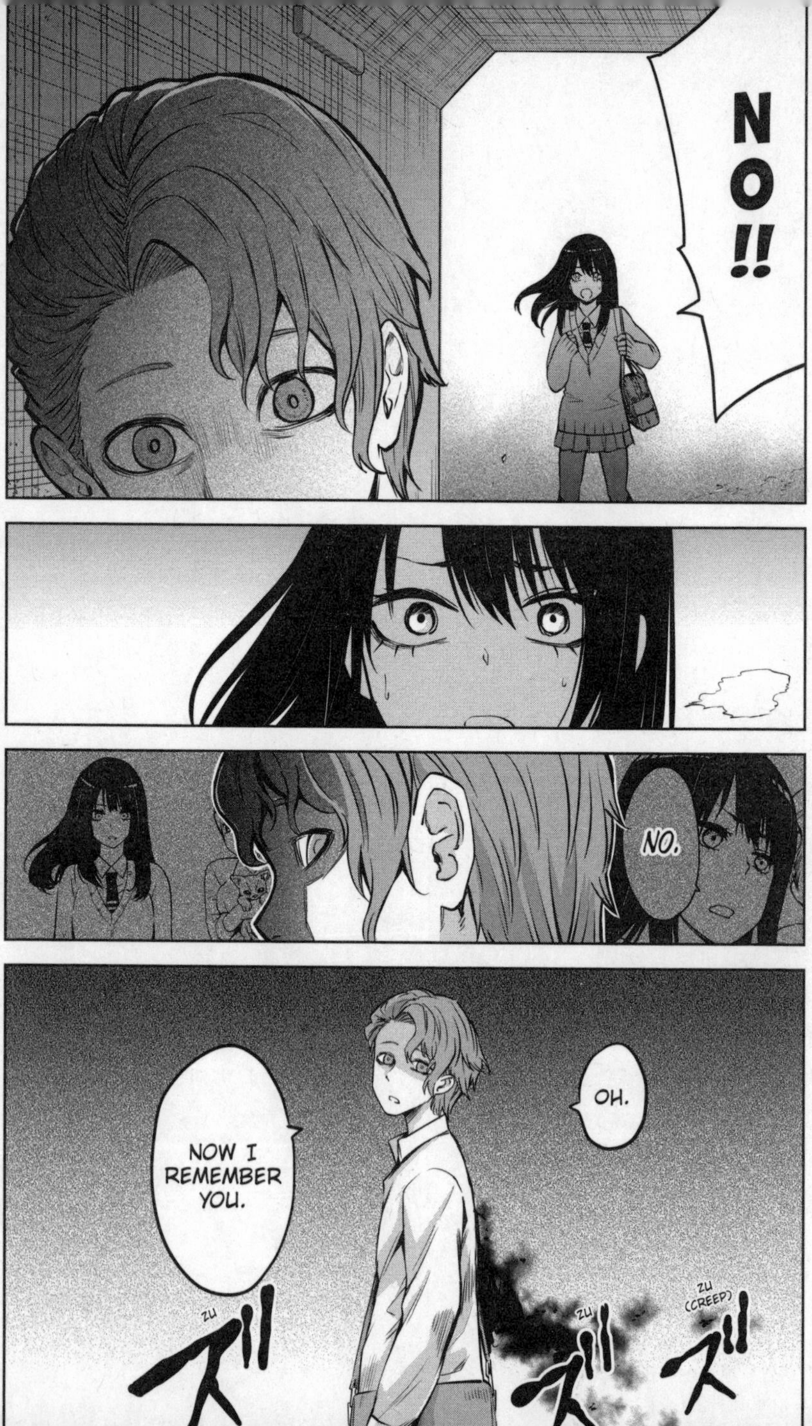
NO!!
NO.
OH.
NOW I REMEMBER YOU.
ZU (CREEP)
ZU
ZU

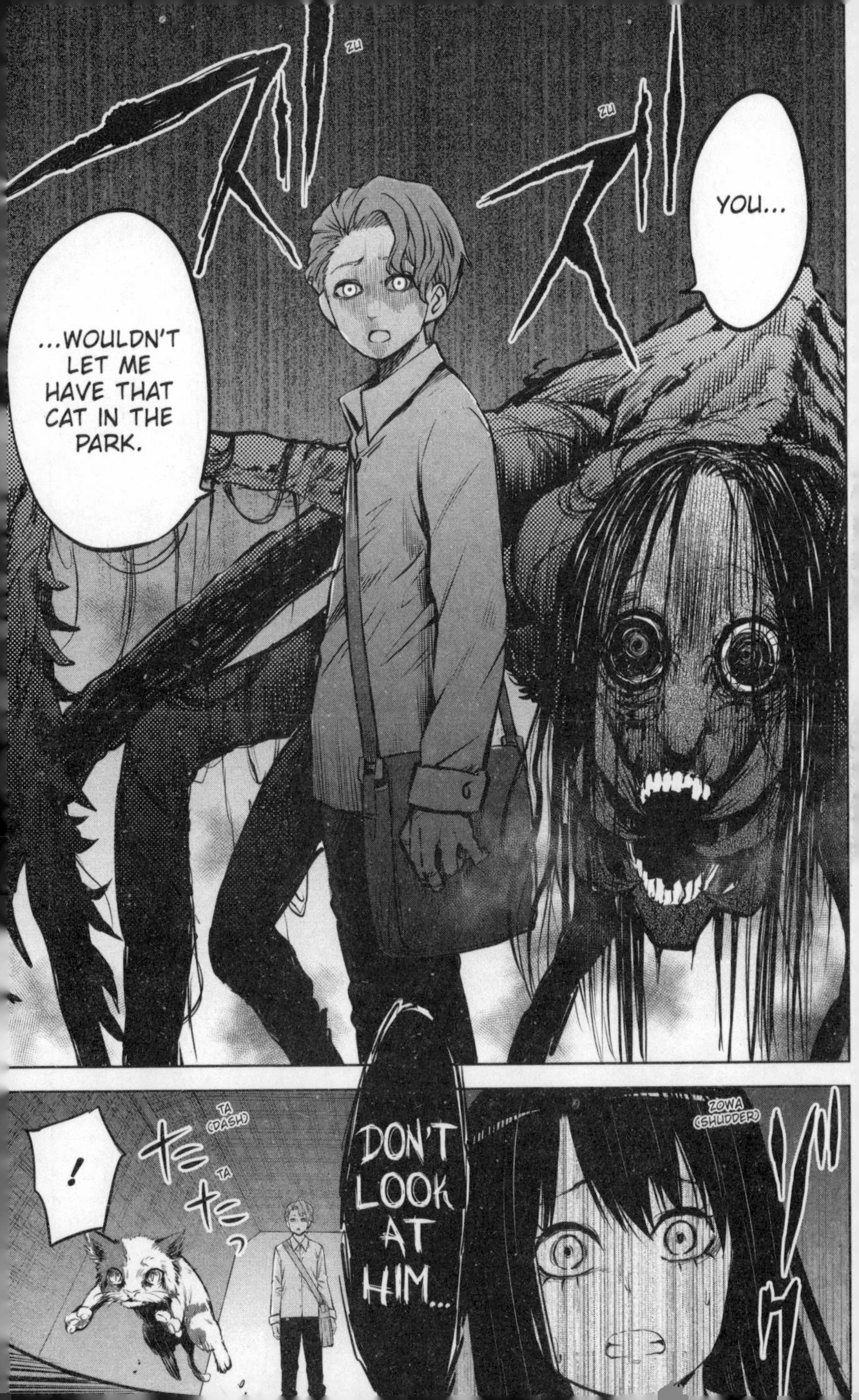
ZU
ZU
YOU...
...WOULDN'T LET ME HAVE THAT CAT IN THE PARK.
ZOWA (SHUDDER)
DON'T LOOK AT HIM...
TA (DASH)
TA
!

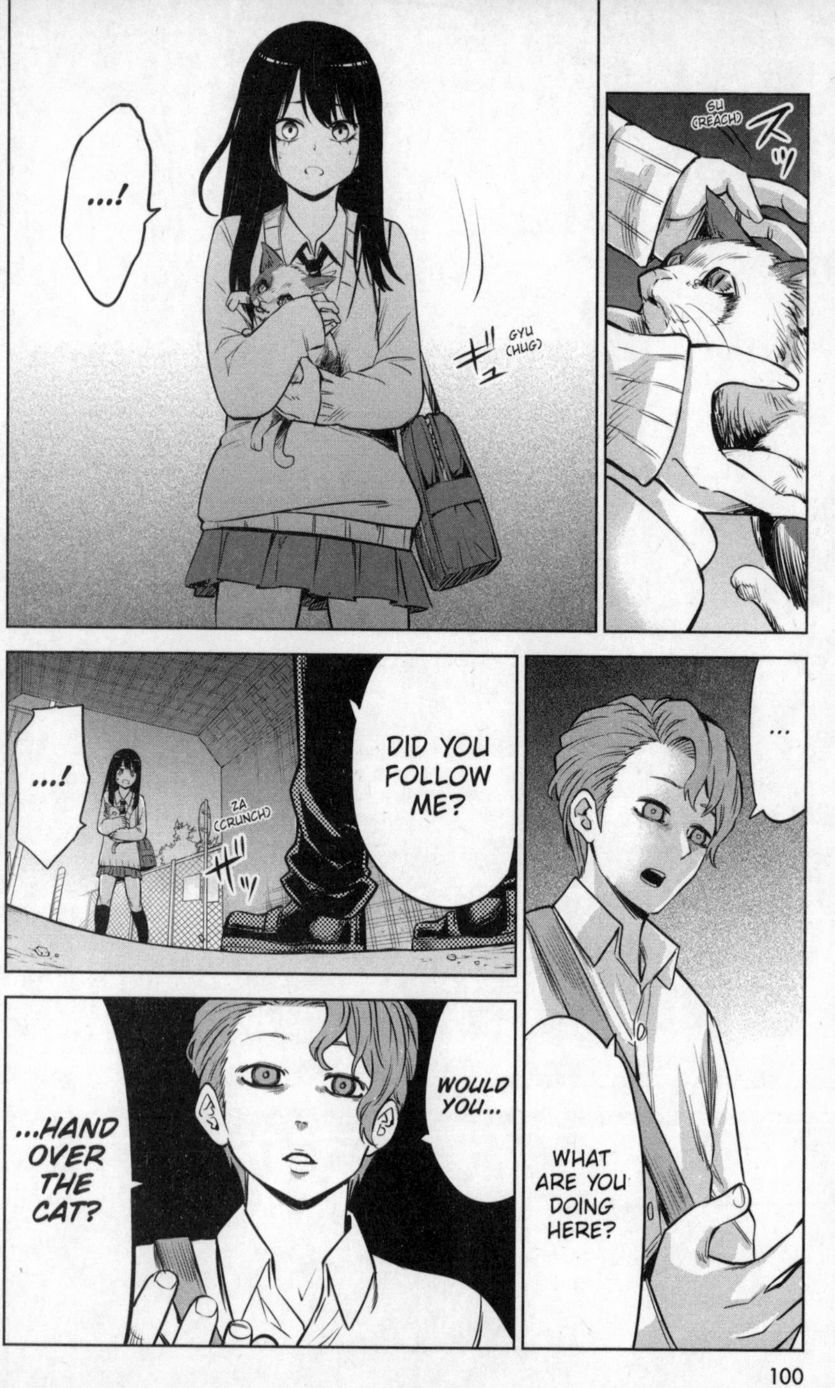
SU (REACH)
スッ
...!
ギュ
GYU (HUG)
...
WHAT ARE YOU DOING HERE?
DID YOU FOLLOW ME?
ZA (CRUNCH)
ザッ
...!
WOULD YOU...
...HAND OVER THE CAT?

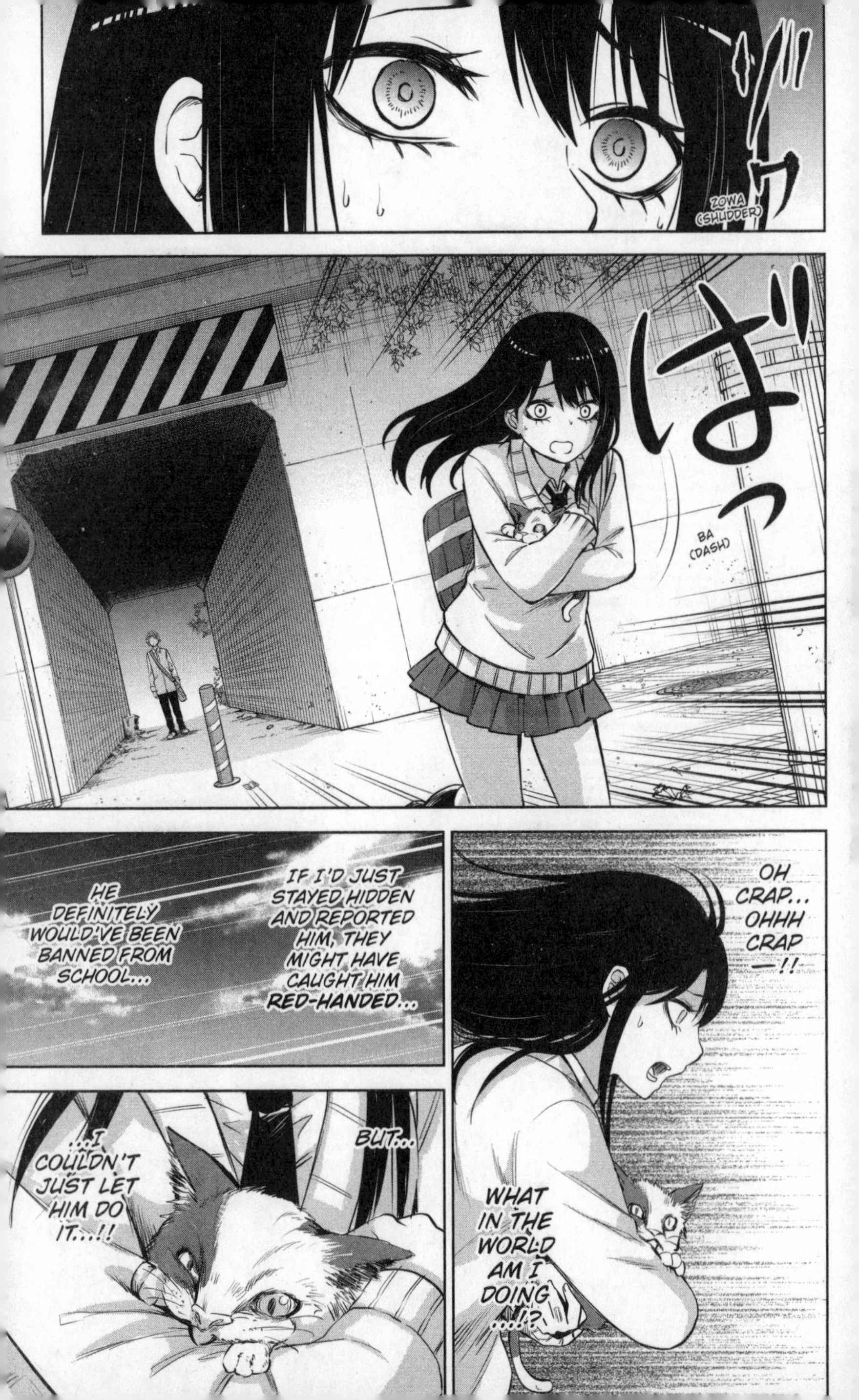
ZOWA (SHUDDER)
ばっ
BA (DASH)
OH CRAP... OHHH CRAP—!!
WHAT IN THE WORLD AM I DOING...!?
IF I'D JUST STAYED HIDDEN AND REPORTED HIM, THEY MIGHT HAVE CAUGHT HIM RED-HANDED...
HE DEFINITELY WOULD'VE BEEN BANNED FROM SCHOOL...
BUT...
...I COULDN'T JUST LET HIM DO IT...!!

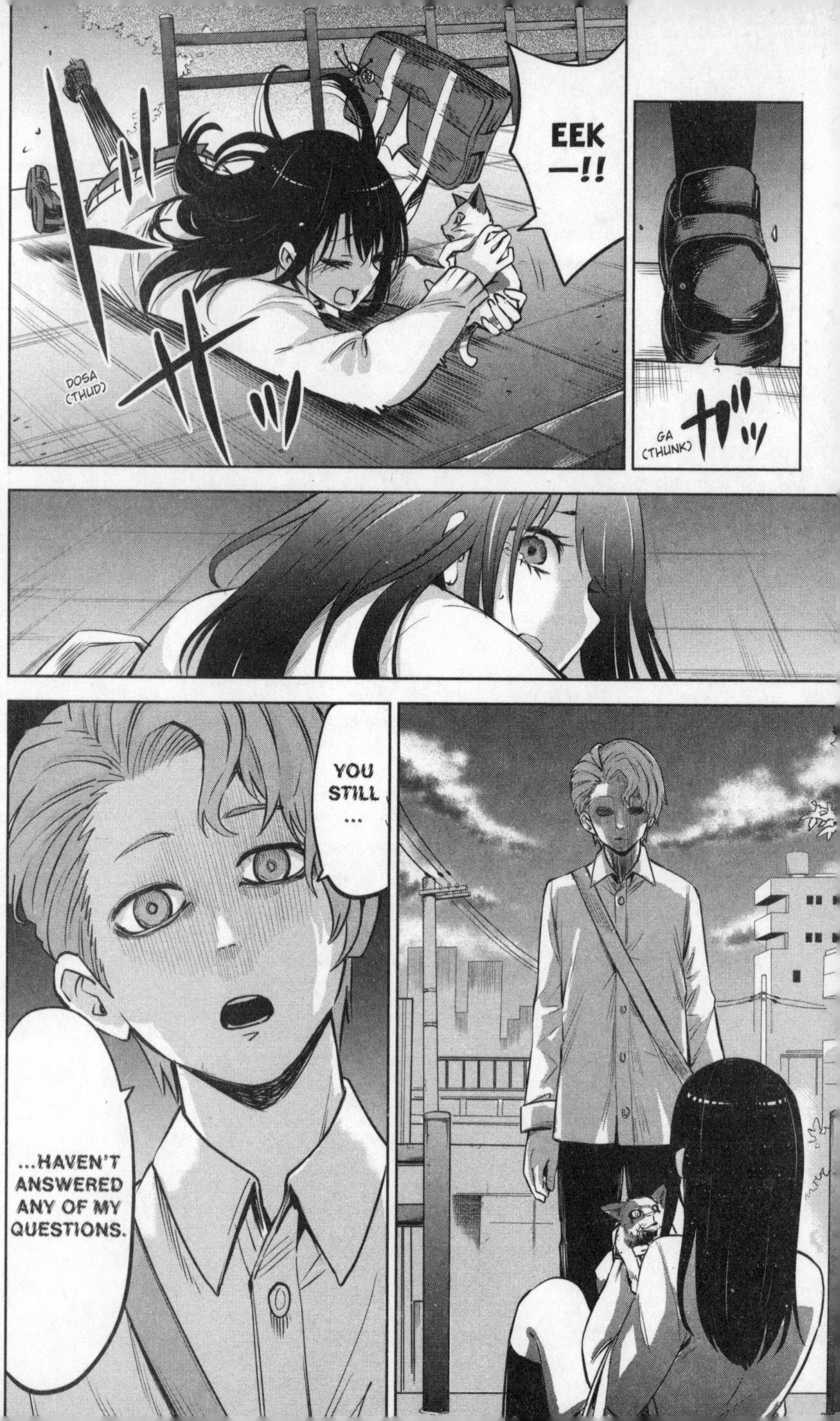
EEK—!!
GA (THUNK)
DOSA (THUD)
YOU STILL...
...HAVEN'T ANSWERED ANY OF MY QUESTIONS.

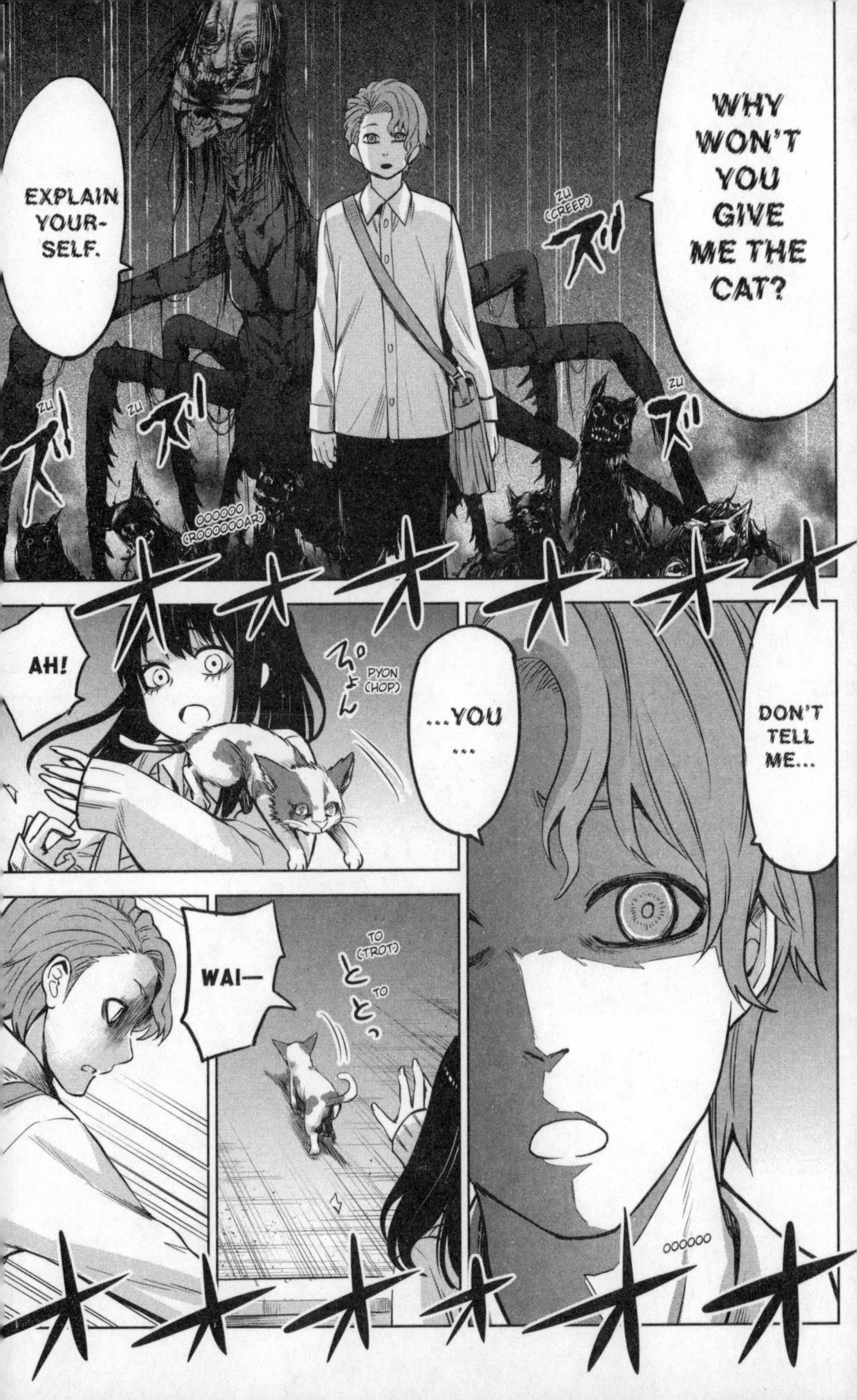
WHY WON'T YOU GIVE ME THE CAT?
ZU (CREEP)
EXPLAIN YOURSELF.
ZU
ZU
ZU
OOOOOO (ROOOOOOAR)
DON'T TELL ME...
...YOU ...
OOOOOO
AH!
PYON (HOP)
WAI—
TO (TROT)
TO

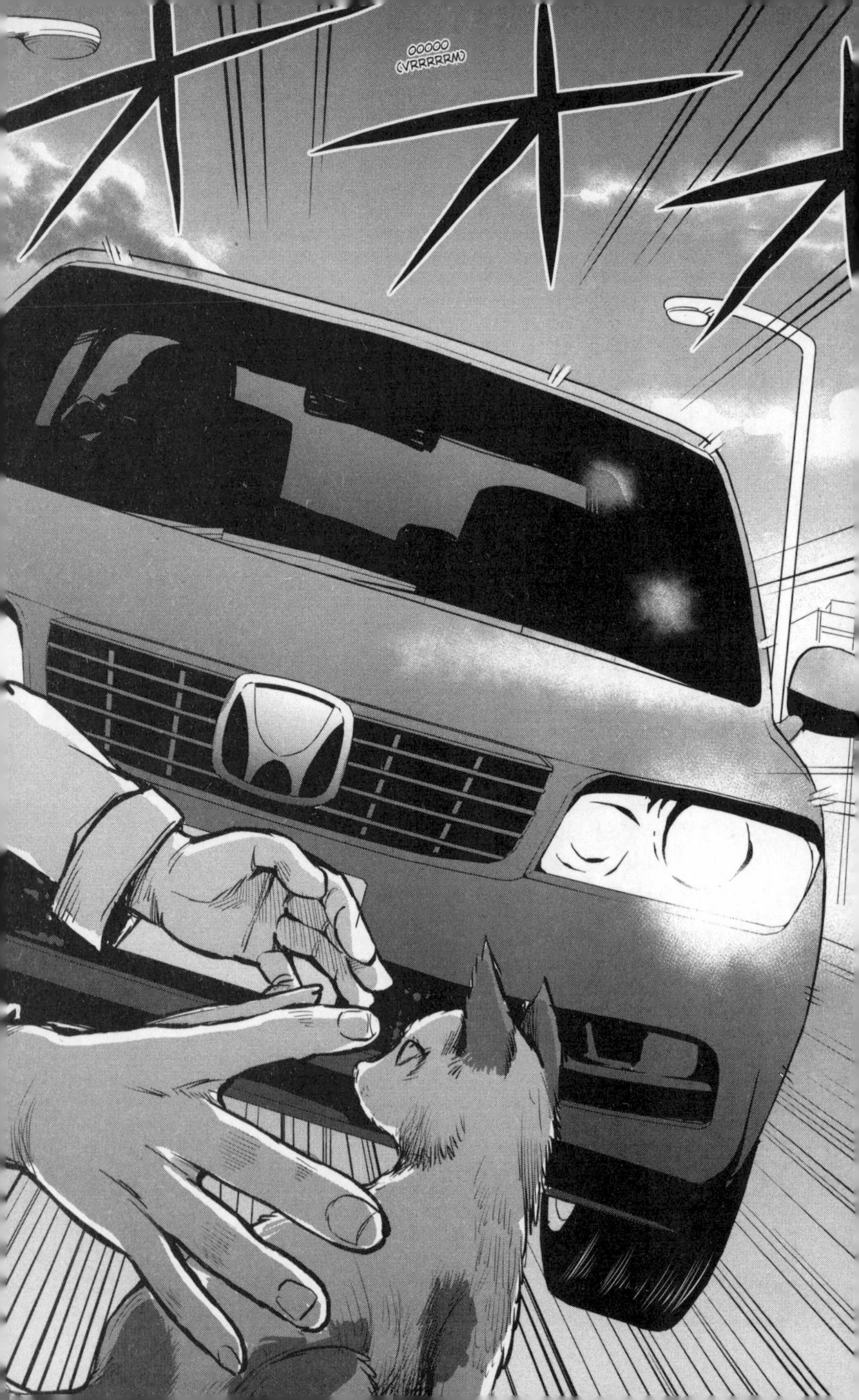
オオオ
OOOOO (VRRRRRM)

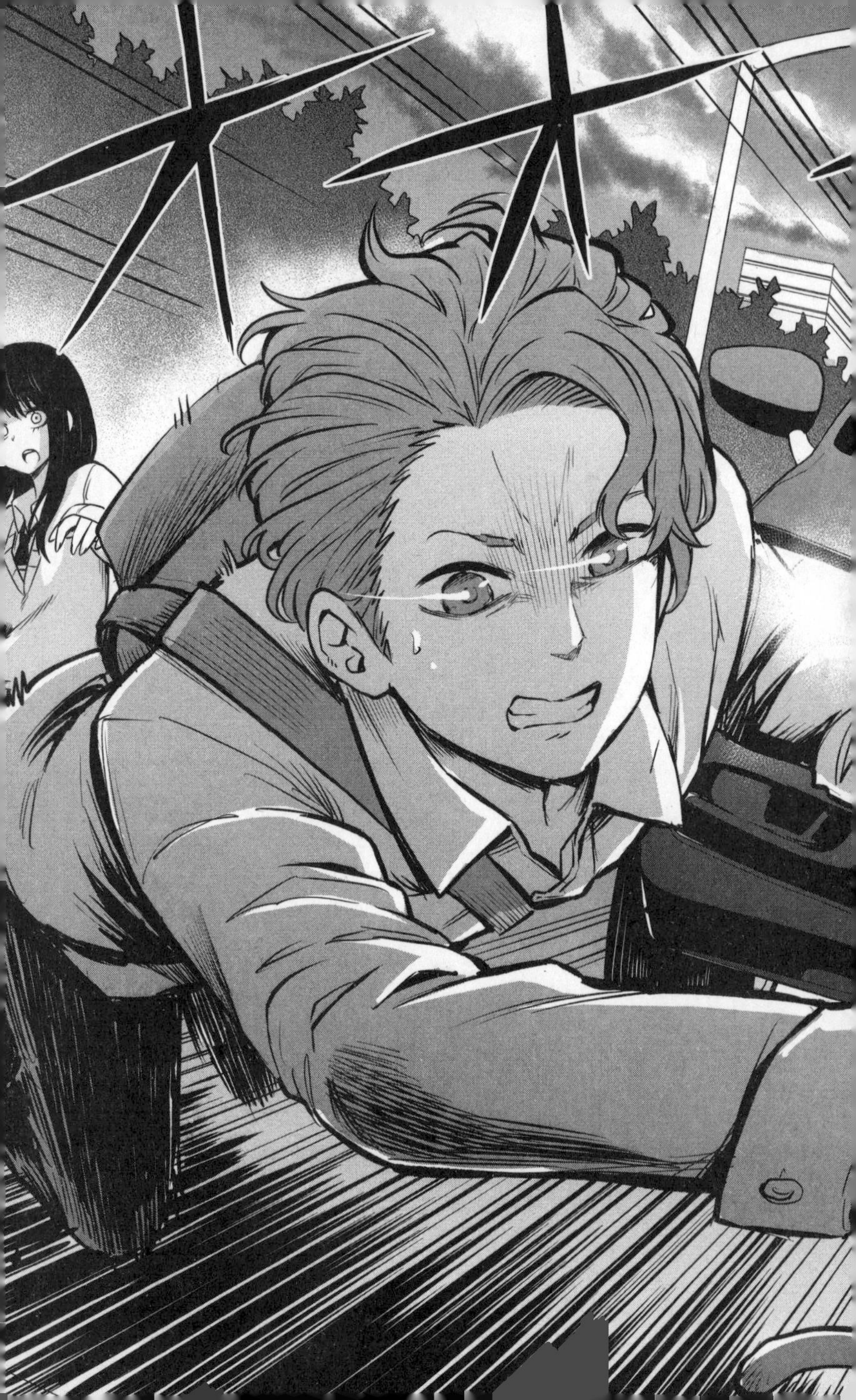

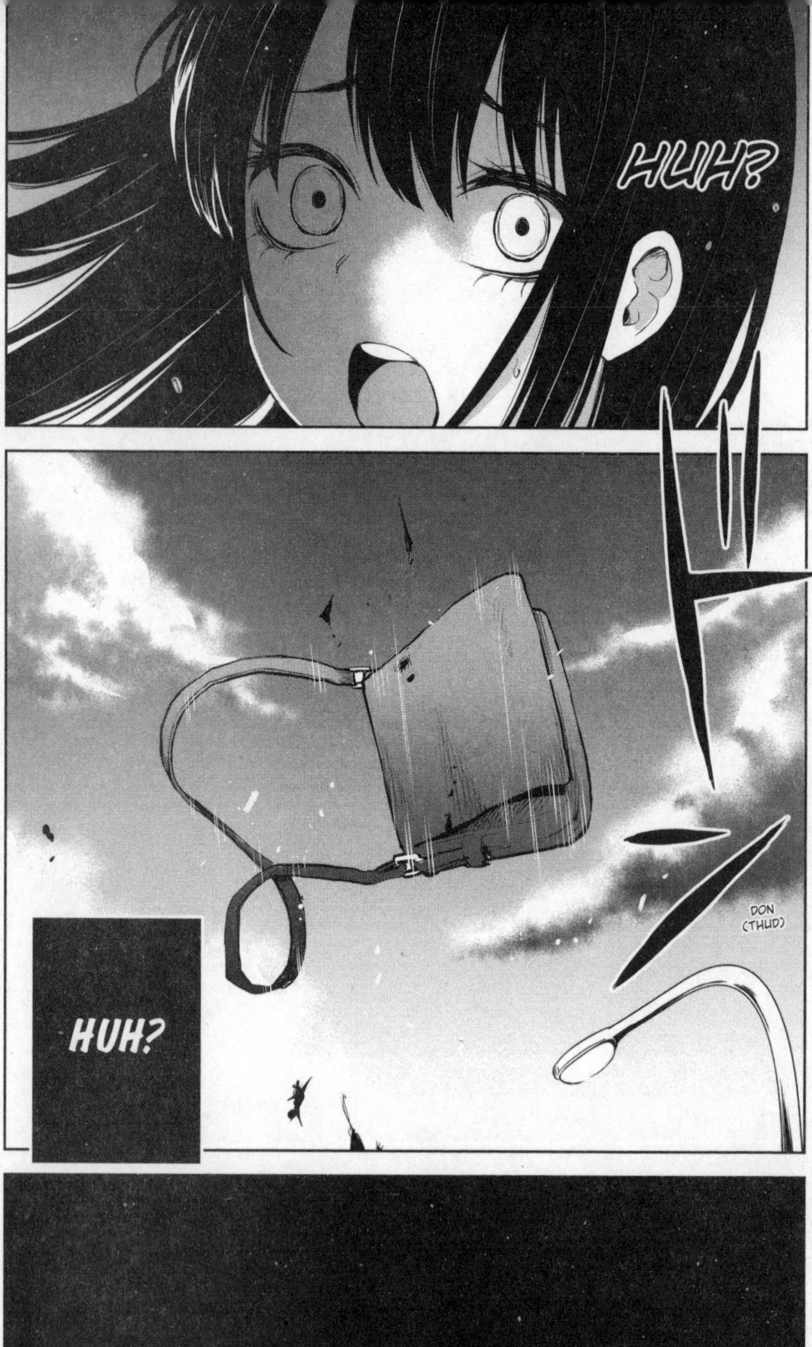
HUH?
DON (THUD)
HUH?

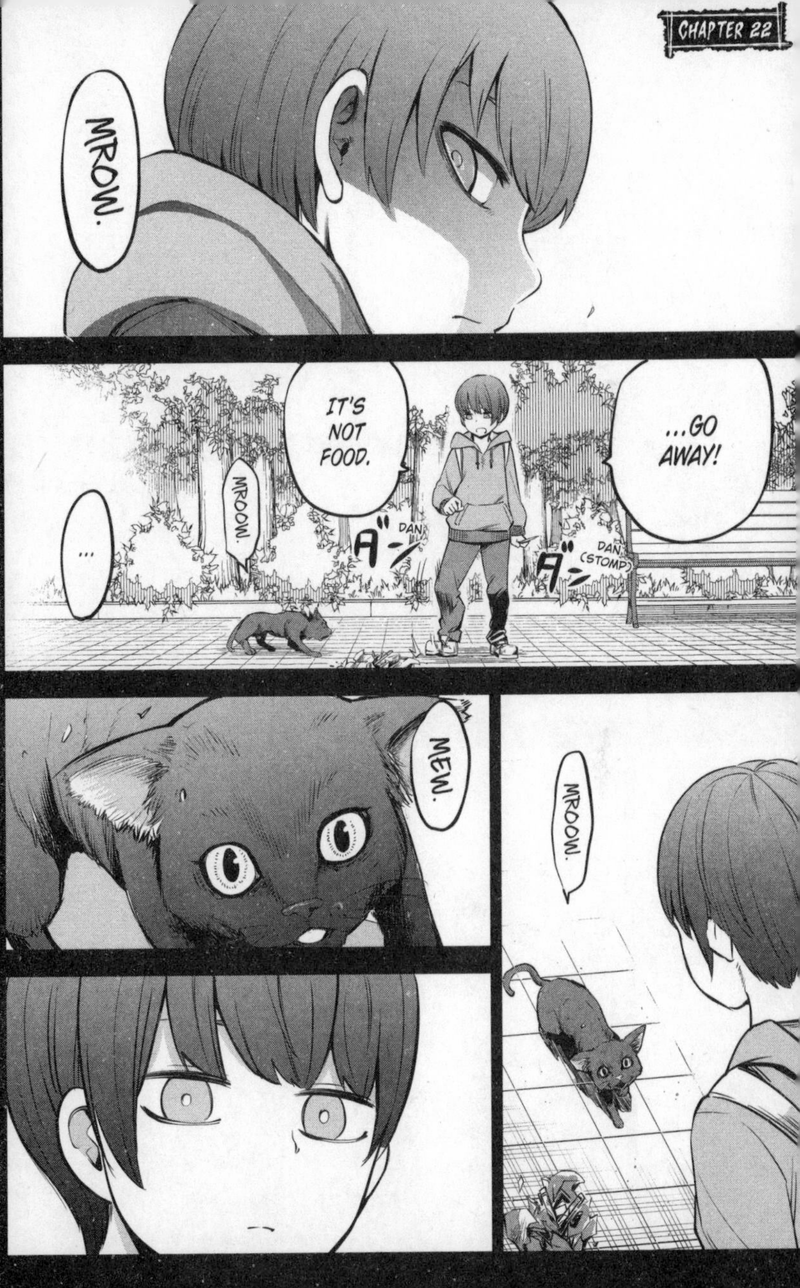
MROW.
...GO AWAY!
IT'S NOT FOOD.
MROOW.
...
DAN
DAN (STOMP)
MEW.
MROOW.

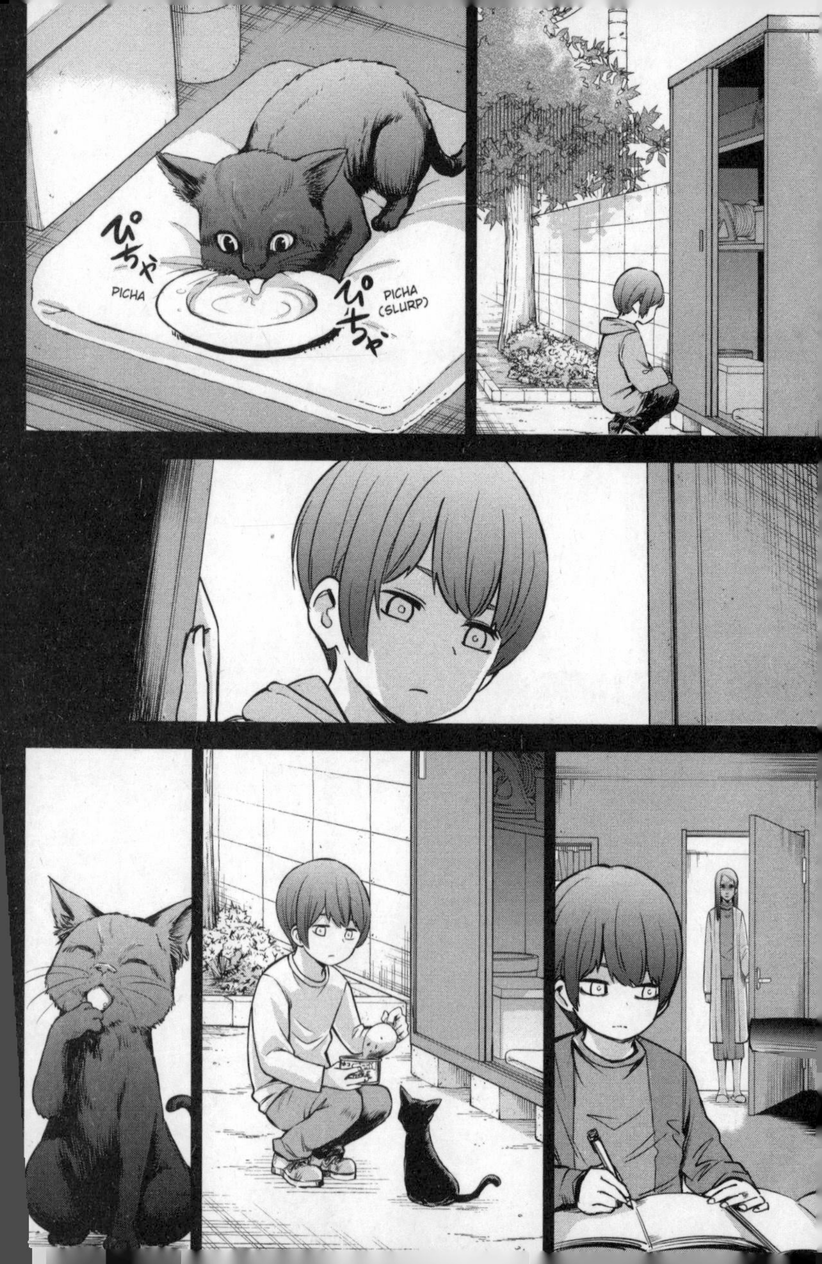
ぴちゃ
PICHA
ぴちゃ
PICHA (SLURP)

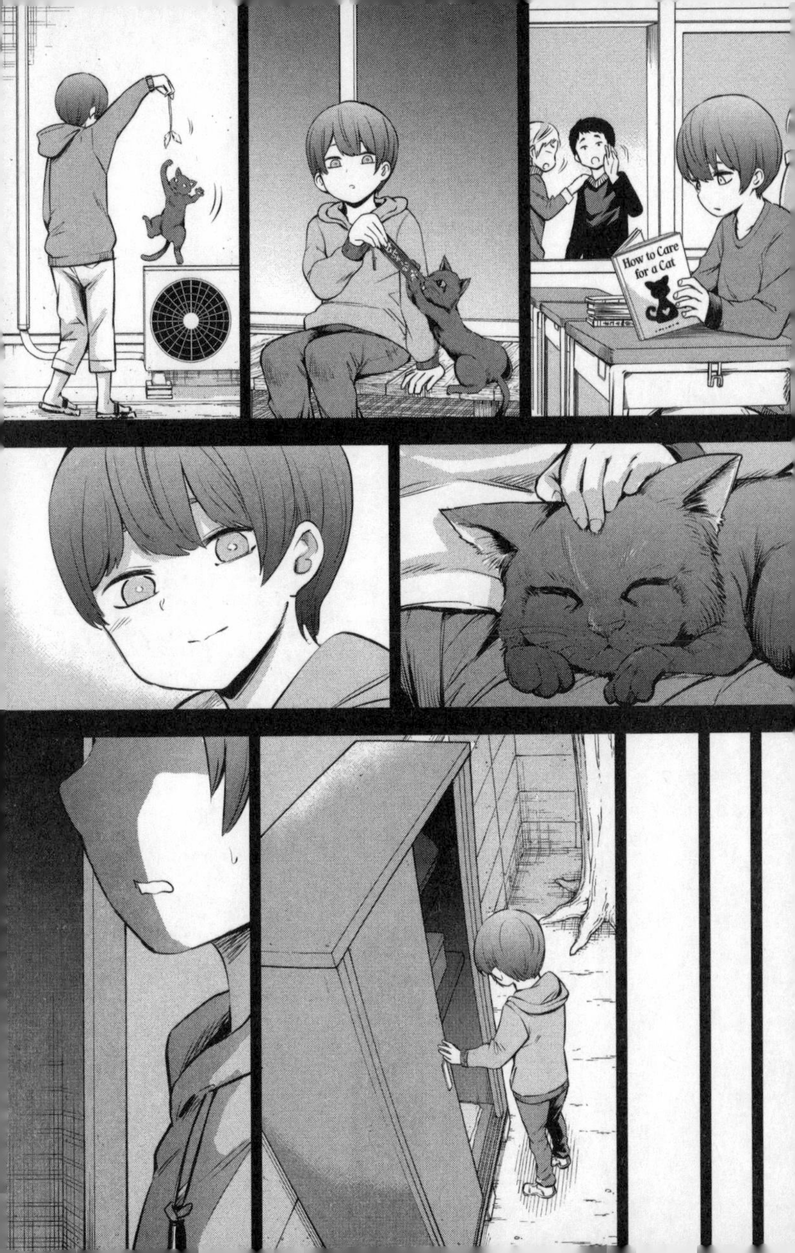
How to Care for a Cat

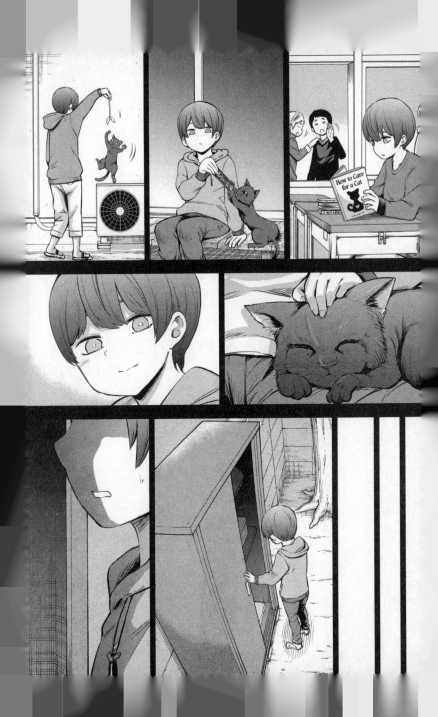

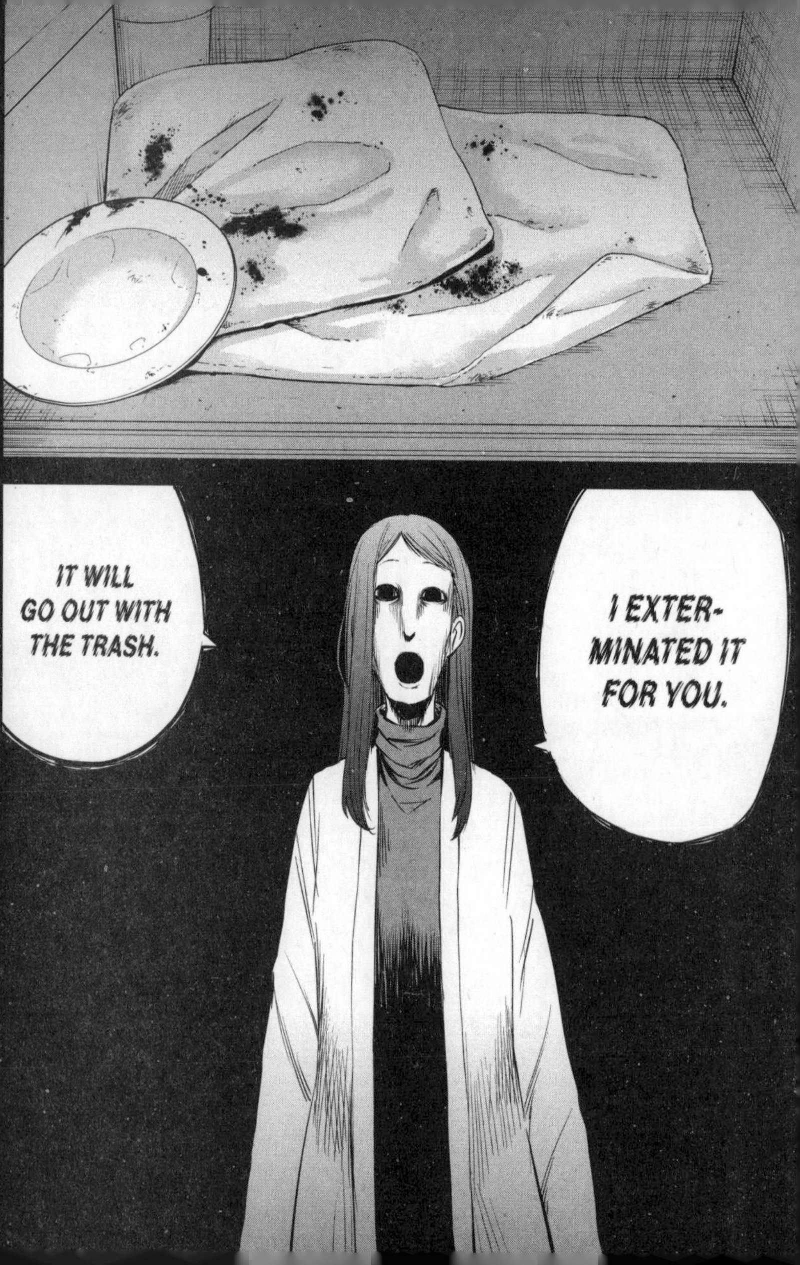
I EXTER-MINATED IT FOR YOU.
IT WILL GO OUT WITH THE TRASH.

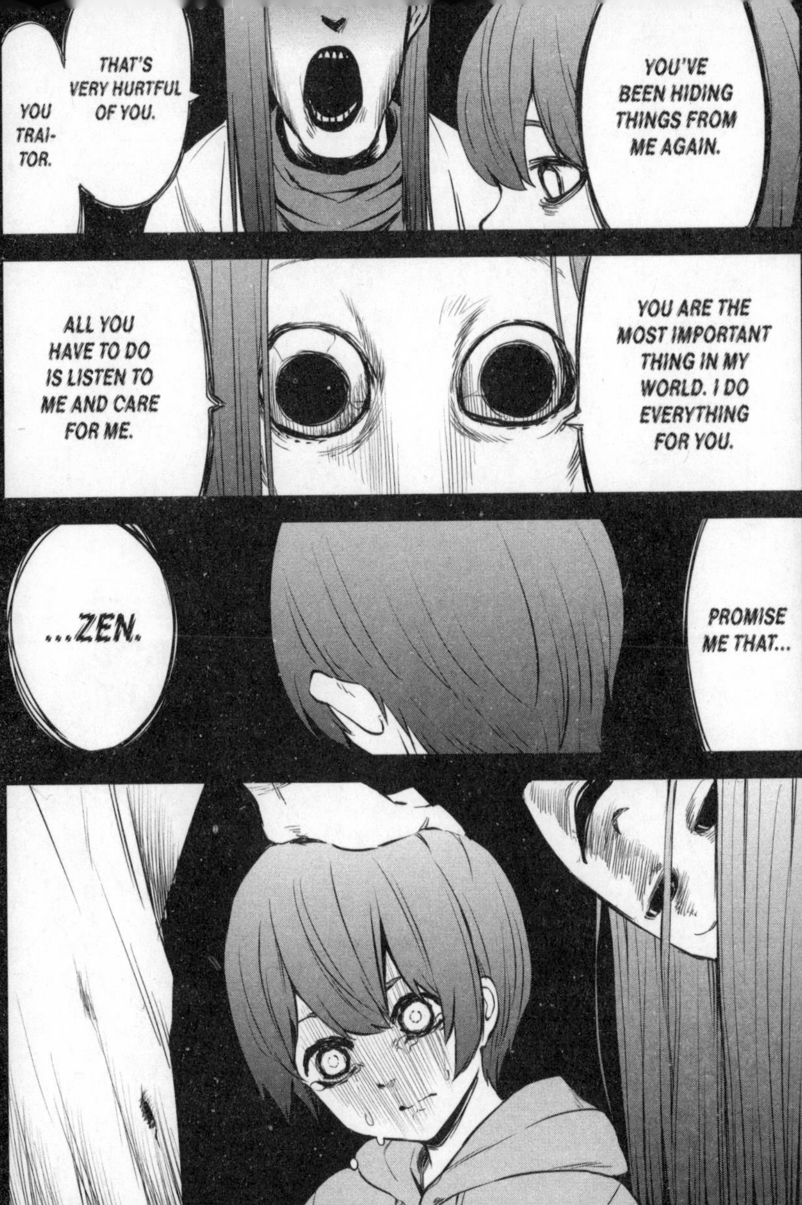
YOU'VE BEEN HIDING THINGS FROM ME AGAIN.
THAT'S VERY HURTFUL OF YOU.
YOU TRAI-TOR.
YOU ARE THE MOST IMPORTANT THING IN MY WORLD. I DO EVERYTHING FOR YOU.
ALL YOU HAVE TO DO IS LISTEN TO ME AND CARE FOR ME.
PROMISE ME THAT...
...ZEN.

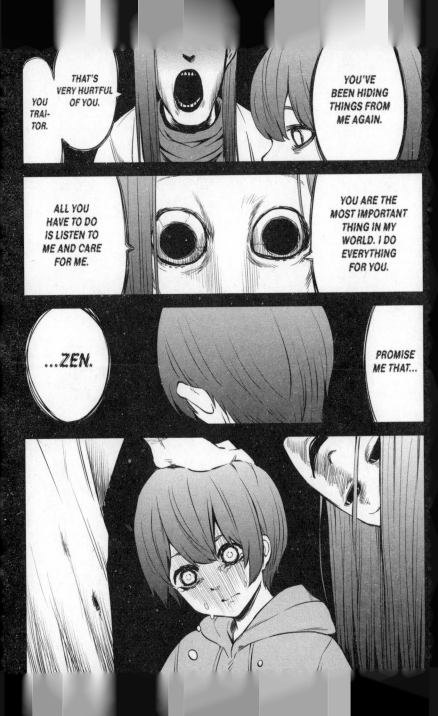

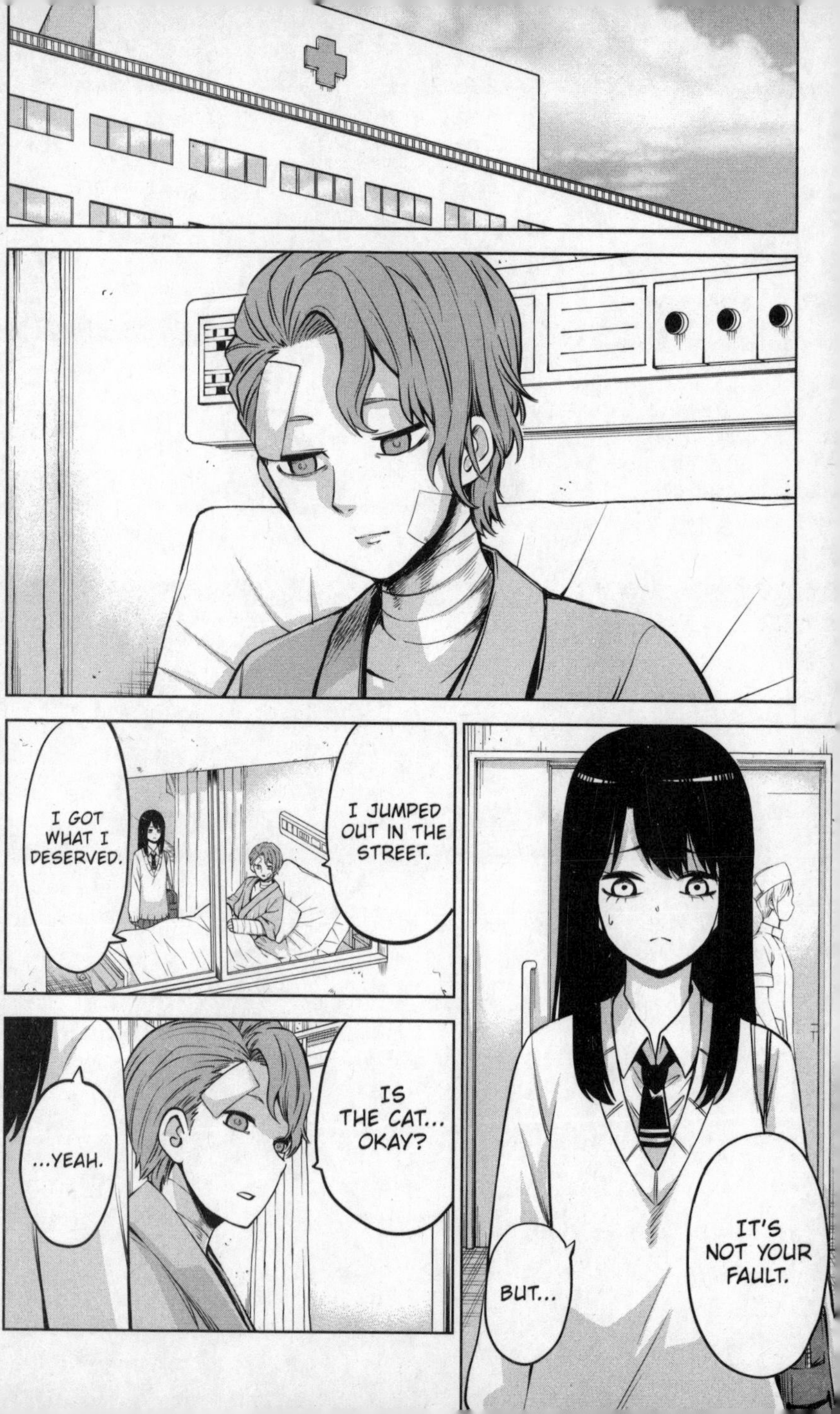
IT'S NOT YOUR FAULT.
BUT...
I JUMPED OUT IN THE STREET.
I GOT WHAT I DESERVED.
IS THE CAT... OKAY?
...YEAH.

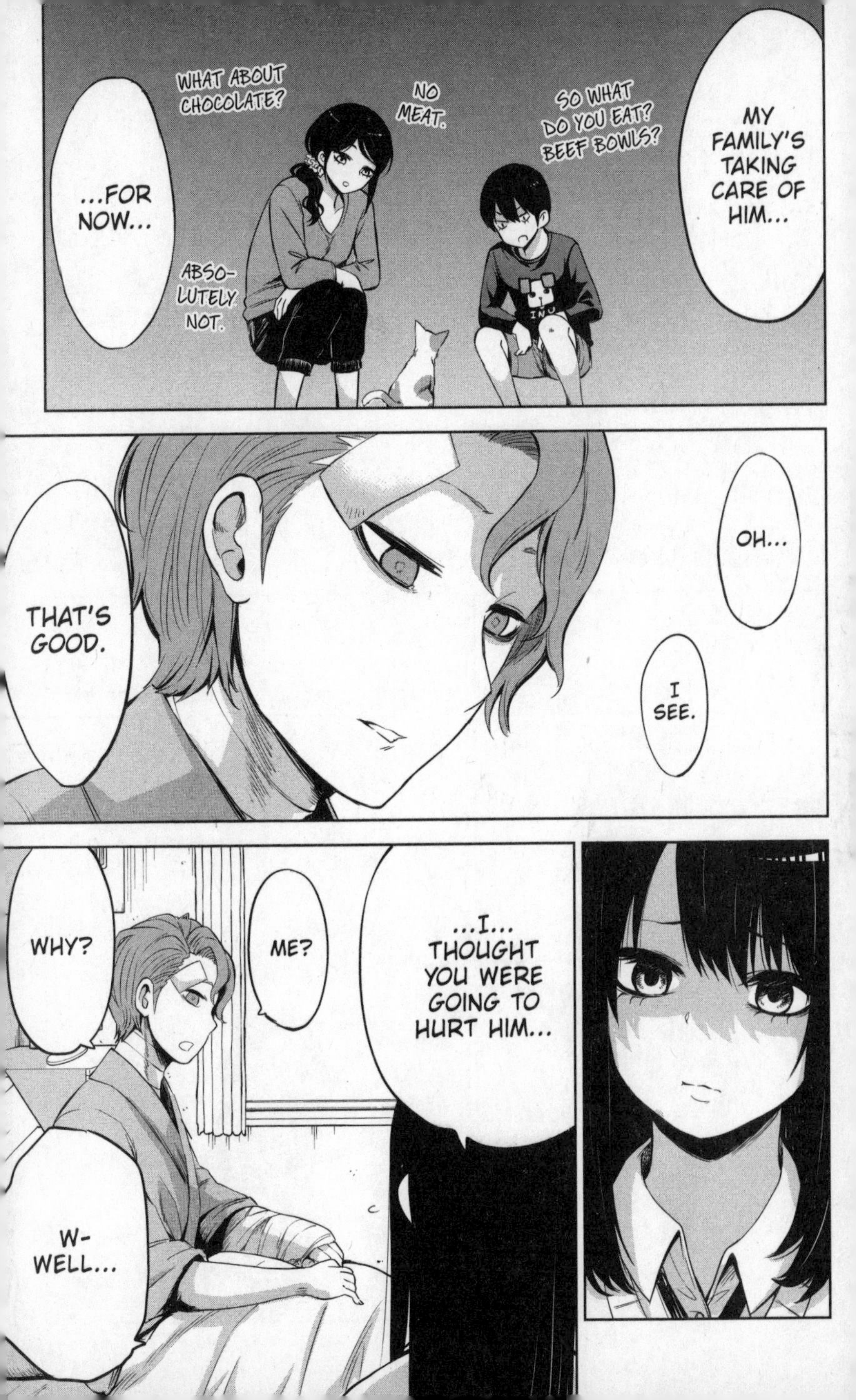
MY FAMILY'S TAKING CARE OF HIM...
SO WHAT DO YOU EAT? BEEF BOWLS?
NO MEAT.
WHAT ABOUT CHOCOLATE?
...FOR NOW...
ABSO-LUTELY NOT.
OH...
I SEE.
THAT'S GOOD.
...I... THOUGHT YOU WERE GOING TO HURT HIM...
ME?
WHY?
W-WELL...

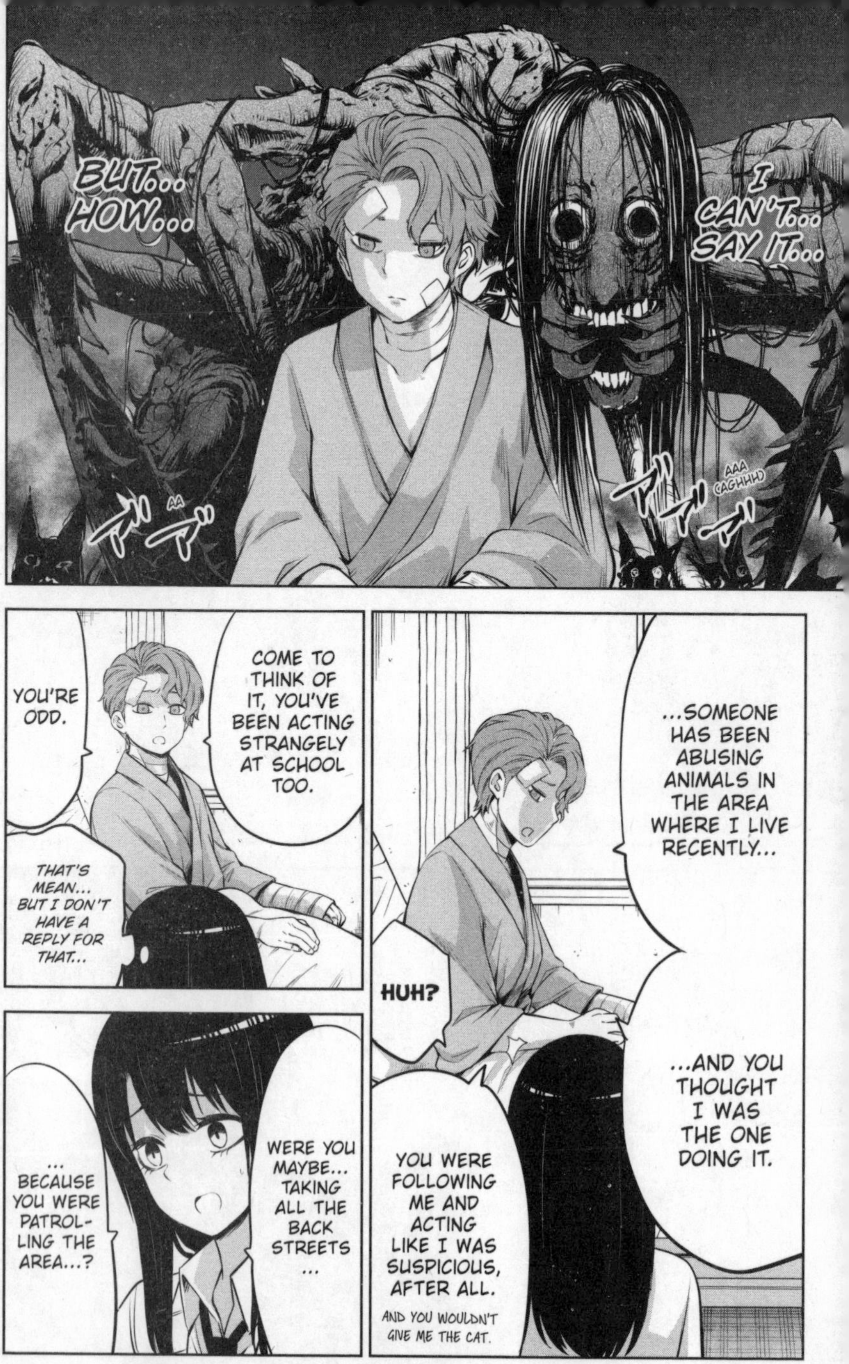
I CAN'T... SAY IT...
AAA (AGHHH)
BUT... HOW...
AA
...SOMEONE HAS BEEN ABUSING ANIMALS IN THE AREA WHERE I LIVE RECENTLY...
HUH?
...AND YOU THOUGHT I WAS THE ONE DOING IT.
YOU WERE FOLLOWING ME AND ACTING LIKE I WAS SUSPICIOUS, AFTER ALL.
AND YOU WOULDN'T GIVE ME THE CAT.
COME TO THINK OF IT, YOU'VE BEEN ACTING STRANGELY AT SCHOOL TOO.
YOU'RE ODD.
THAT'S MEAN... BUT I DON'T HAVE A REPLY FOR THAT...
WERE YOU MAYBE... TAKING ALL THE BACK STREETS ...
... BECAUSE YOU WERE PATROL-LING THE AREA...?

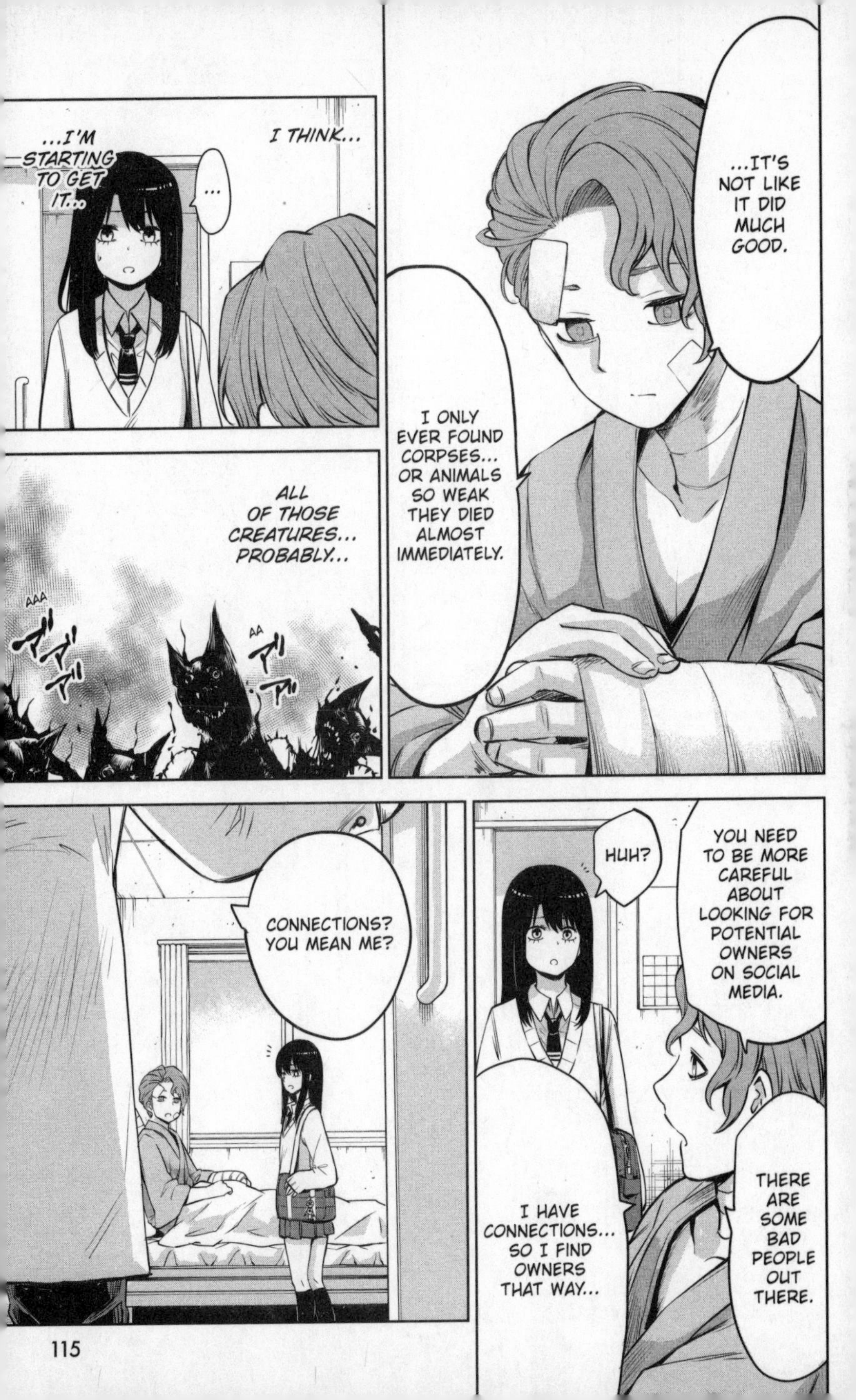
...IT'S NOT LIKE IT DID MUCH GOOD.
I ONLY EVER FOUND CORPSES... OR ANIMALS SO WEAK THEY DIED ALMOST IMMEDIATELY.
I THINK...
...
...I'M STARTING TO GET IT...
ALL OF THOSE CREATURES... PROBABLY...
AA
AAA
YOU NEED TO BE MORE CAREFUL ABOUT LOOKING FOR POTENTIAL OWNERS ON SOCIAL MEDIA.
HUH?
THERE ARE SOME BAD PEOPLE OUT THERE.
I HAVE CONNECTIONS... SO I FIND OWNERS THAT WAY...
CONNECTIONS? YOU MEAN ME?

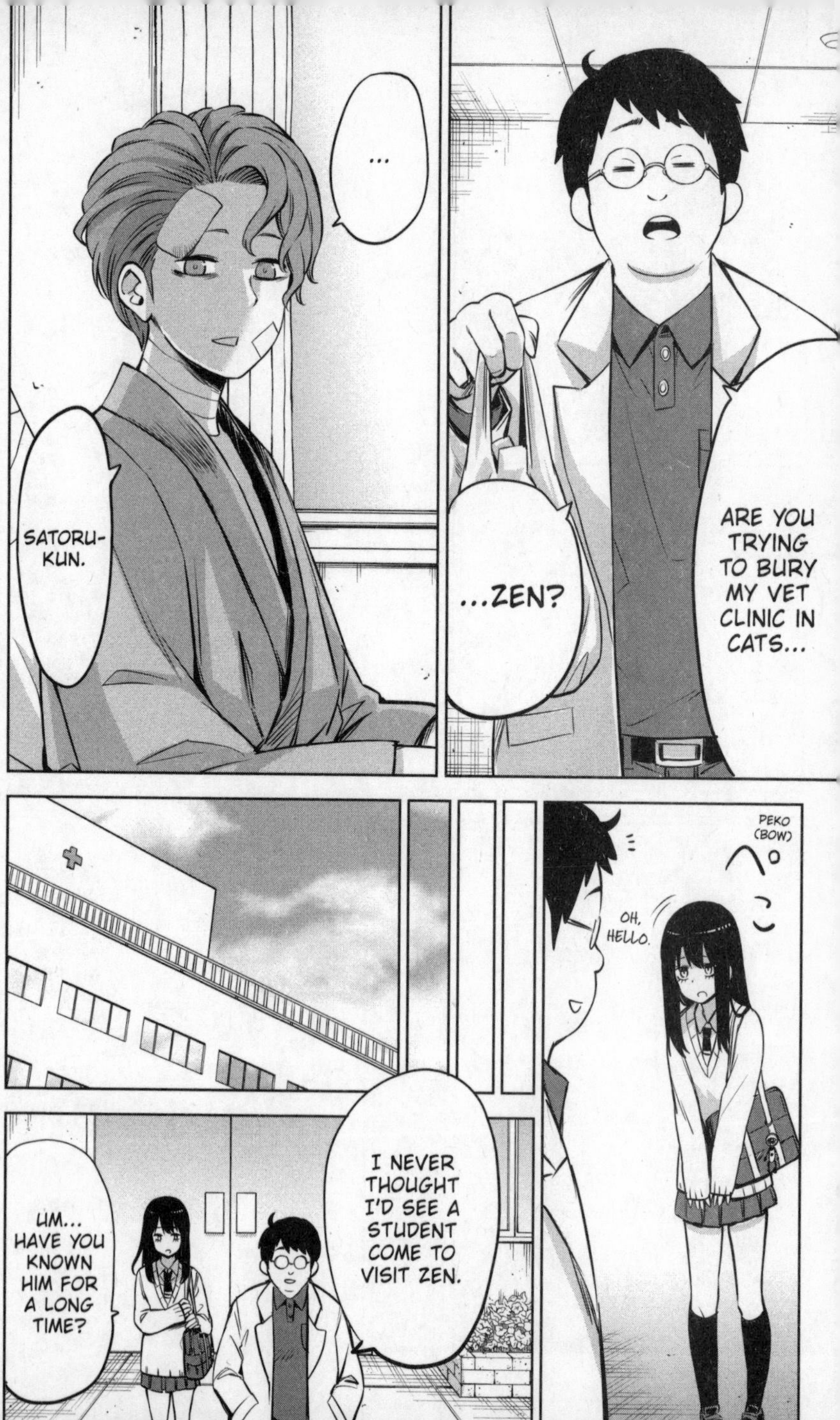
ARE YOU TRYING TO BURY MY VET CLINIC IN CATS...
...ZEN?
...
SATORU-KUN.
PEKO (BOW)
OH, HELLO.
I NEVER THOUGHT I'D SEE A STUDENT COME TO VISIT ZEN.
UM... HAVE YOU KNOWN HIM FOR A LONG TIME?

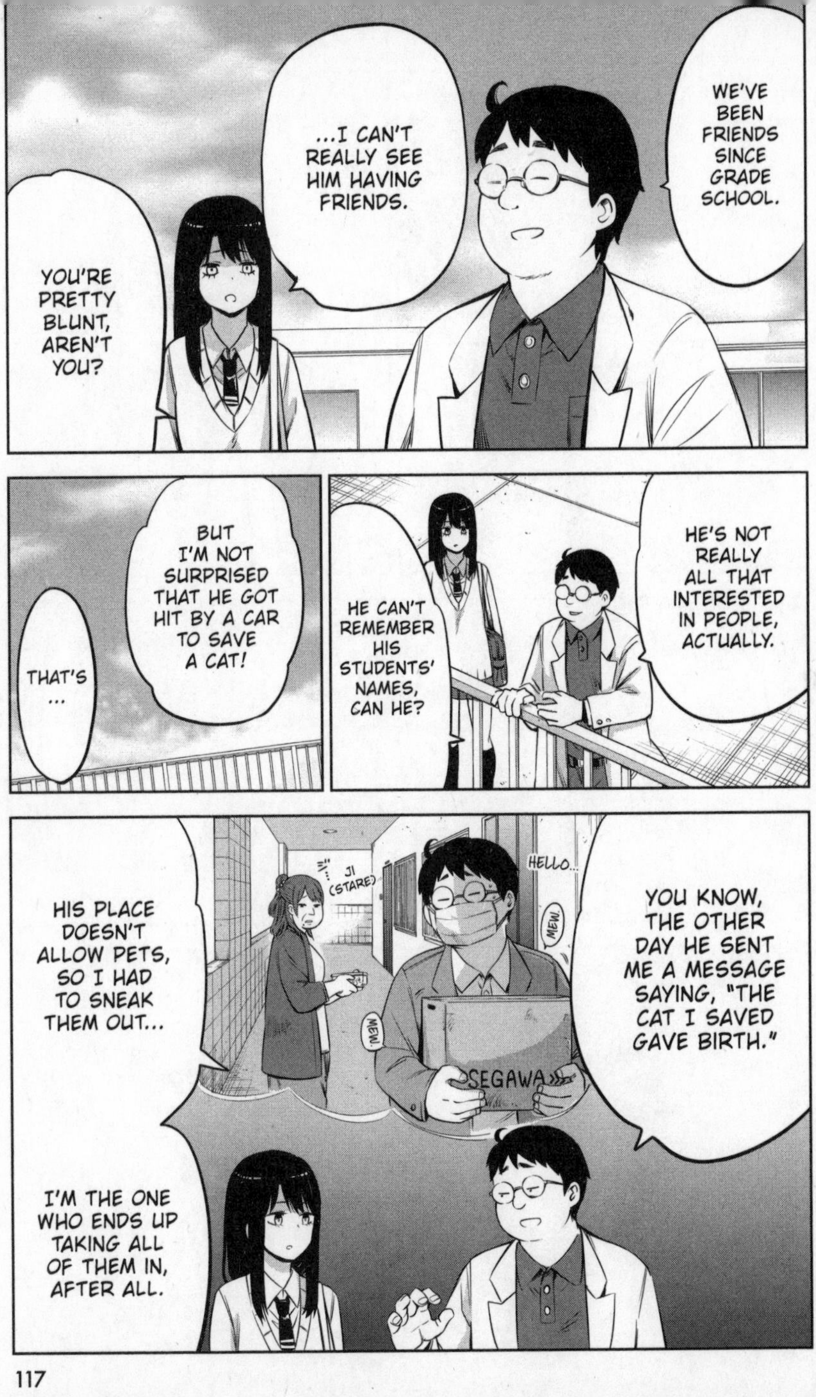
WE'VE BEEN FRIENDS SINCE GRADE SCHOOL.
...I CAN'T REALLY SEE HIM HAVING FRIENDS.
YOU'RE PRETTY BLUNT, AREN'T YOU?
HE'S NOT REALLY ALL THAT INTERESTED IN PEOPLE, ACTUALLY.
HE CAN'T REMEMBER HIS STUDENTS' NAMES, CAN HE?
BUT I'M NOT SURPRISED THAT HE GOT HIT BY A CAR TO SAVE A CAT!
THAT'S ...
YOU KNOW, THE OTHER DAY HE SENT ME A MESSAGE SAYING, "THE CAT I SAVED GAVE BIRTH."
HELLO...
MEW.
JI (STARE)
MEW.
SEGAWA
HIS PLACE DOESN'T ALLOW PETS, SO I HAD TO SNEAK THEM OUT...
I'M THE ONE WHO ENDS UP TAKING ALL OF THEM IN, AFTER ALL.

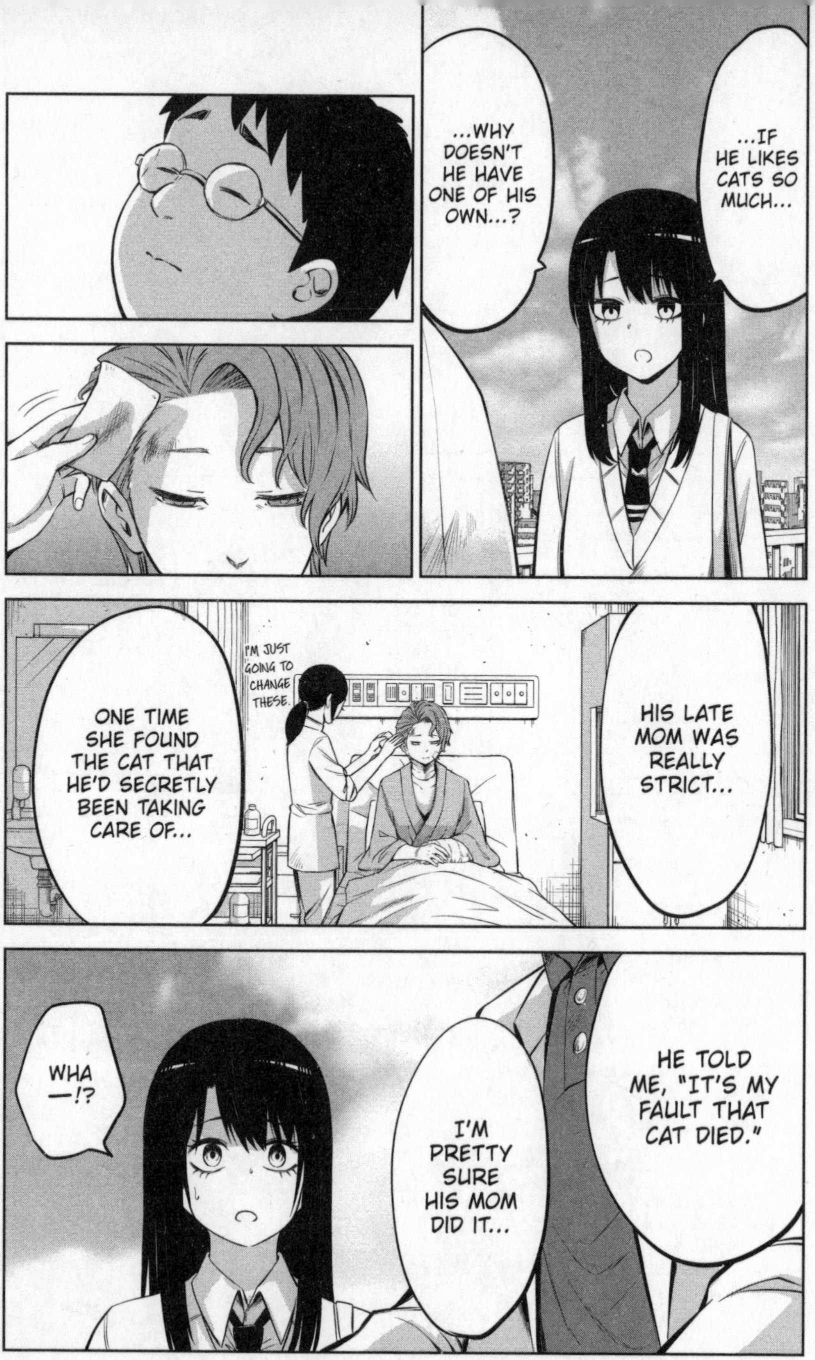
...IF HE LIKES CATS SO MUCH...
...WHY DOESN'T HE HAVE ONE OF HIS OWN...?
HIS LATE MOM WAS REALLY STRICT...
I'M JUST GOING TO CHANGE THESE.
ONE TIME SHE FOUND THE CAT THAT HE'D SECRETLY BEEN TAKING CARE OF...
HE TOLD ME, "IT'S MY FAULT THAT CAT DIED."
I'M PRETTY SURE HIS MOM DID IT...
WHA—!?

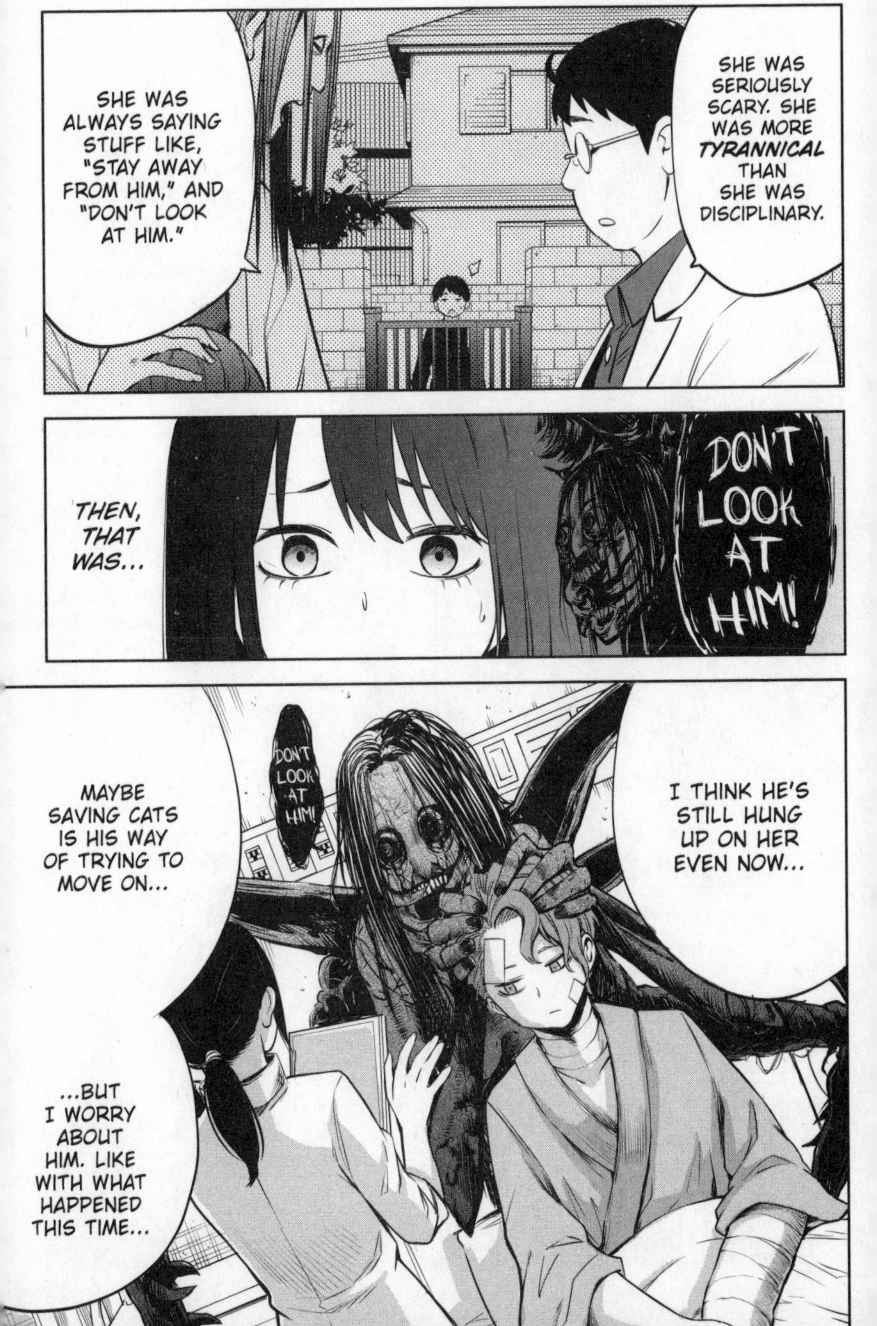
SHE WAS SERIOUSLY SCARY. SHE WAS MORE *TYRANNICAL* THAN SHE WAS DISCIPLINARY.
SHE WAS ALWAYS SAYING STUFF LIKE, "STAY AWAY FROM HIM," AND "DON'T LOOK AT HIM."
DON'T LOOK AT HIM!
THEN, THAT WAS...
I THINK HE'S STILL HUNG UP ON HER EVEN NOW...
DON'T LOOK AT HIM!
MAYBE SAVING CATS IS HIS WAY OF TRYING TO MOVE ON...
...BUT I WORRY ABOUT HIM. LIKE WITH WHAT HAPPENED THIS TIME...

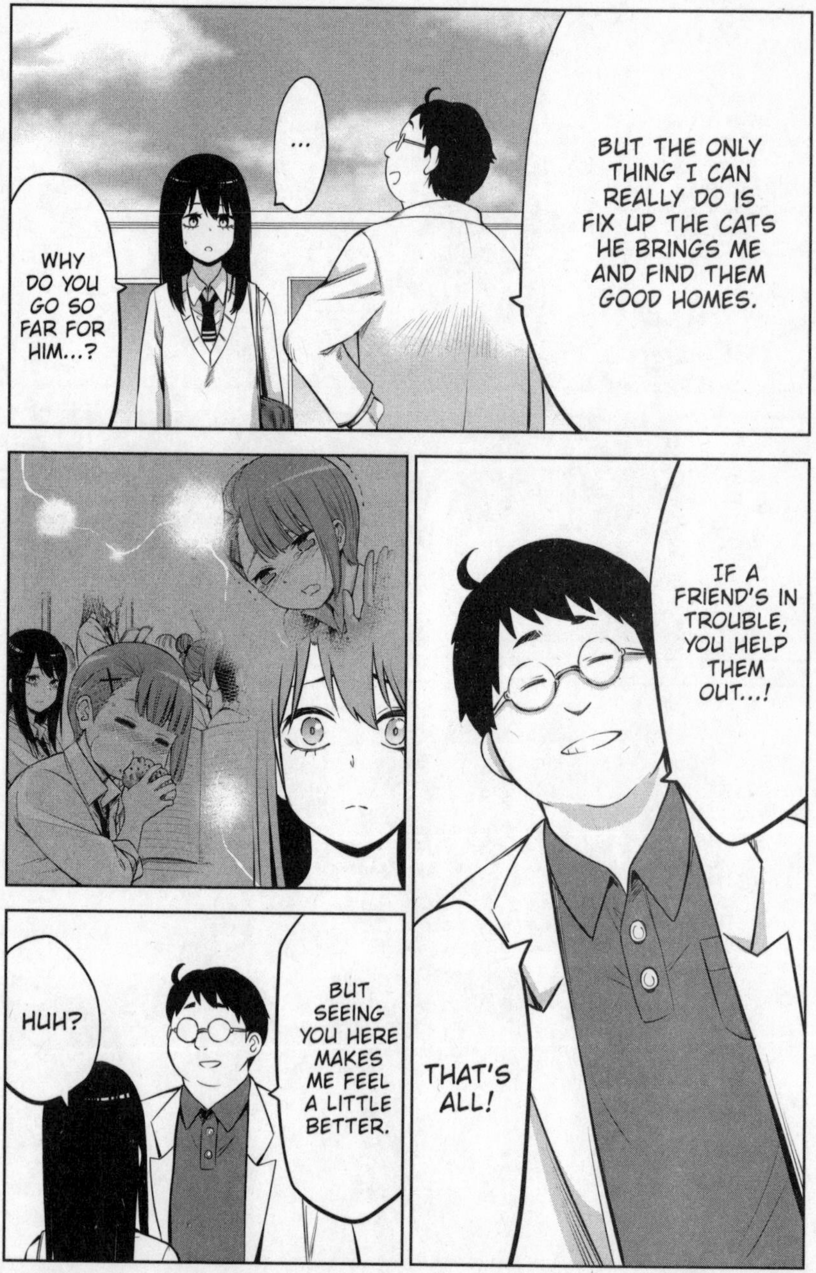
BUT THE ONLY THING I CAN REALLY DO IS FIX UP THE CATS HE BRINGS ME AND FIND THEM GOOD HOMES.
...
WHY DO YOU GO SO FAR FOR HIM...?
IF A FRIEND'S IN TROUBLE, YOU HELP THEM OUT...!
THAT'S ALL!
BUT SEEING YOU HERE MAKES ME FEEL A LITTLE BETTER.
HUH?

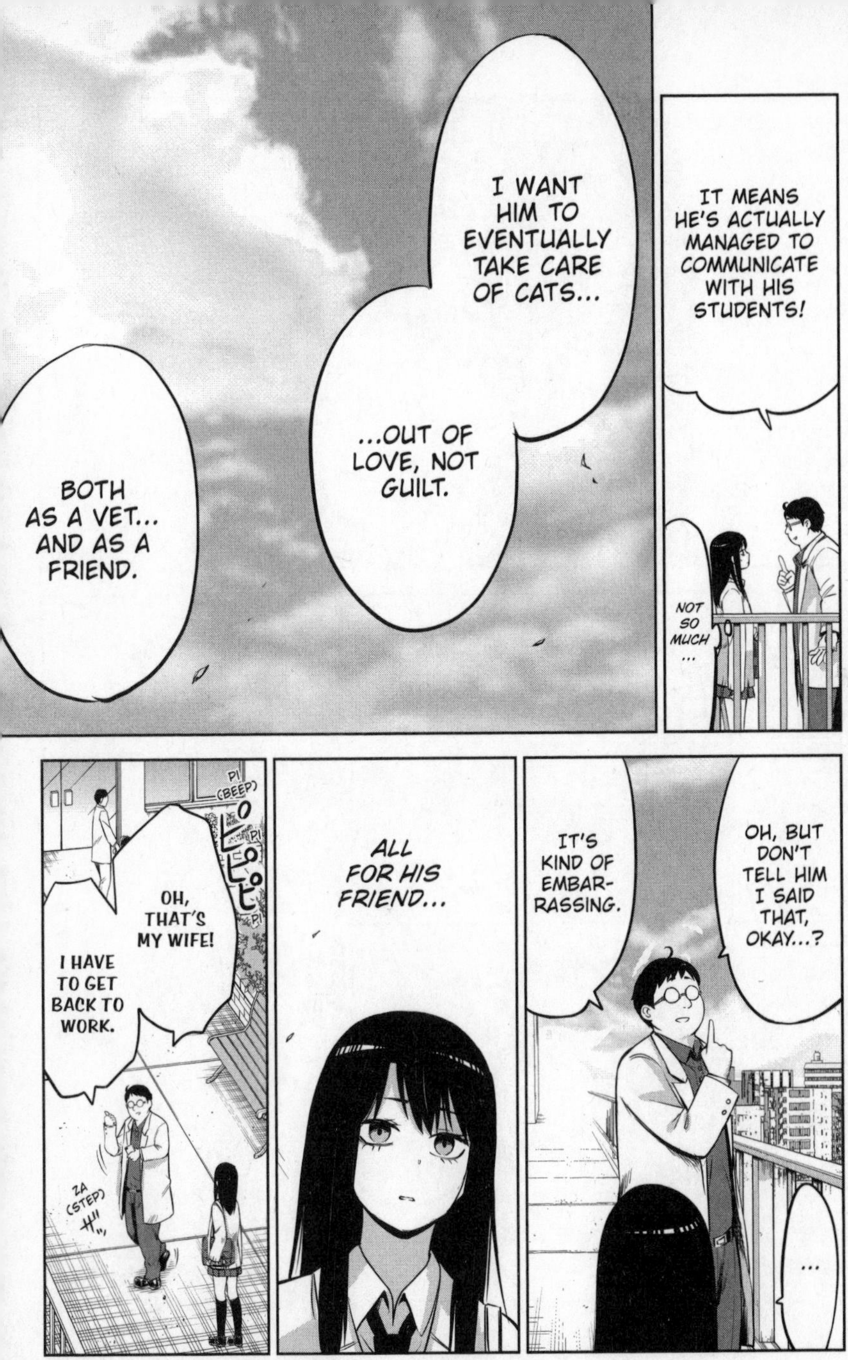
IT MEANS HE'S ACTUALLY MANAGED TO COMMUNICATE WITH HIS STUDENTS!
NOT SO MUCH...
I WANT HIM TO EVENTUALLY TAKE CARE OF CATS...
...OUT OF LOVE, NOT GUILT.
BOTH AS A VET... AND AS A FRIEND.
OH, BUT DON'T TELL HIM I SAID THAT, OKAY...?
IT'S KIND OF EMBAR-RASSING.
...
ALL FOR HIS FRIEND...
PI (BEEP)
PI
PI
OH, THAT'S MY WIFE!
I HAVE TO GET BACK TO WORK.
ZA (STEP)

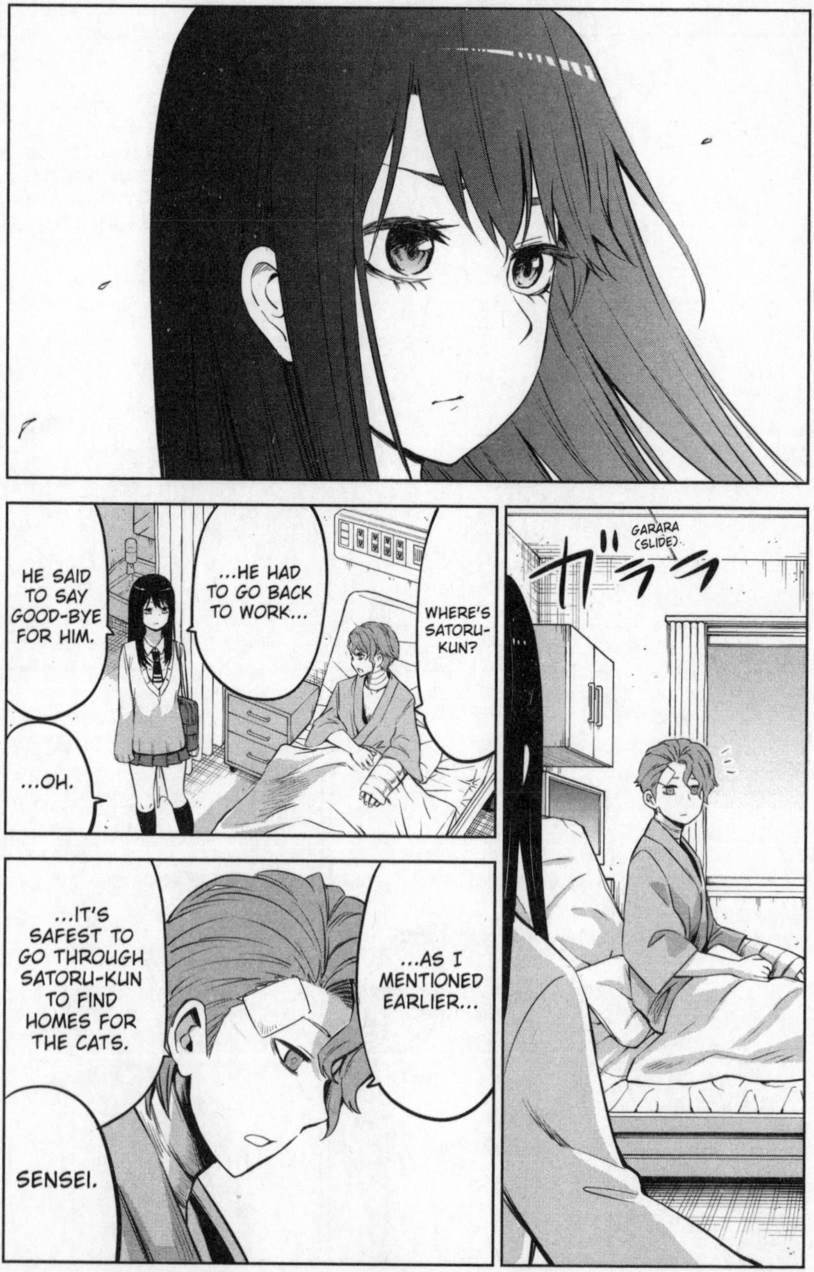
ガララ
GARARA (SLIDE)
WHERE'S SATORU-KUN?
...HE HAD TO GO BACK TO WORK...
HE SAID TO SAY GOOD-BYE FOR HIM.
...OH.
...AS I MENTIONED EARLIER...
...IT'S SAFEST TO GO THROUGH SATORU-KUN TO FIND HOMES FOR THE CATS.
SENSEI.

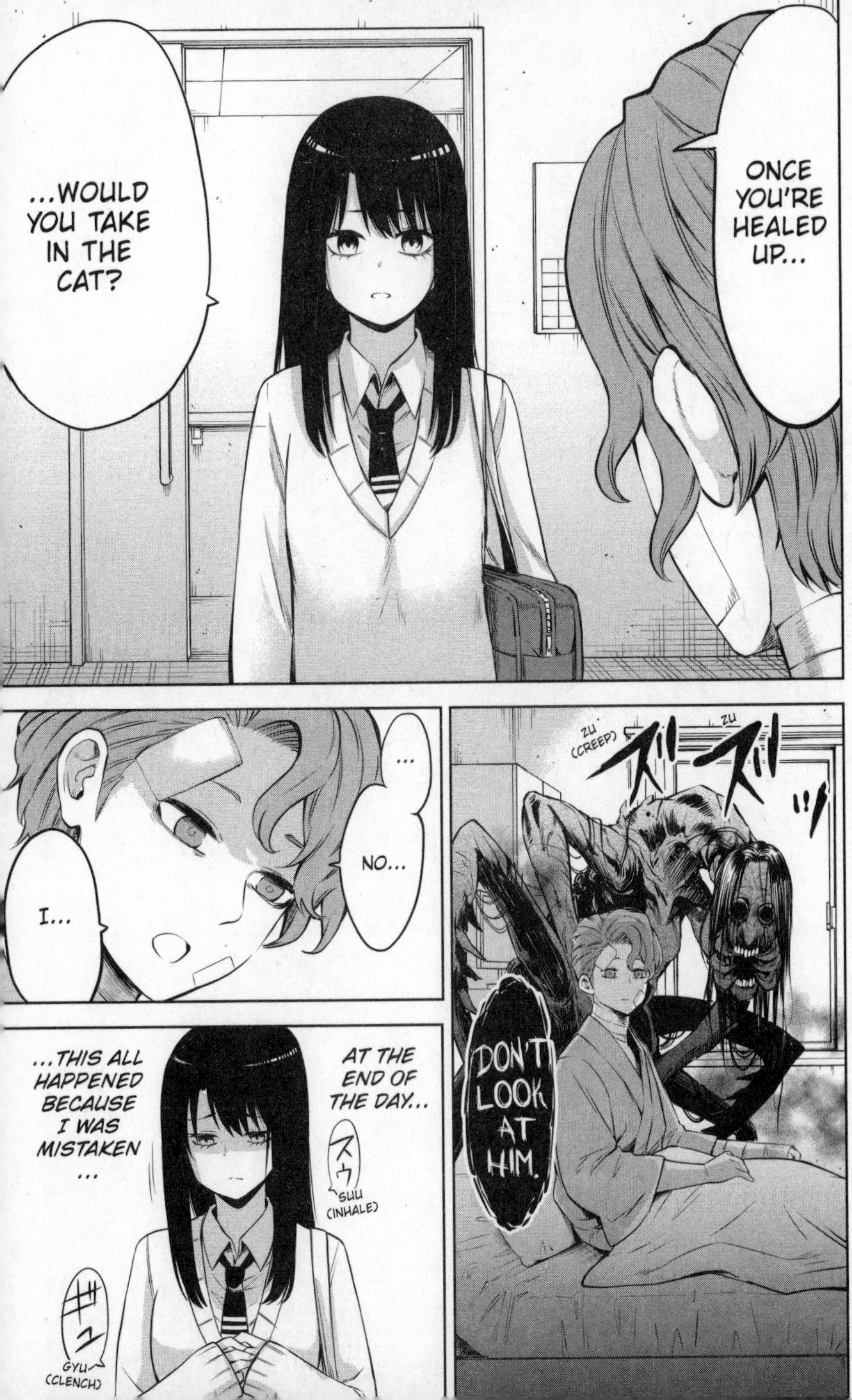
ONCE YOU'RE HEALED UP...
...WOULD YOU TAKE IN THE CAT?
ズリ
ZU (CREEP)
ズリ
ZU
DON'T LOOK AT HIM.
...
NO...
I...
AT THE END OF THE DAY...
...THIS ALL HAPPENED BECAUSE I WAS MISTAKEN ...
スウ
SUU (INHALE)
ギュ
GYU (CLENCH)

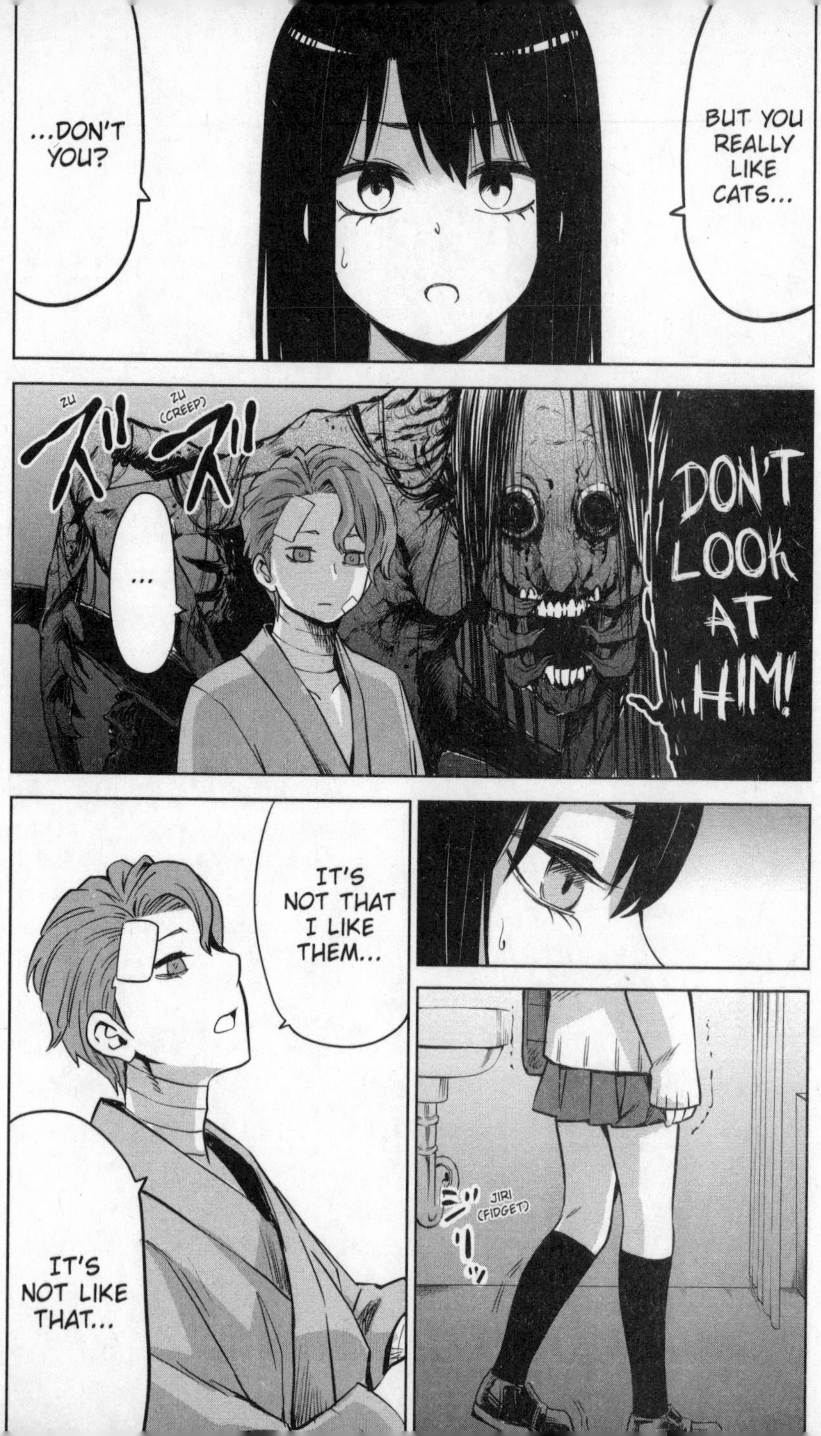
BUT YOU REALLY LIKE CATS...
...DON'T YOU?
DON'T LOOK AT HIM!
ZU
ZU (CREEP)
...
JIRI (FIDGET)
IT'S NOT THAT I LIKE THEM...
IT'S NOT LIKE THAT...

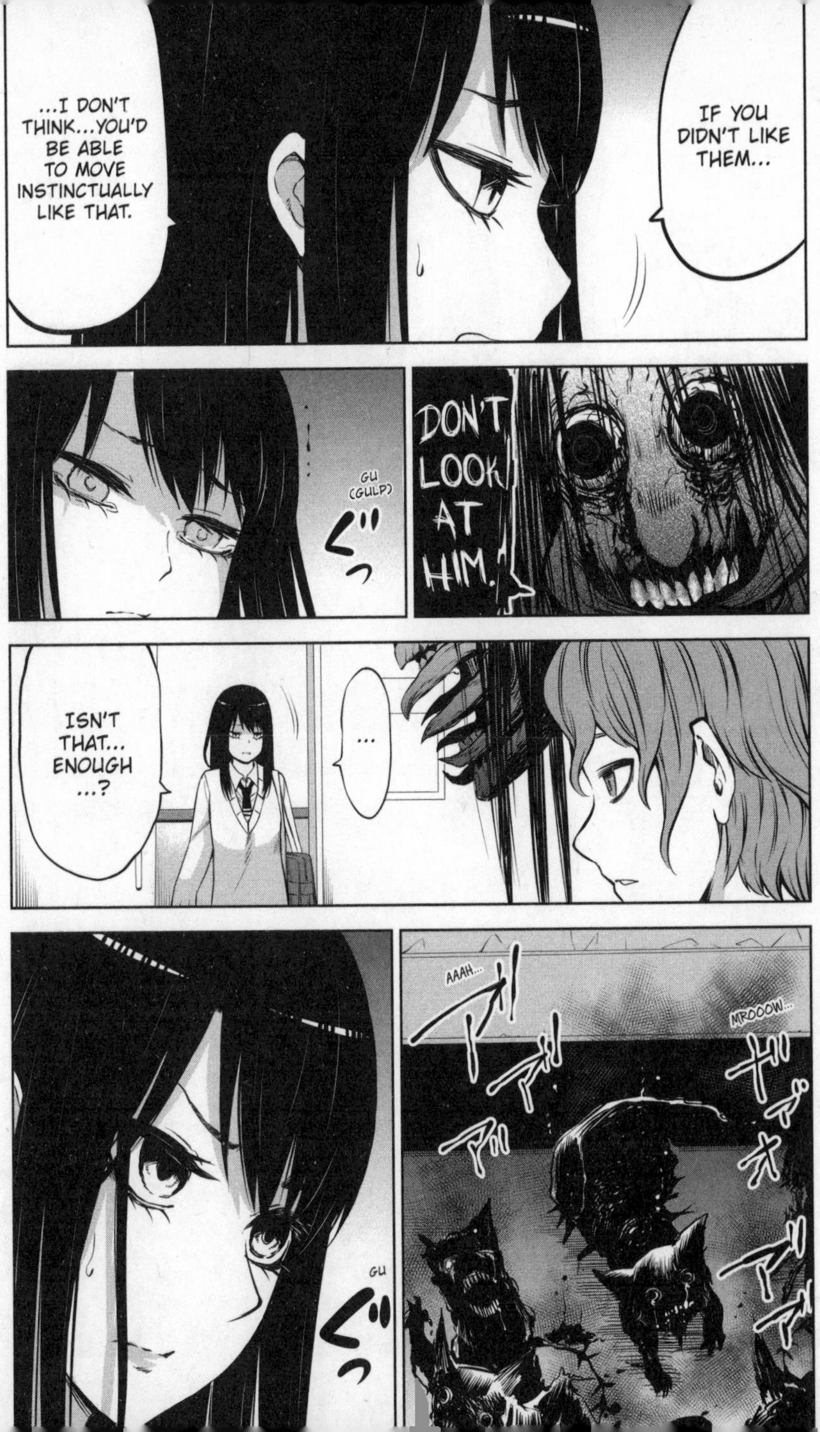

IF YOU DIDN'T LIKE THEM...
...I DON'T THINK...YOU'D BE ABLE TO MOVE INSTINCTUALLY LIKE THAT.
DON'T LOOK AT HIM.
GU (GULP)
ぐっ
...
ISN'T THAT... ENOUGH ...?
MROOOW...
AAAH...
GU
ぐっ

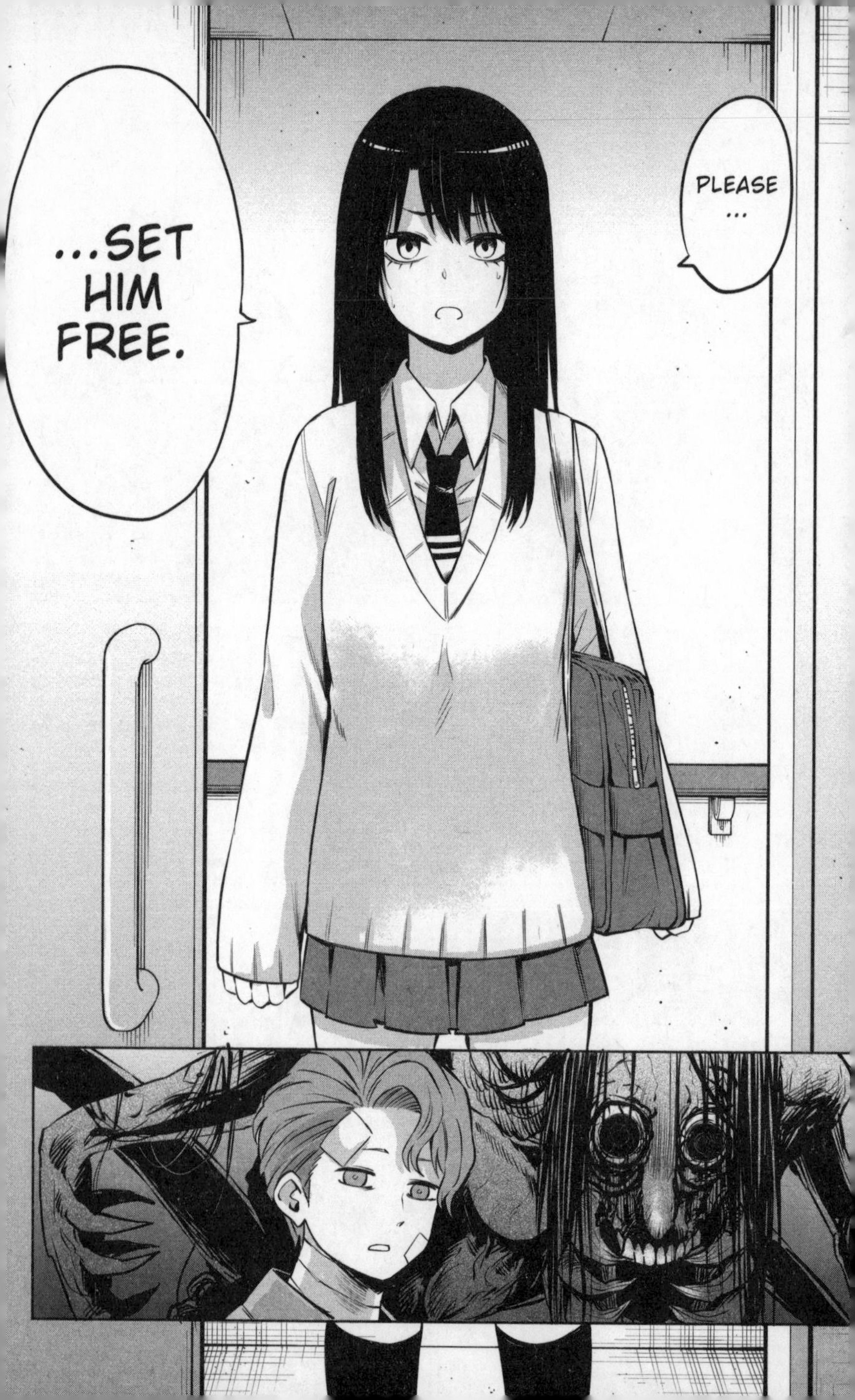
PLEASE ...
...SET HIM FREE.

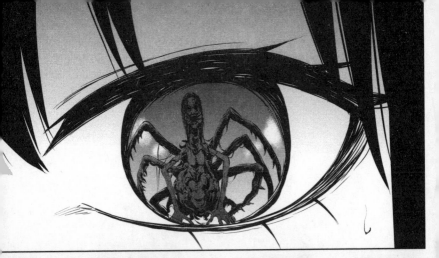

ス_ッ

SU
(FWISH)

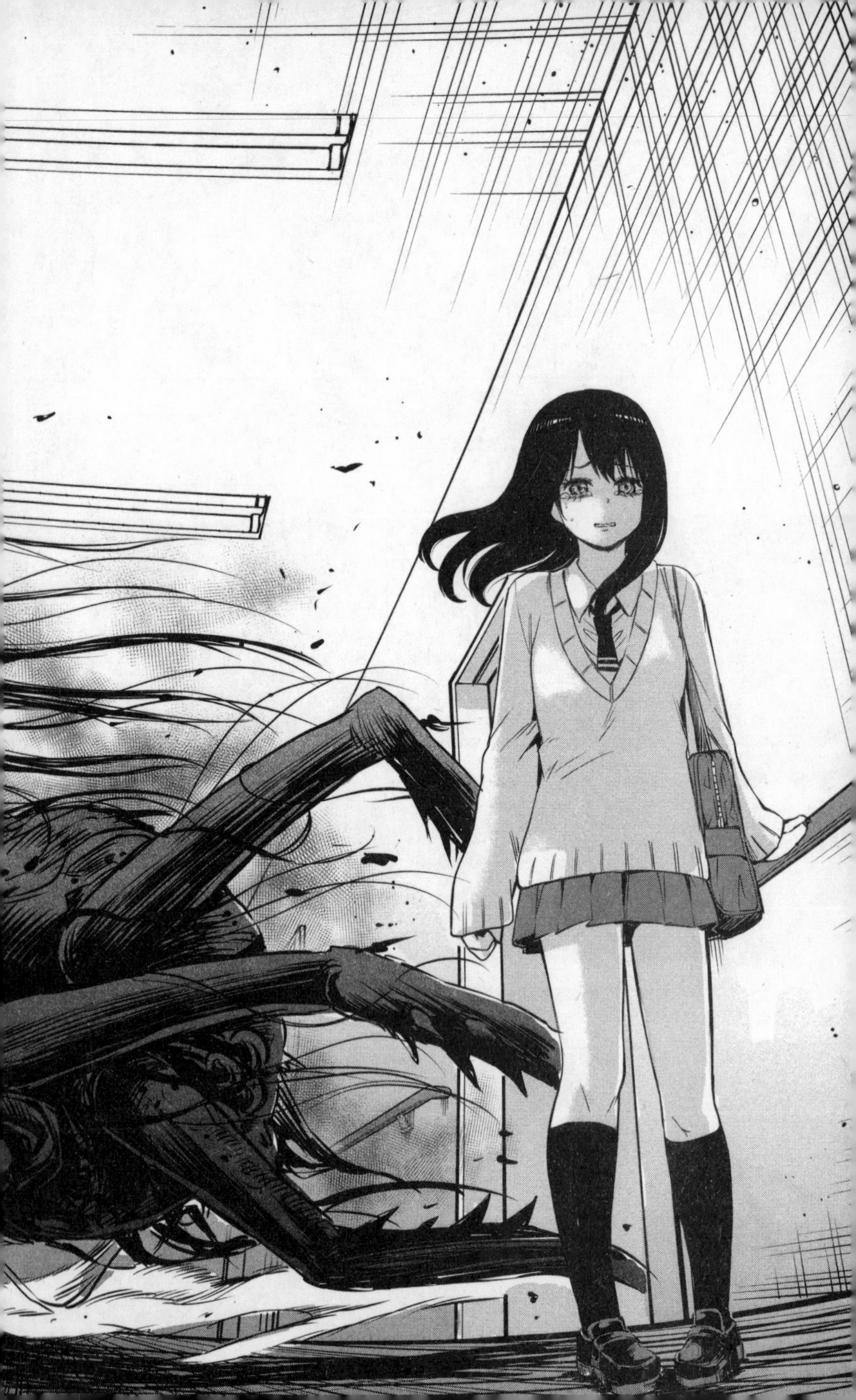

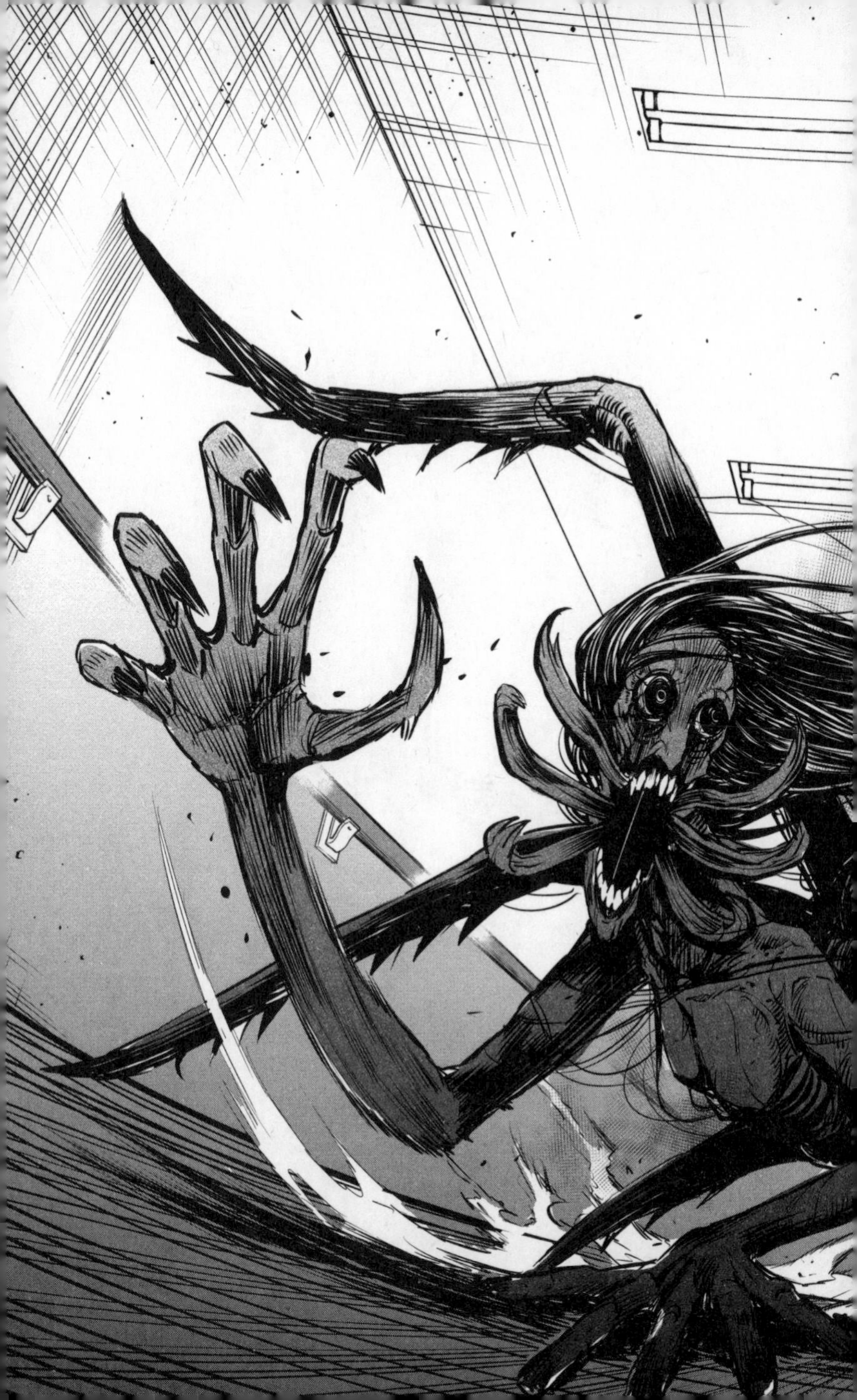

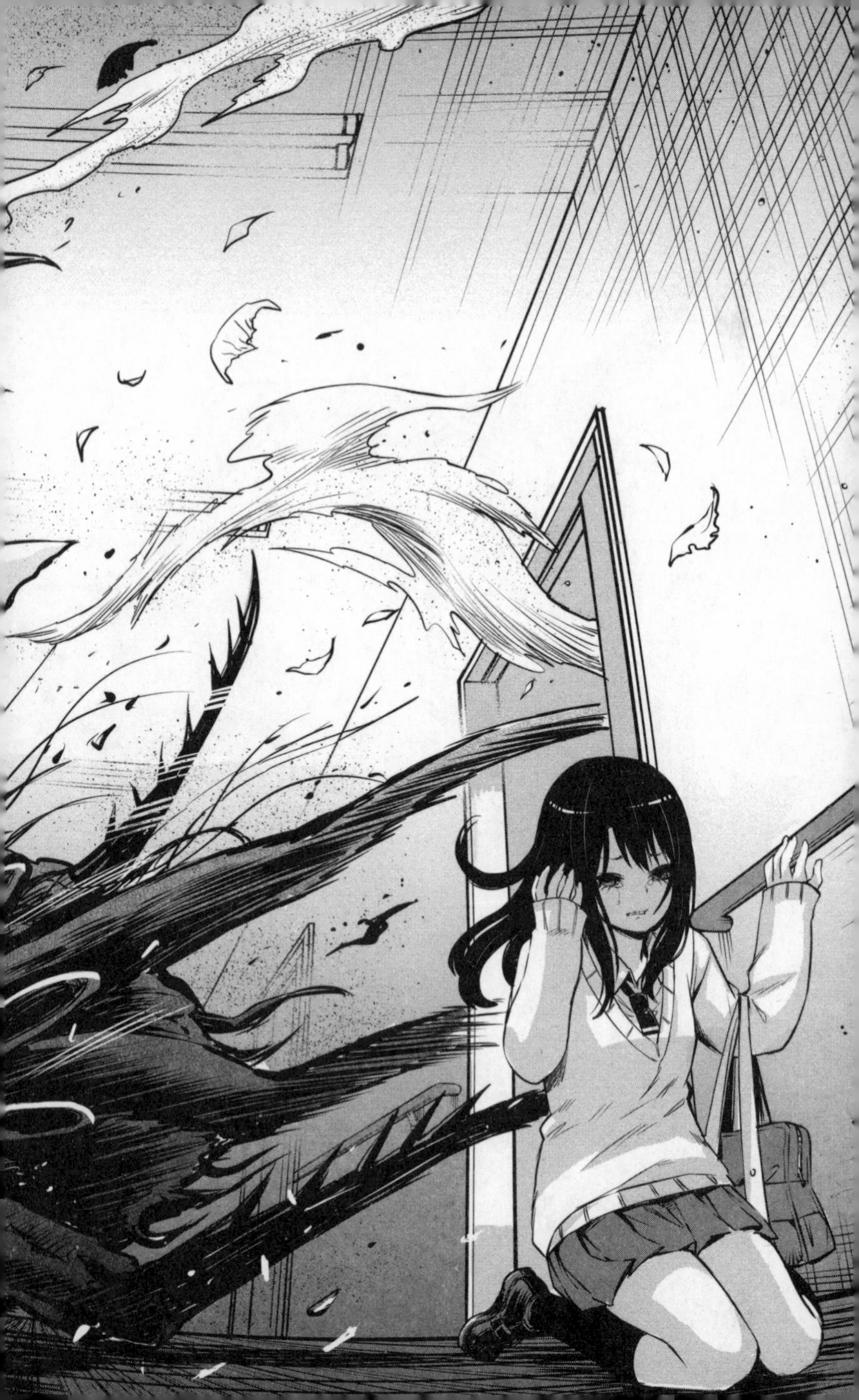

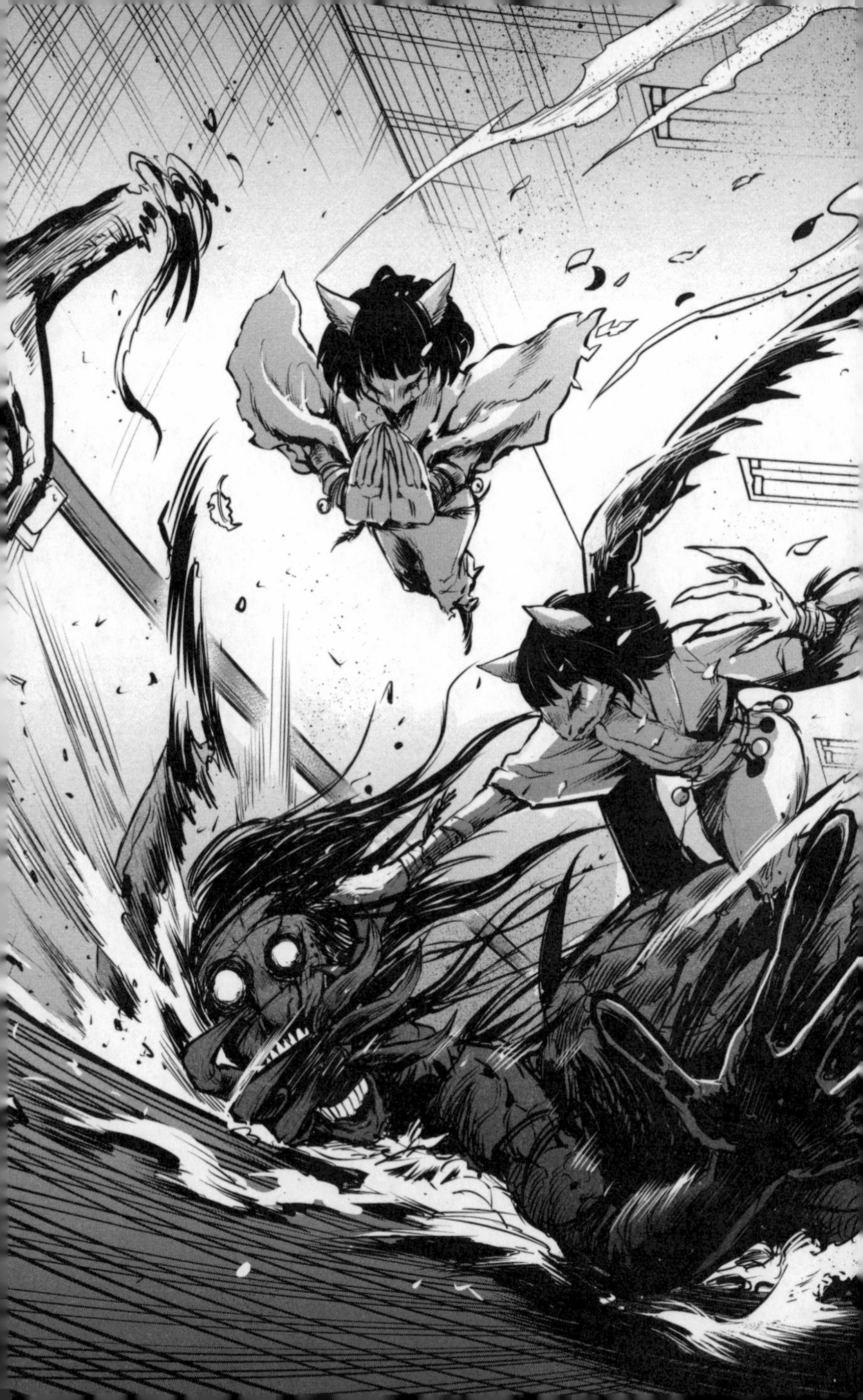

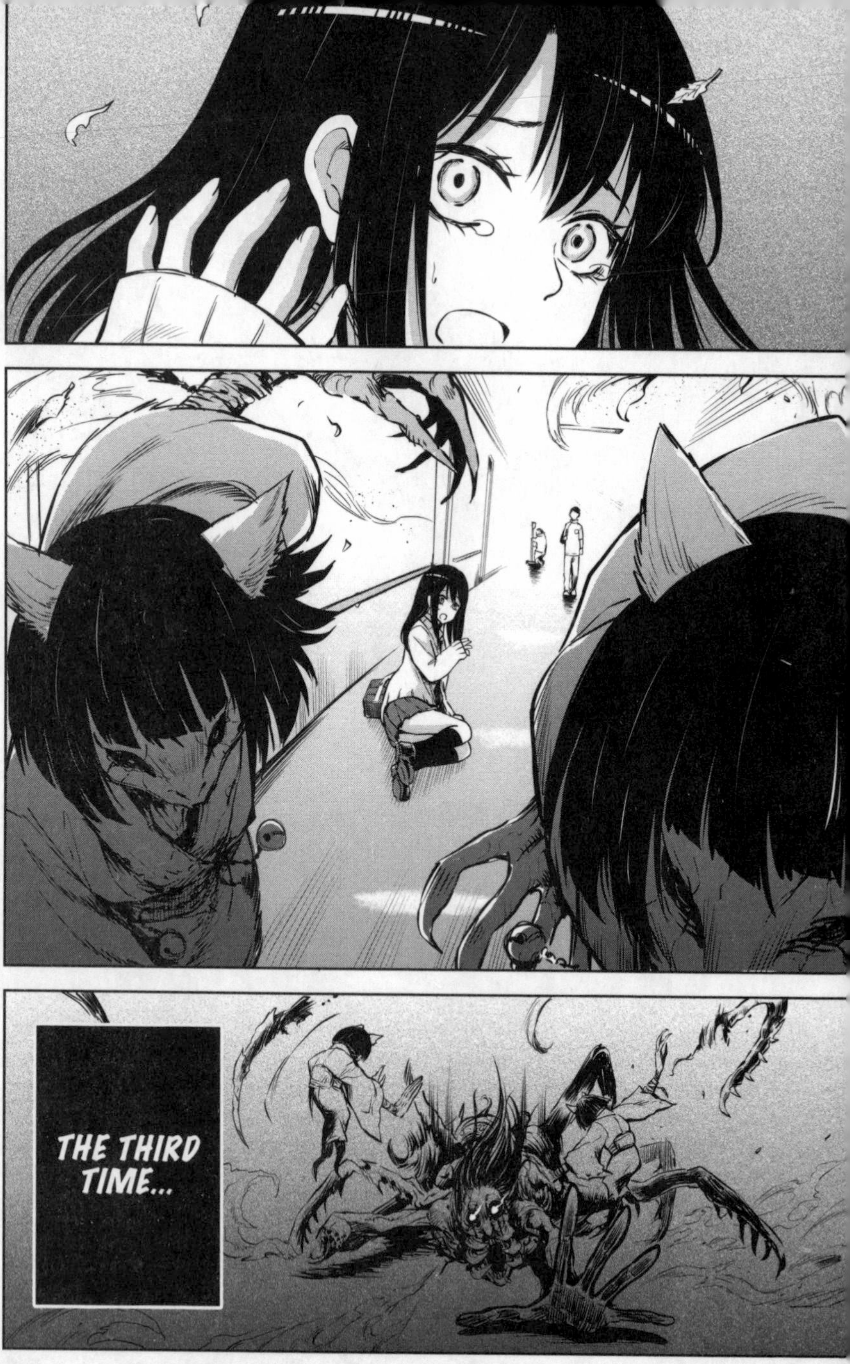
THE THIRD TIME...

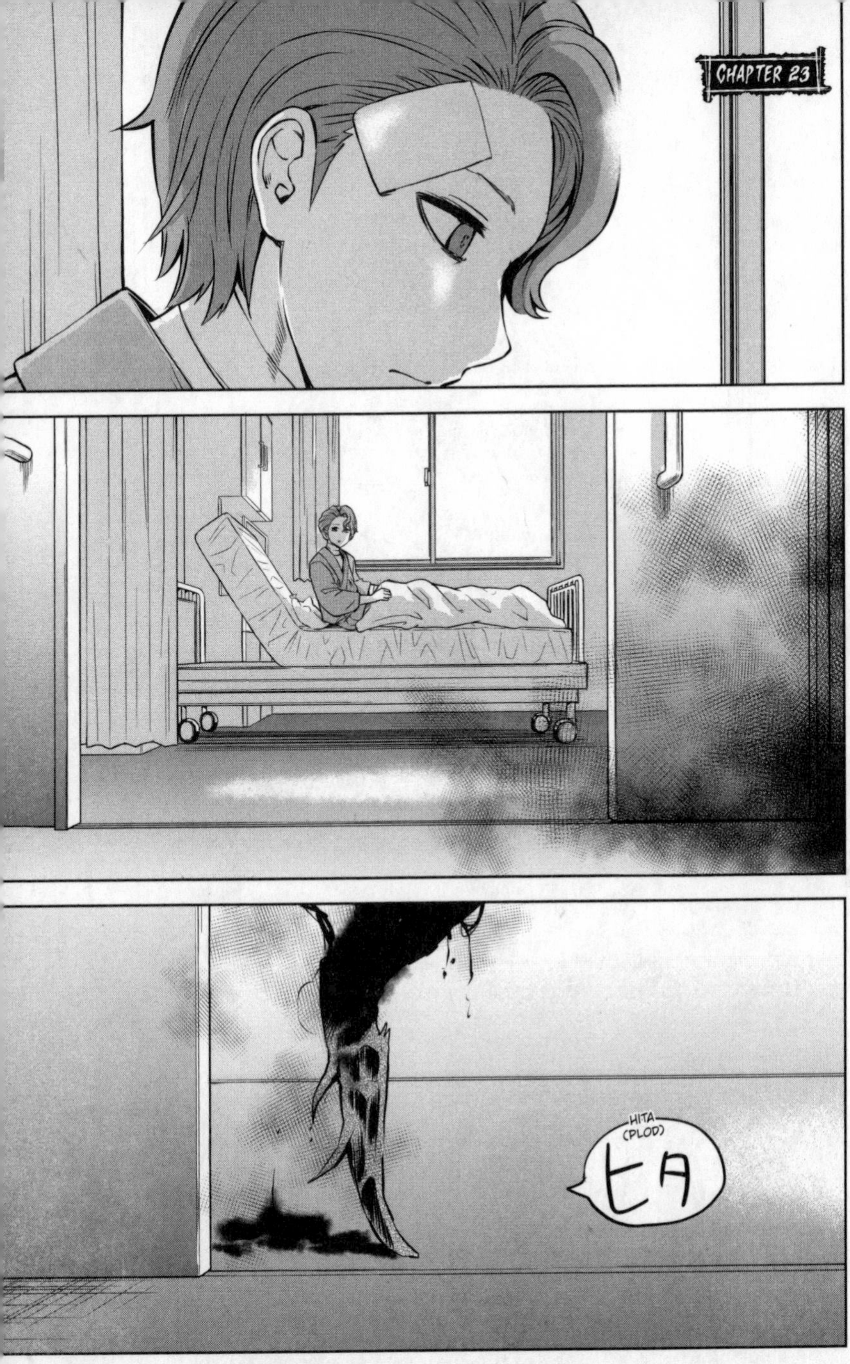
CHAPTER 23
HITA (PLOD)
ヒタ

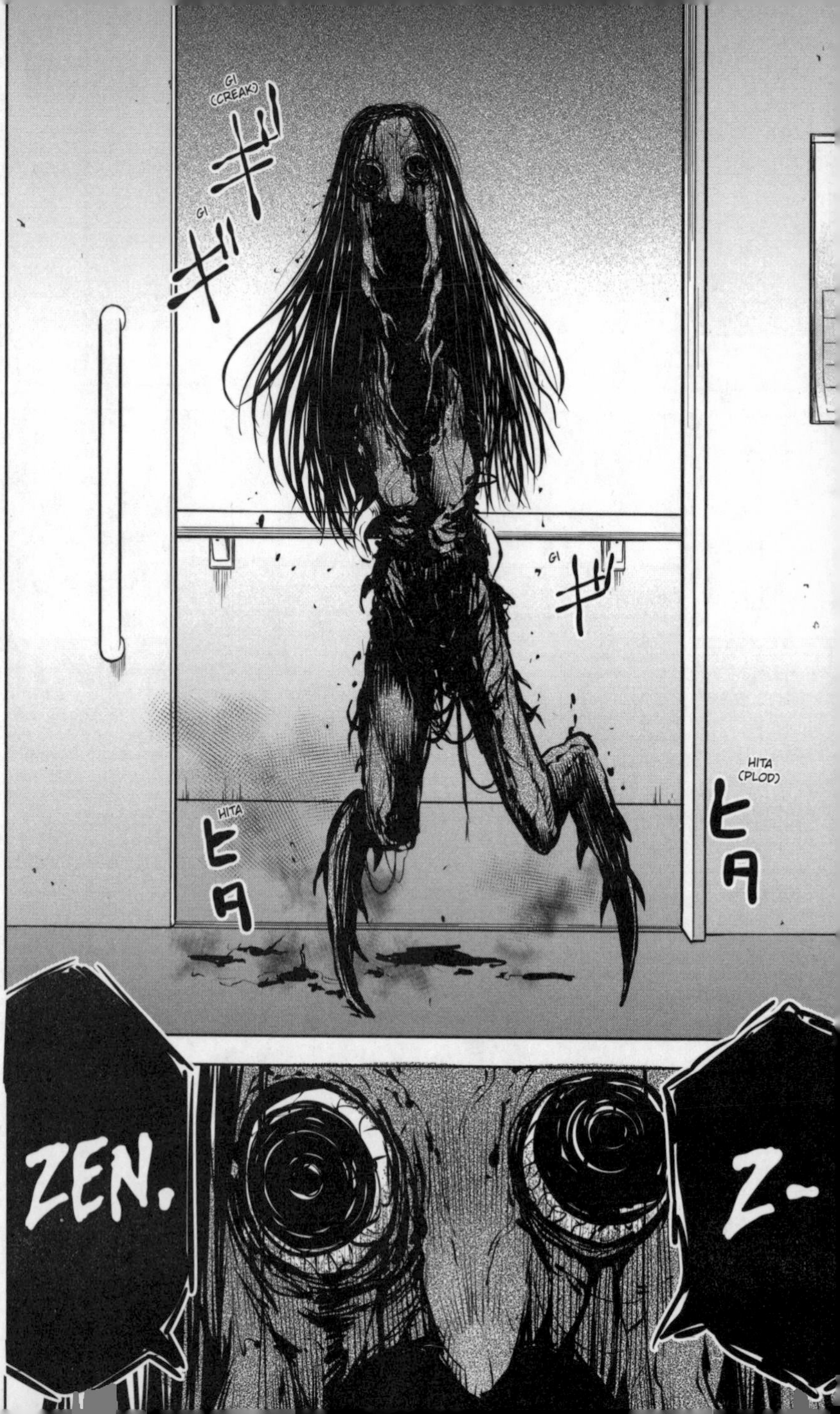
ギ
GI
(CREAK)
ギ
GI
ギ
GI
ヒタ
HITA
(PLOD)
ヒタ
HITA
Z-
ZEN.

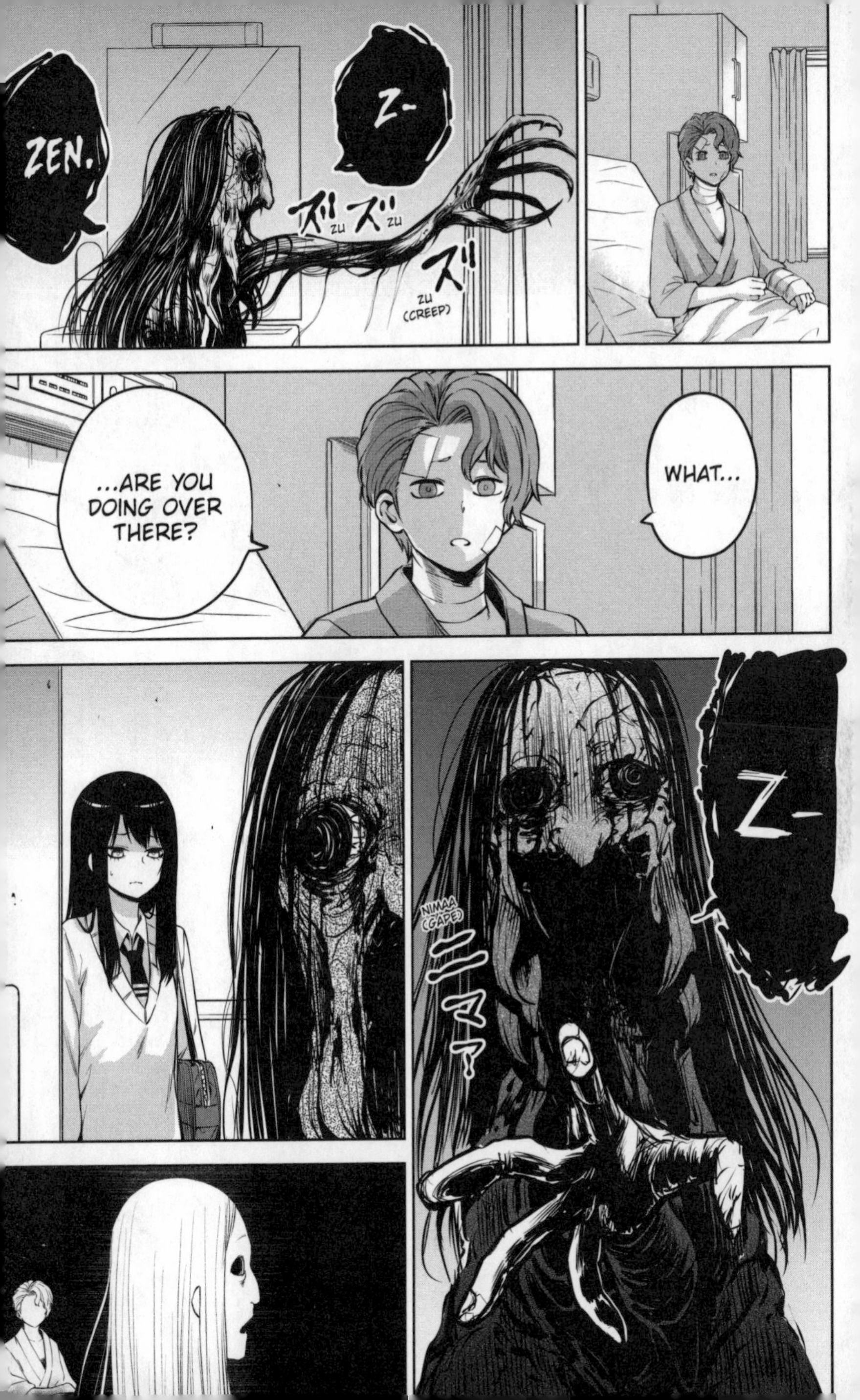
Z-
ZEN.
ズ ZU ズ ZU ズ ZU (CREEP)
WHAT...
...ARE YOU DOING OVER THERE?
Z-
ニマァ NIMAA (GAPE)

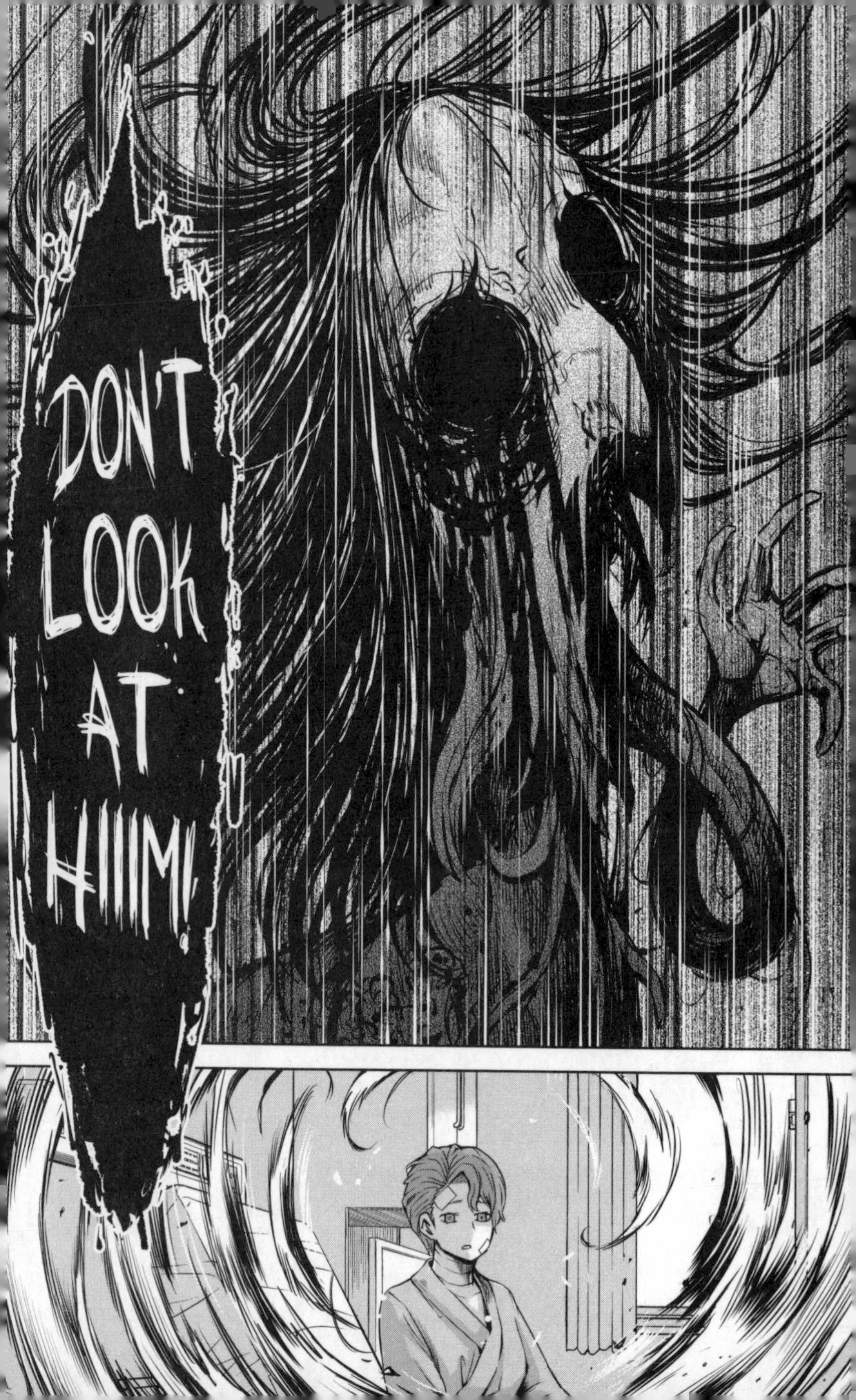
DON'T LOOK AT HIIIM!

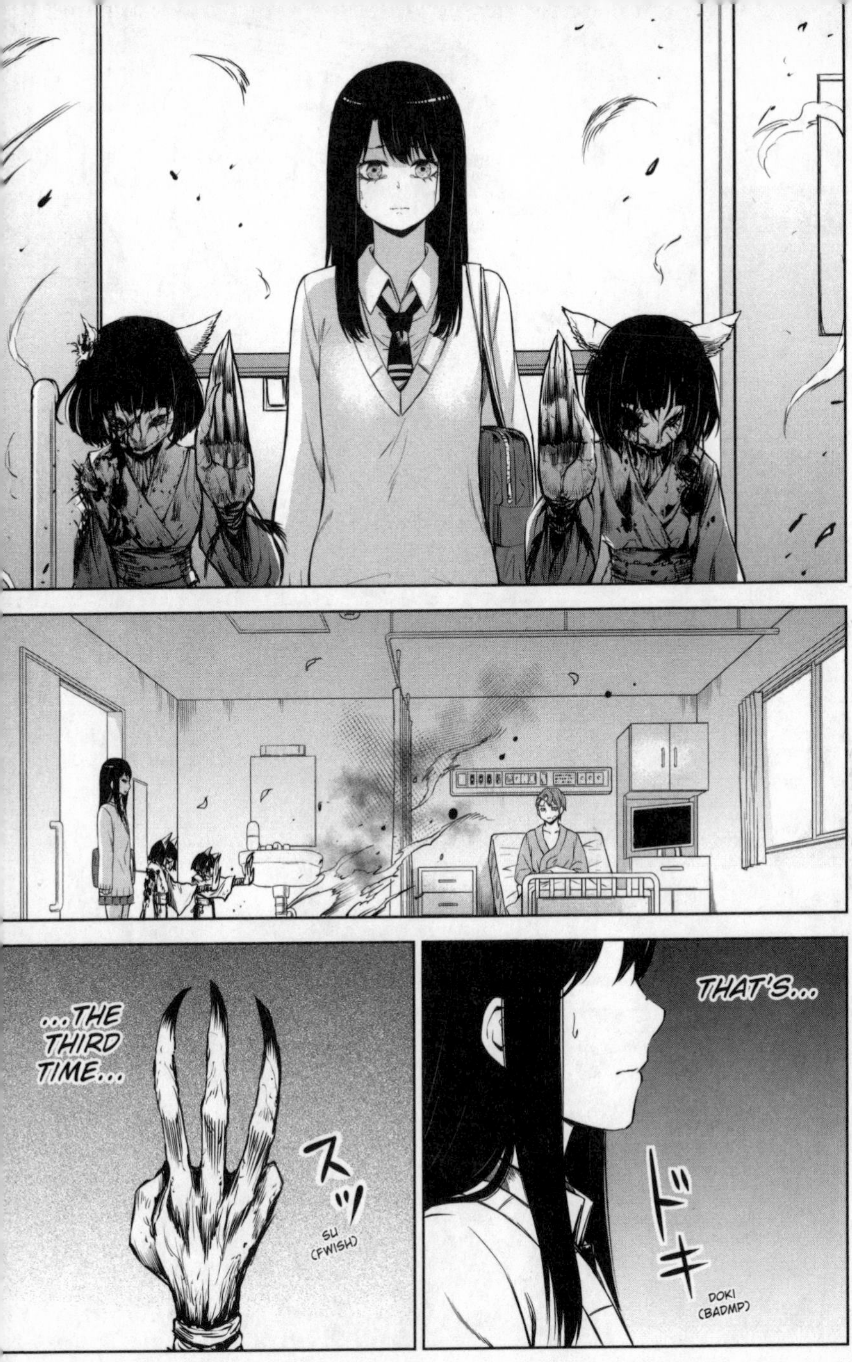
THAT'S...
ドキ
DOKI (BADMP)
...THE THIRD TIME...
スッ
SU (FWISH)

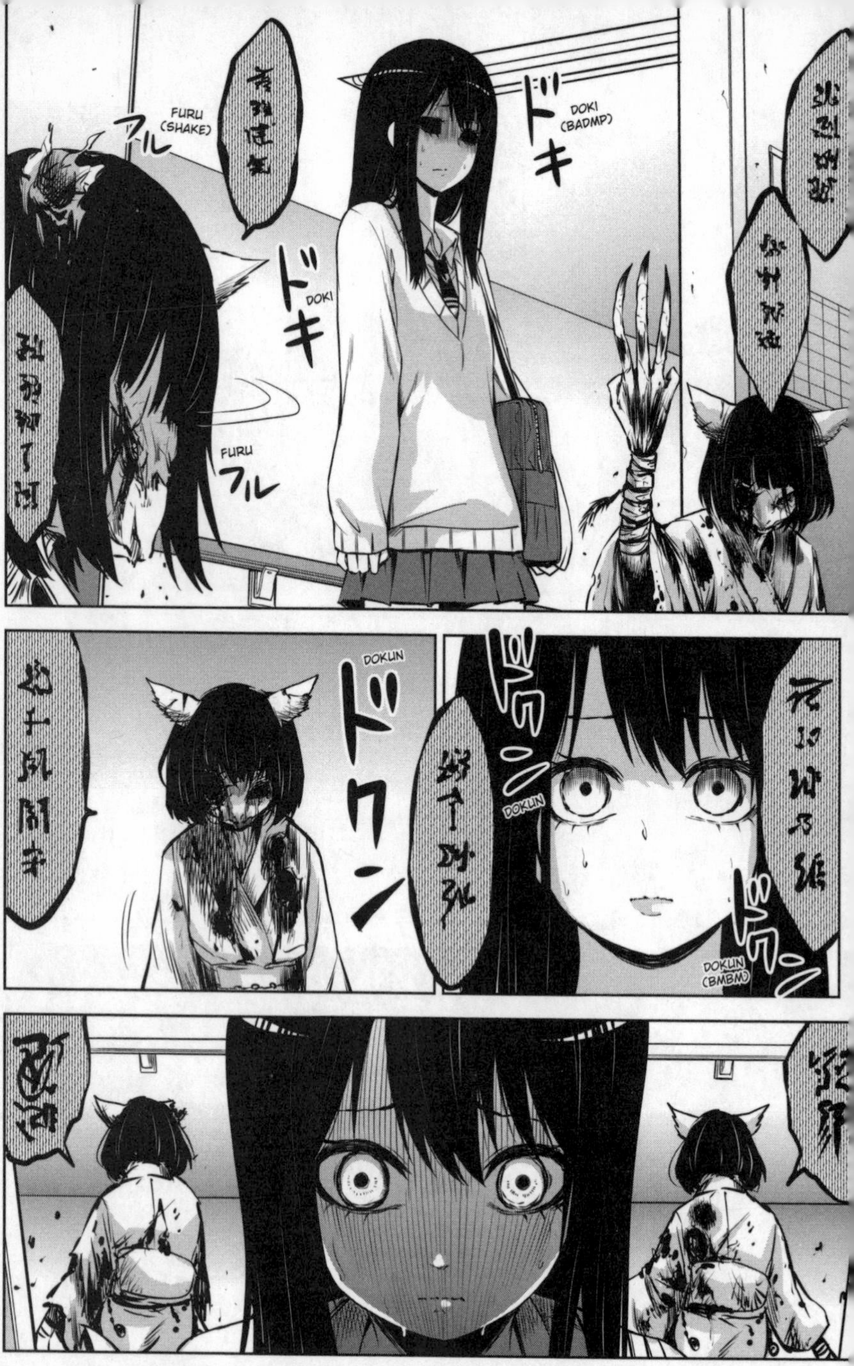
ドキ
DOKI (BADMP)
ドキ
DOKI
フル
FURU (SHAKE)
フル
FURU
ドクン
DOKUN
ドクン
DOKUN (BMBM)
ドクン
DOKUN

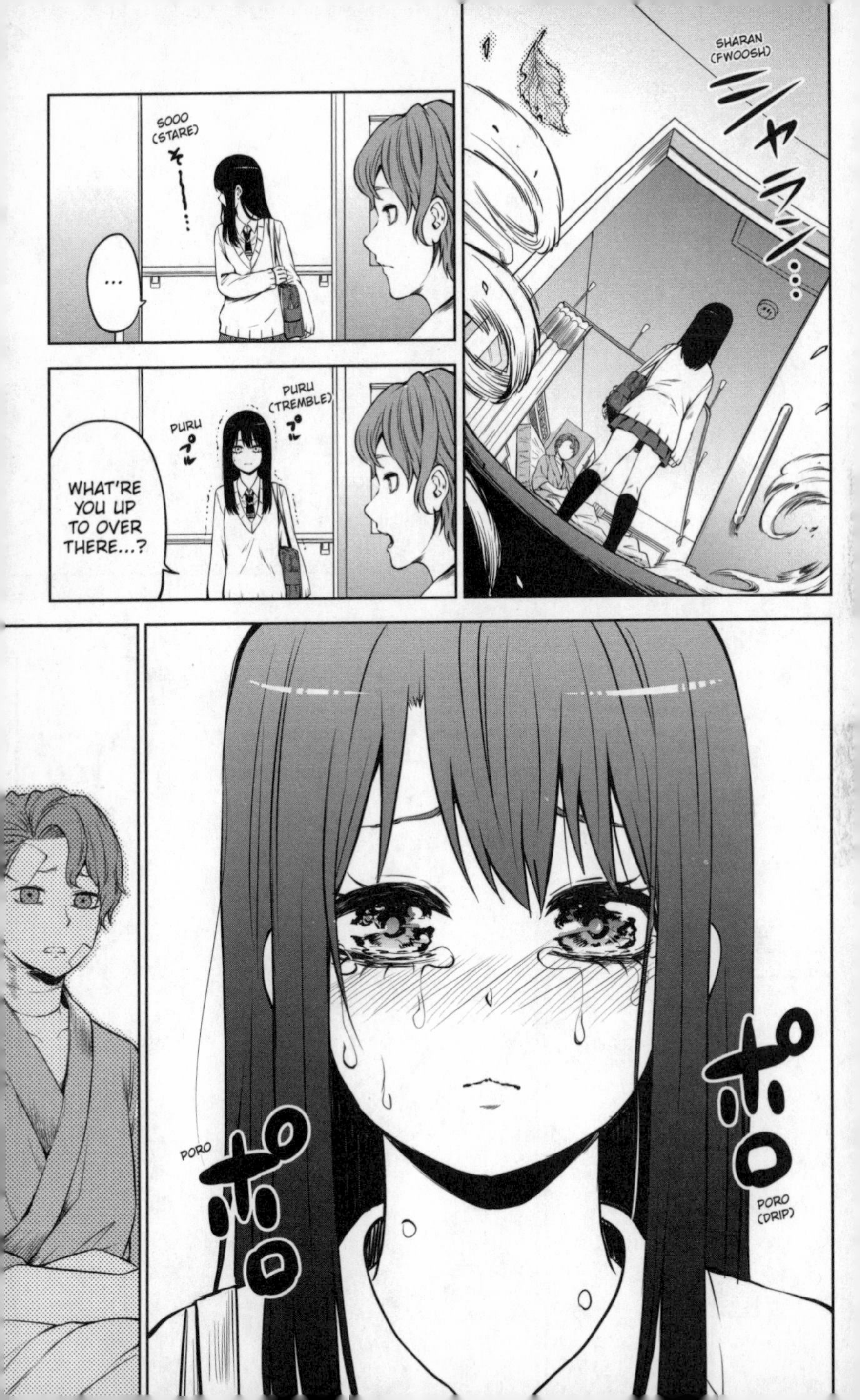
SHARAN (FWOOSH)
シャラン…
SOOO (STARE)
そ～…
...
PURU (TREMBLE)
プル
PURU
プル
WHAT'RE YOU UP TO OVER THERE...?
ポロ
PORO (DRIP)
PORO
ポロ

BAN (SLAM)
ばん

BIKU (JOLT)
ビク

OH!

I MADE IIIIIT!

SHE REALLY IS A STRANGE ONE.

OH...! WHAT'RE YOU TWO DOING HERE...?

SORRY!

H-HANA-CHAN WANTED TO...

DOKI (BADMP)
ド キ

DOKI
ド キ

THERE YOU ARE!!

HANA-CHAN! WE'RE AT THE HOSPITAL. KEEP IT DOWN...!

TANAKA...

MIKI... MIKA...?

YOU OKAY, SENSEI?

IT'S HANA YURI-KAWA.

NOT TANAKA.

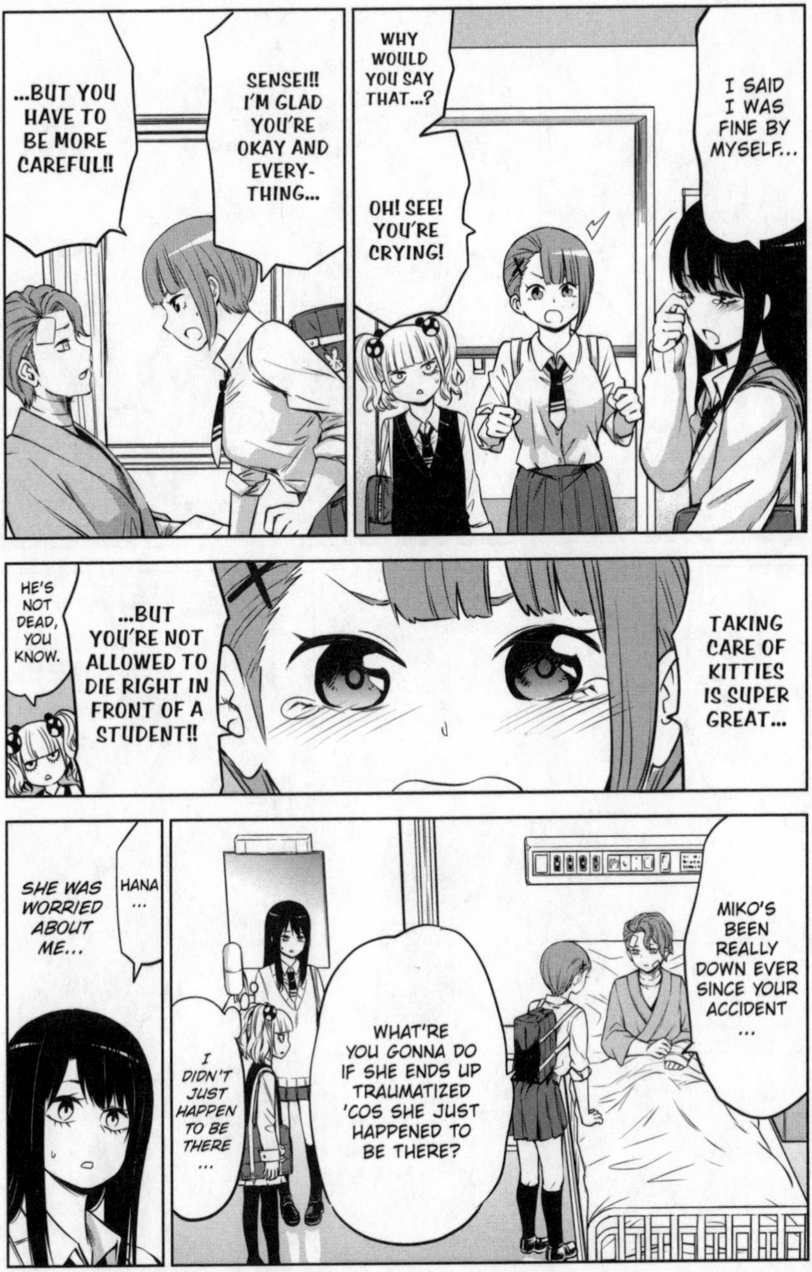
I SAID I WAS FINE BY MYSELF...
WHY WOULD YOU SAY THAT...?
OH! SEE! YOU'RE CRYING!
SENSEI!! I'M GLAD YOU'RE OKAY AND EVERY-THING...
...BUT YOU HAVE TO BE MORE CAREFUL!!
TAKING CARE OF KITTIES IS SUPER GREAT...
...BUT YOU'RE NOT ALLOWED TO DIE RIGHT IN FRONT OF A STUDENT!!
HE'S NOT DEAD, YOU KNOW.
MIKO'S BEEN REALLY DOWN EVER SINCE YOUR ACCIDENT ...
WHAT'RE YOU GONNA DO IF SHE ENDS UP TRAUMATIZED 'COS SHE JUST HAPPENED TO BE THERE?
I DIDN'T JUST HAPPEN TO BE THERE ...
HANA ...
SHE WAS WORRIED ABOUT ME...

...

THIS... ISN'T ABOUT *THAT*...

BUT YOU'RE CRYING!

YOU CAN'T SAY STUFF LIKE THAT...

YOU'RE HERE TO VISIT HIM.

HE MADE YOU CRY OVER SOMETHING ELSE!?

...I GOT WHAT I DESERVED.

AS I MENTIONED EARLIER...

...I DON'T REALLY KNOW WHAT'S GOING ON...

YOU DID NOTHING WRONG...

OH...

I'M FINE NOW...

...BUT I'M SORRY FOR MAKING YOU WORRY.

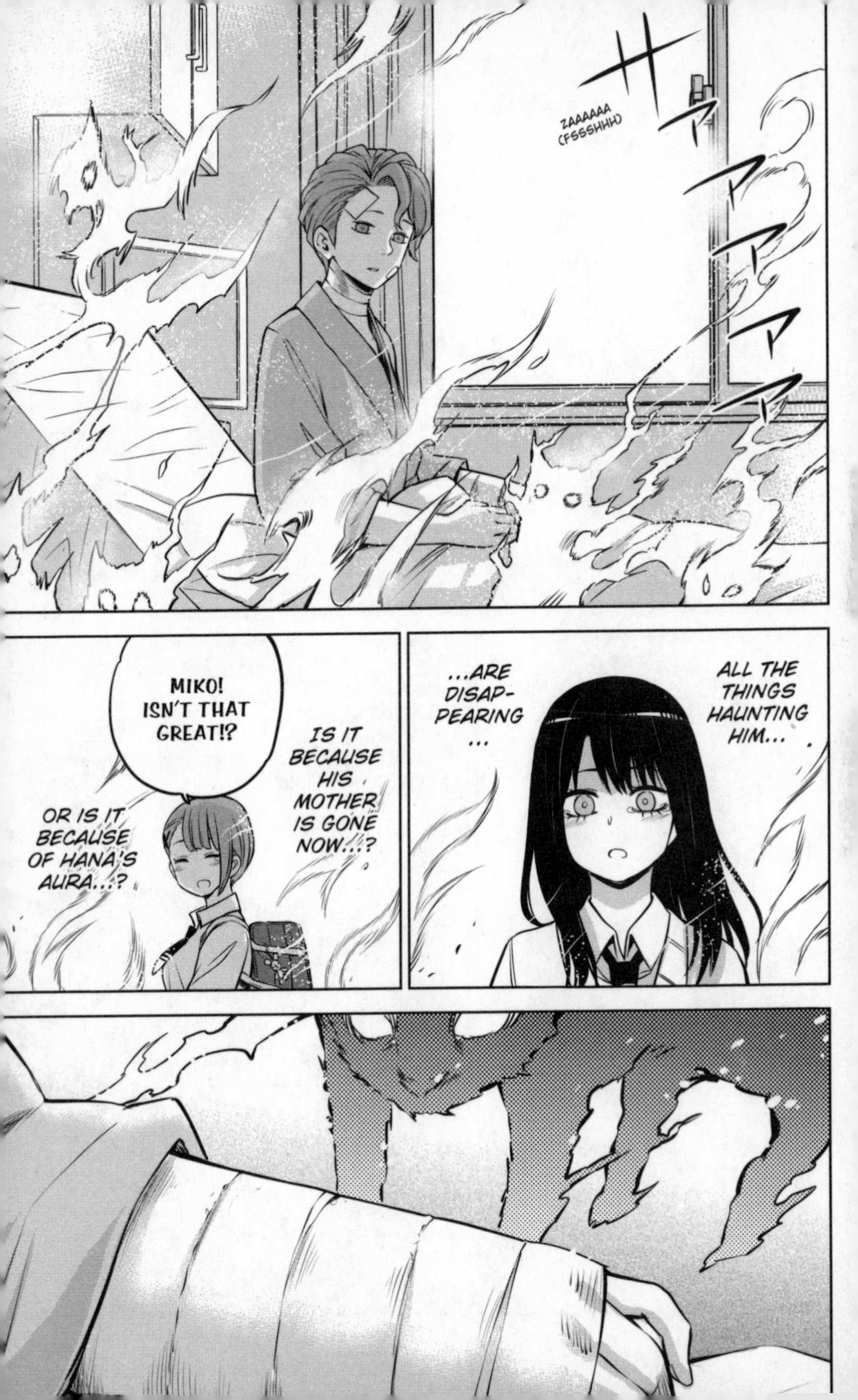
ZAAAAAA (FSSSHHH)
ALL THE THINGS HAUNTING HIM...
...ARE DISAP-PEARING ...
MIKO! ISN'T THAT GREAT!?
IS IT BECAUSE HIS MOTHER IS GONE NOW...?
OR IS IT BECAUSE OF HANA'S AURA...?

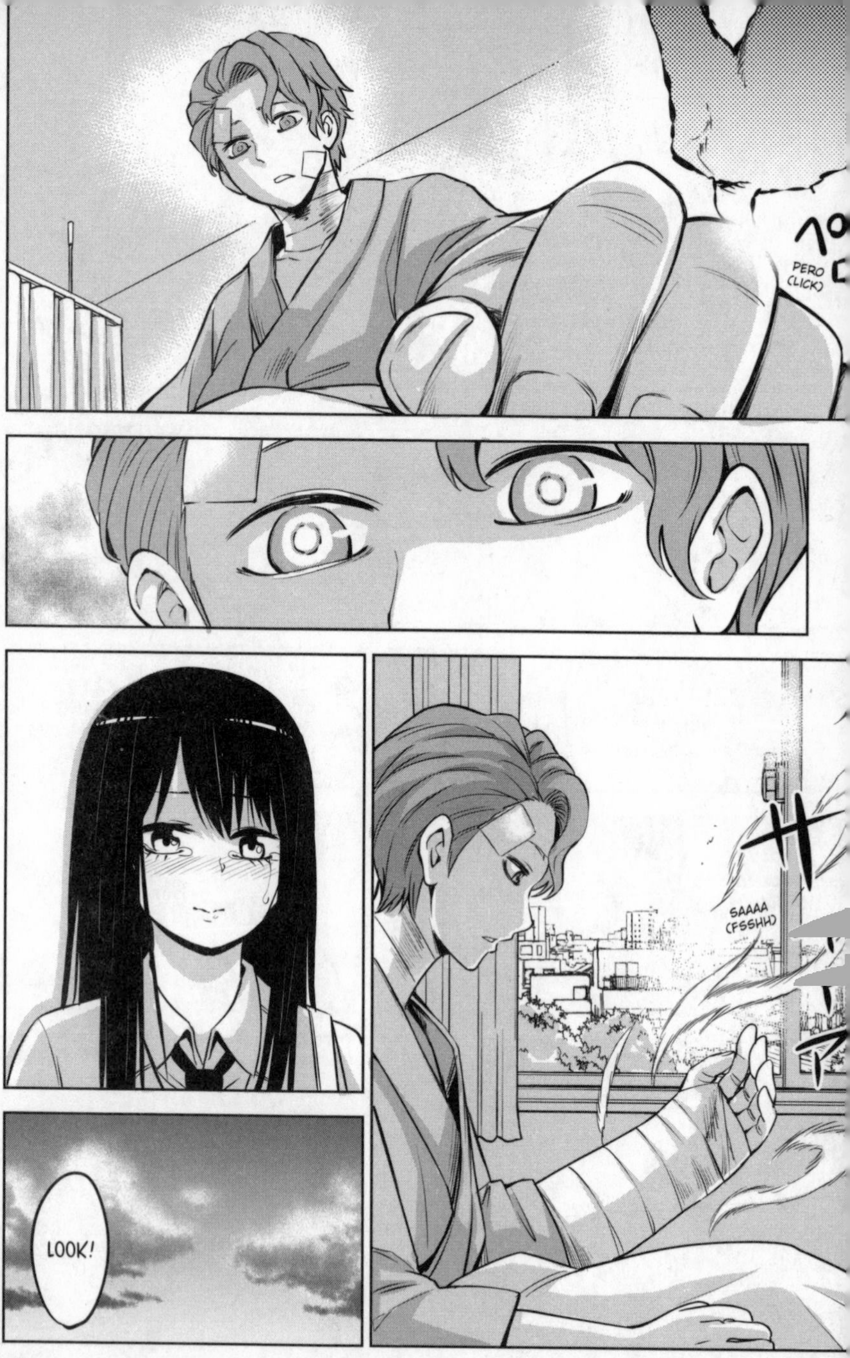
PERO
(LICK)
SAAAA
(FSSHH)
LOOK!

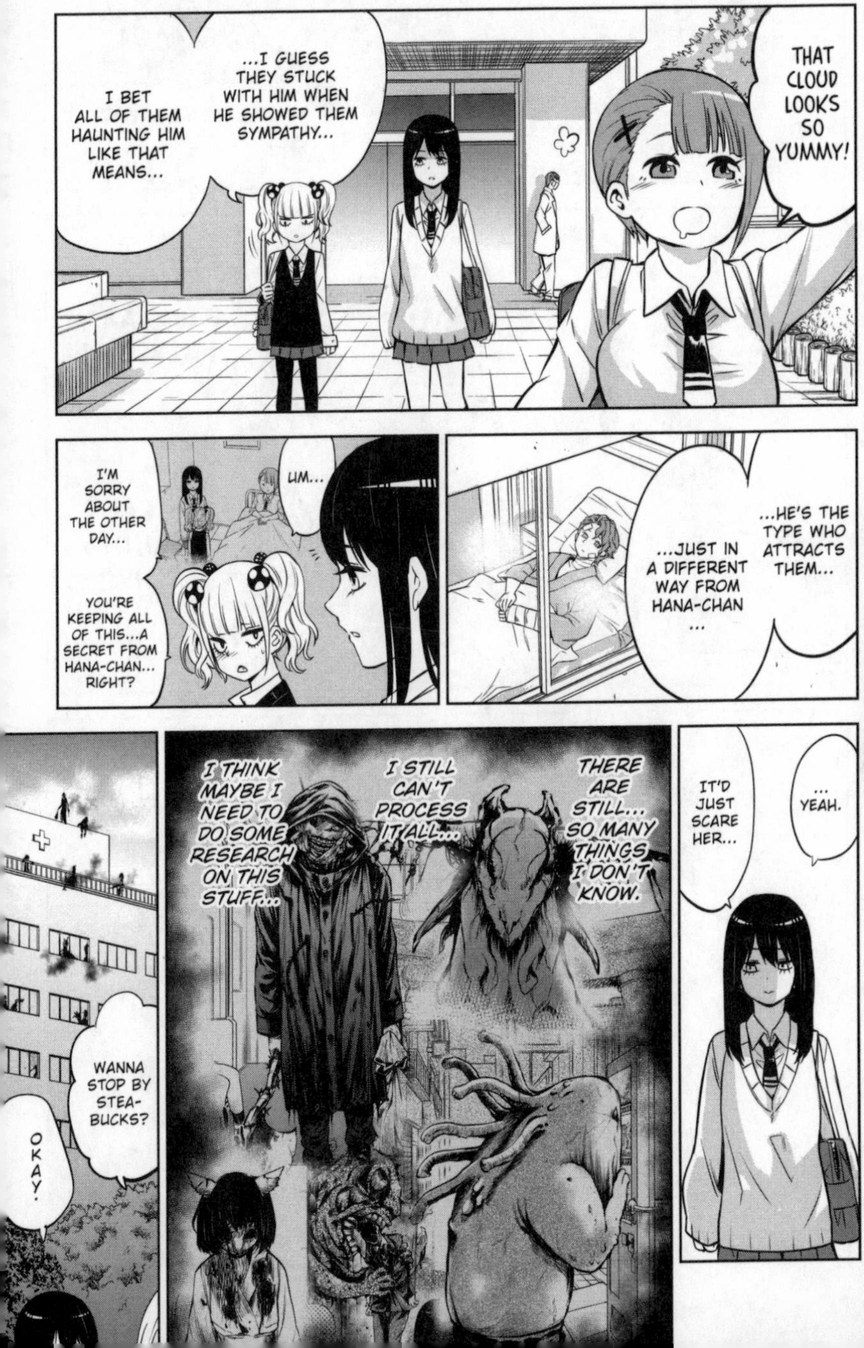
THAT CLOUD LOOKS SO YUMMY!
...I GUESS THEY STUCK WITH HIM WHEN HE SHOWED THEM SYMPATHY...
I BET ALL OF THEM HAUNTING HIM LIKE THAT MEANS...
...HE'S THE TYPE WHO ATTRACTS THEM...
...JUST IN A DIFFERENT WAY FROM HANA-CHAN ...
UM...
I'M SORRY ABOUT THE OTHER DAY...
YOU'RE KEEPING ALL OF THIS...A SECRET FROM HANA-CHAN... RIGHT?
... YEAH.
IT'D JUST SCARE HER...
THERE ARE STILL... SO MANY THINGS I DON'T KNOW.
I STILL CAN'T PROCESS IT ALL...
I THINK MAYBE I NEED TO DO SOME RESEARCH ON THIS STUFF...
WANNA STOP BY STEA-BUCKS?
OKAY.

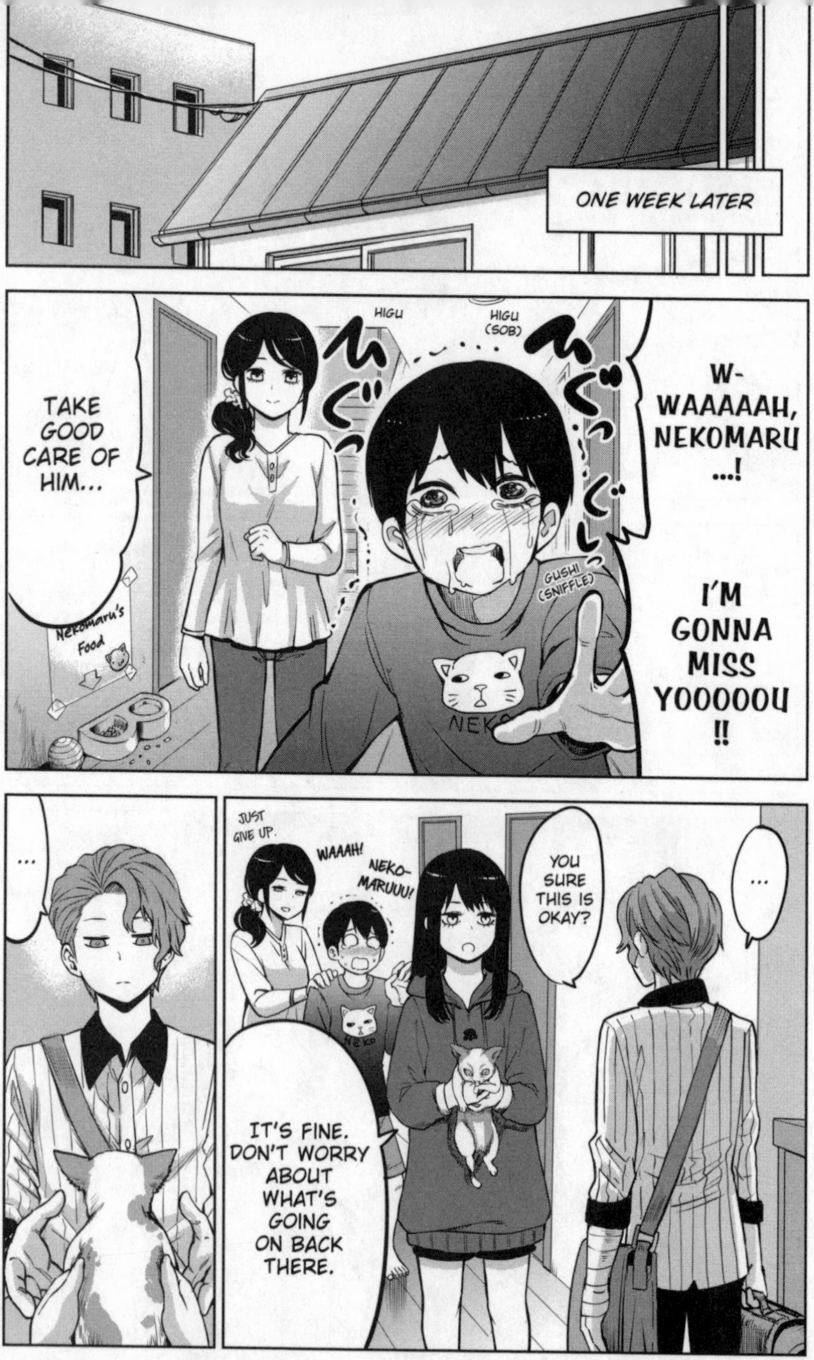
ONE WEEK LATER
W-WAAAAAH, NEKOMARU...!
I'M GONNA MISS YOOOOOU!!
HIGU (SOB)
HIGU
GUSHI (SNIFFLE)
TAKE GOOD CARE OF HIM...
Nekomaru's Food
...
YOU SURE THIS IS OKAY?
NEKO-MARUUU!
WAAAH!
JUST GIVE UP.
IT'S FINE. DON'T WORRY ABOUT WHAT'S GOING ON BACK THERE.
...

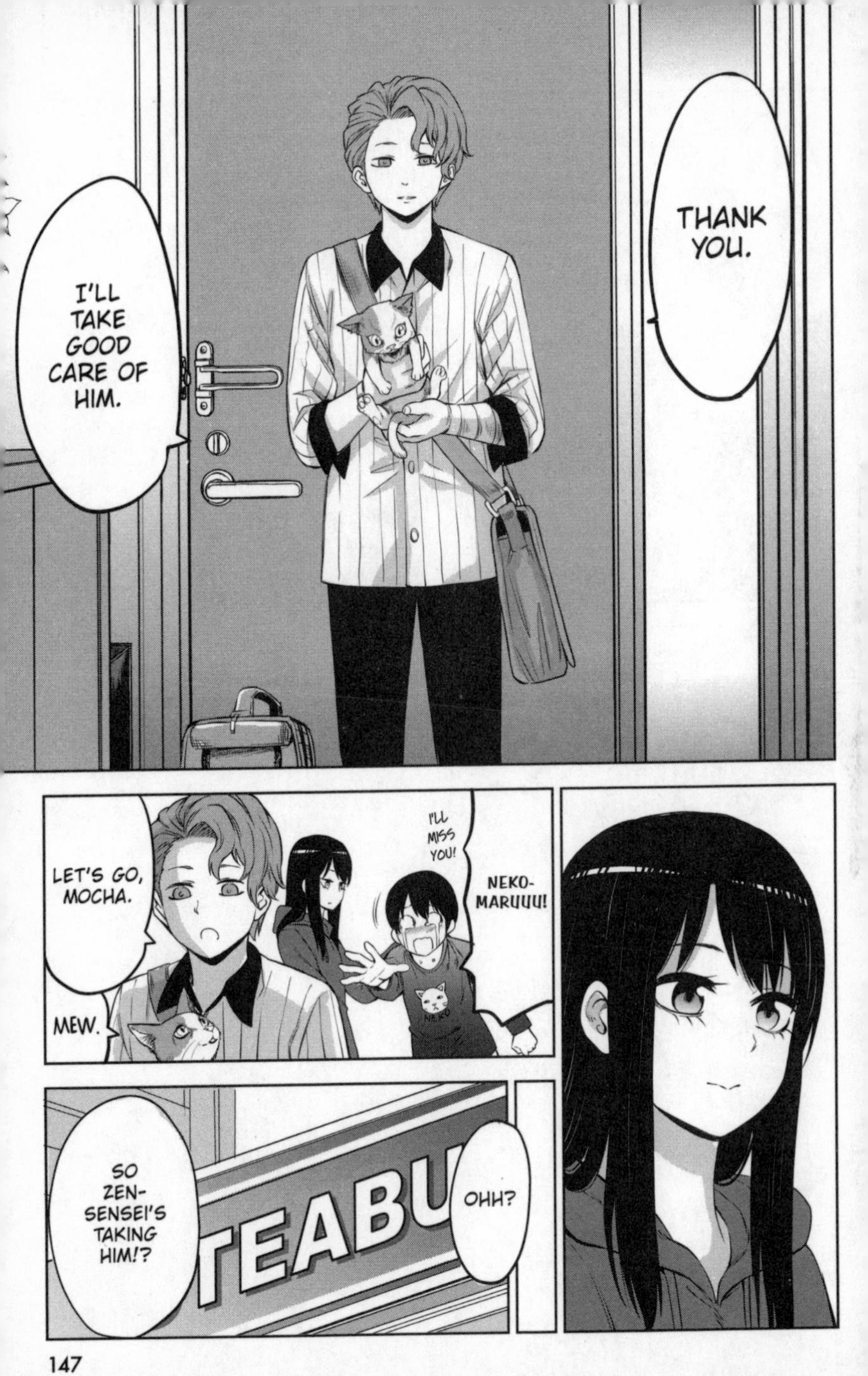
THANK YOU.
I'LL TAKE GOOD CARE OF HIM.
NEKO-MARUUU!
I'LL MISS YOU!
LET'S GO, MOCHA.
MEW.
NEKO
OHH?
TEABU
SO ZEN-SENSEI'S TAKING HIM!?

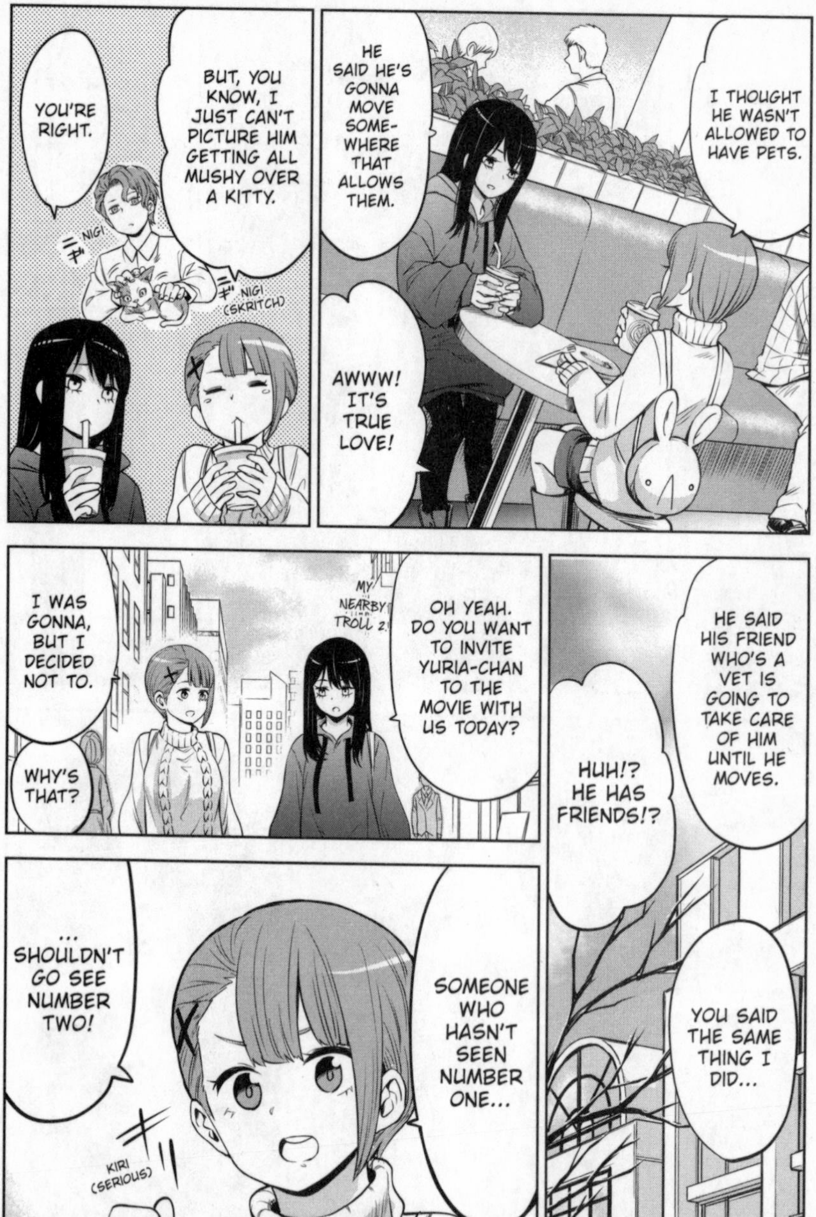

I THOUGHT HE WASN'T ALLOWED TO HAVE PETS.
HE SAID HE'S GONNA MOVE SOME-WHERE THAT ALLOWS THEM.
AWWW! IT'S TRUE LOVE!
BUT, YOU KNOW, I JUST CAN'T PICTURE HIM GETTING ALL MUSHY OVER A KITTY.
YOU'RE RIGHT.
NIGI
NIGI (SKRITCH)
HE SAID HIS FRIEND WHO'S A VET IS GOING TO TAKE CARE OF HIM UNTIL HE MOVES.
HUH!? HE HAS FRIENDS!?
YOU SAID THE SAME THING I DID...
OH YEAH. DO YOU WANT TO INVITE YURIA-CHAN TO THE MOVIE WITH US TODAY?
MY NEARBY TROLL 2!
I WAS GONNA, BUT I DECIDED NOT TO.
WHY'S THAT?
SOMEONE WHO HASN'T SEEN NUMBER ONE...
... SHOULDN'T GO SEE NUMBER TWO!
KIRI (SERIOUS)

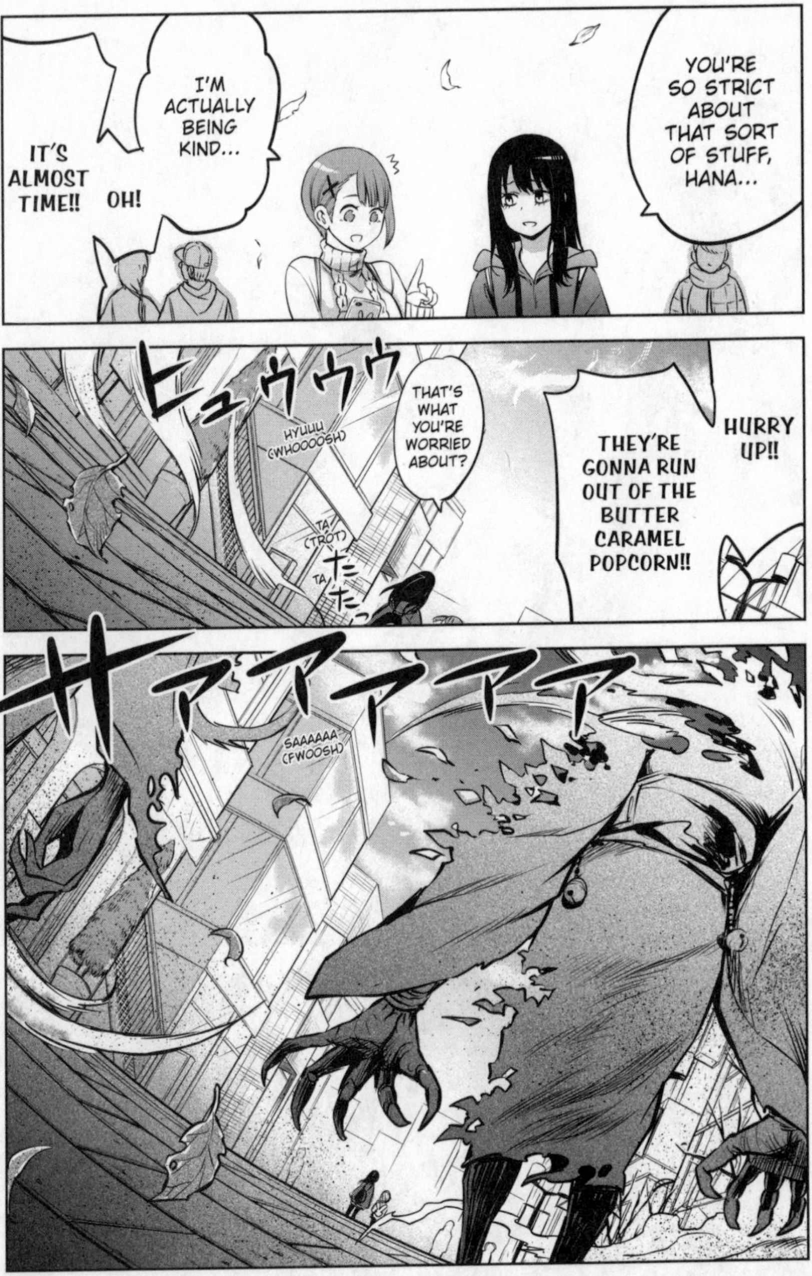
YOU'RE SO STRICT ABOUT THAT SORT OF STUFF, HANA...
I'M ACTUALLY BEING KIND...
OH!
IT'S ALMOST TIME!!
HURRY UP!!
THEY'RE GONNA RUN OUT OF THE BUTTER CARAMEL POPCORN!!
THAT'S WHAT YOU'RE WORRIED ABOUT?
ヒュウウウ
HYUUU (WHOOOOSH)
たたっ
TA (TROT) TA
サアアアアア
SAAAAAA (FWOOSH)

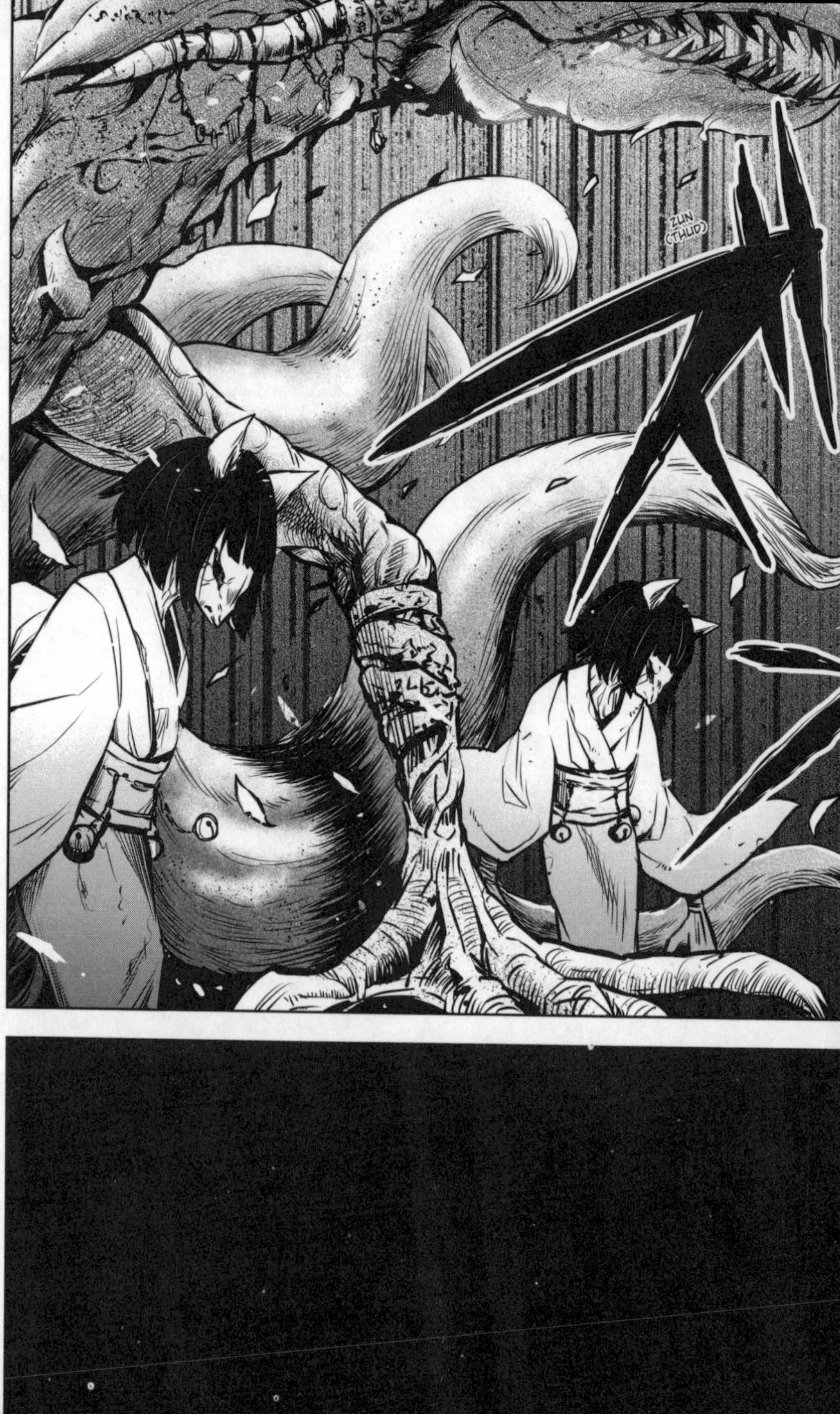
ZUN
(THUD)

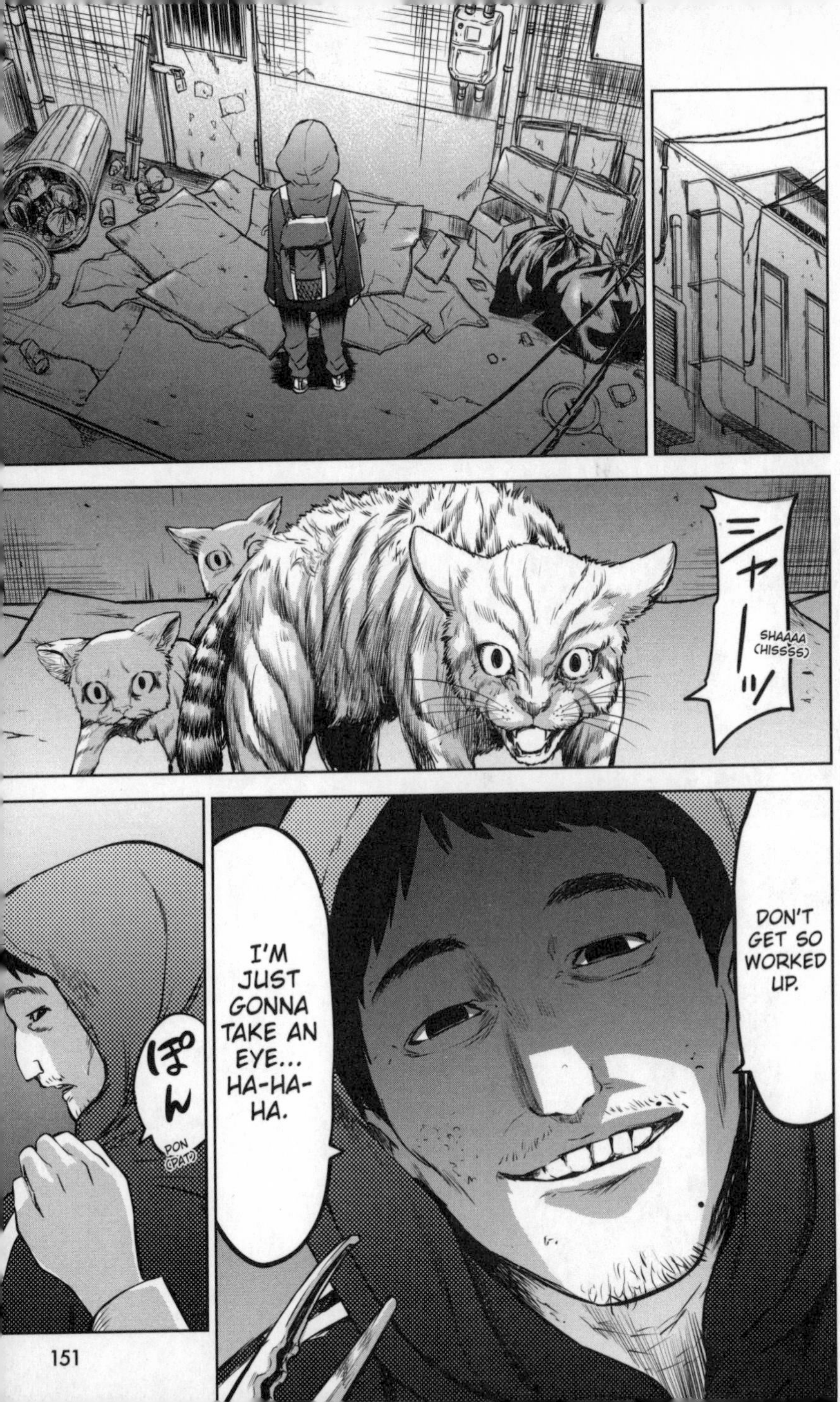
シャーッ
SHAAAA (HISSSS)
DON'T GET SO WORKED UP.
I'M JUST GONNA TAKE AN EYE... HA-HA-HA.
ぽん
PON (PAT)

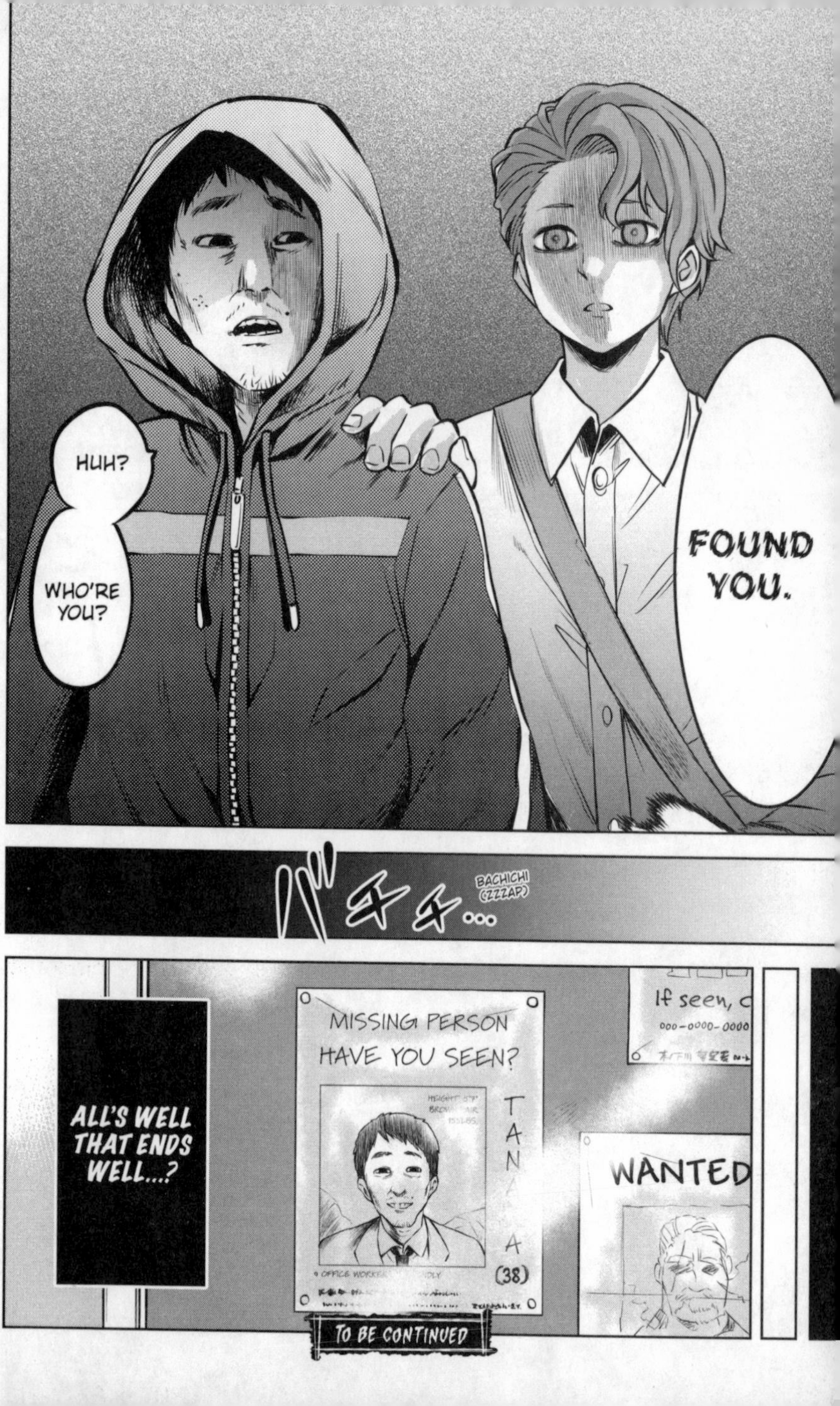
FOUND YOU.
HUH?
WHO'RE YOU?
BACHICHI (ZZZAP)
If seen,
000-0000-0000
WANTED
MISSING PERSON
HAVE YOU SEEN?
TANAKA
(38)
ALL'S WELL THAT ENDS WELL...?
TO BE CONTINUED

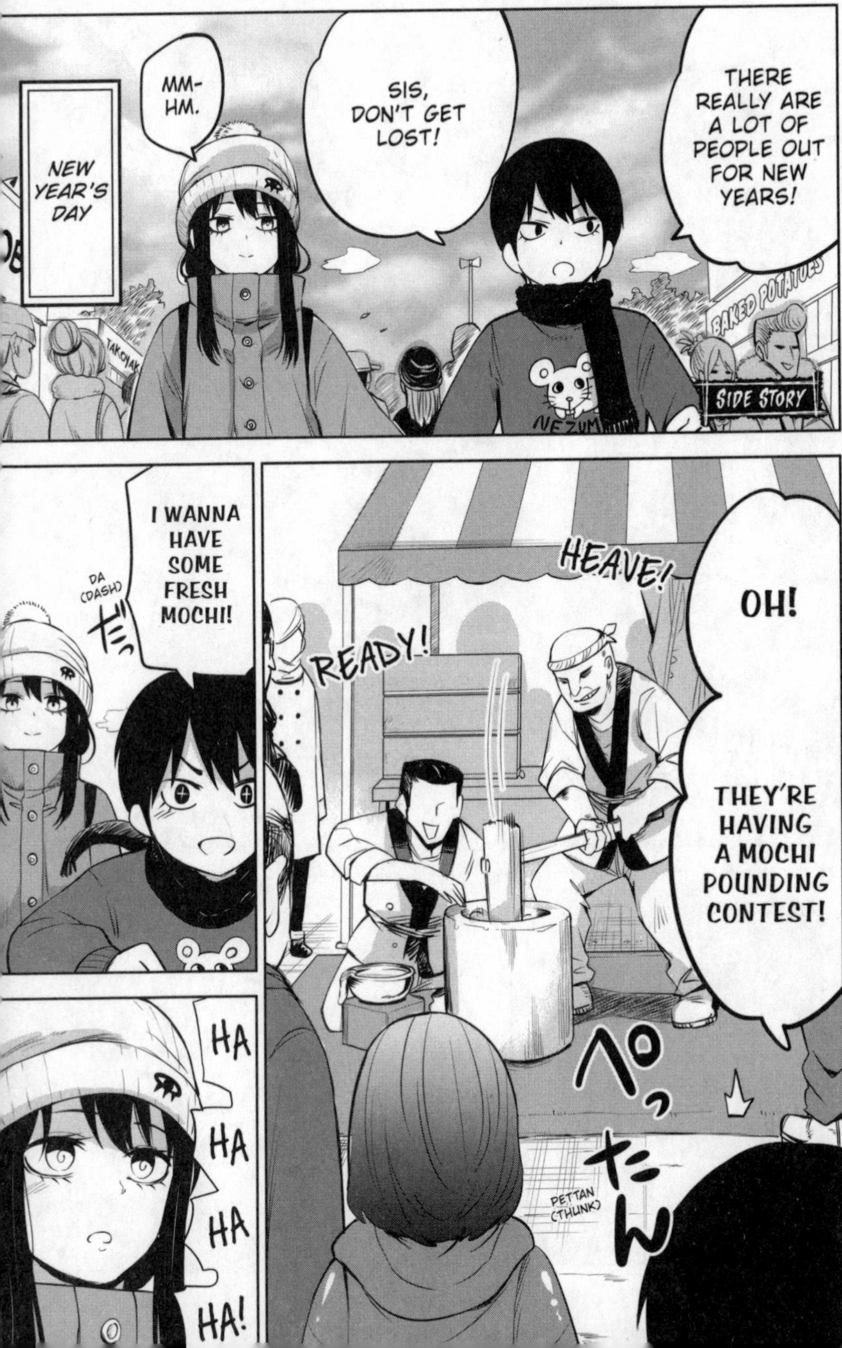
THERE REALLY ARE A LOT OF PEOPLE OUT FOR NEW YEARS!
BAKED POTATOES
SIDE STORY
SIS, DON'T GET LOST!
MM-HM.
NEW YEAR'S DAY
TAKOYAK
HEAVE!
OH!
READY!
THEY'RE HAVING A MOCHI POUNDING CONTEST!
PETTAN (THUNK)
I WANNA HAVE SOME FRESH MOCHI!
DA (DASH)
HA
HA
HA
HA!

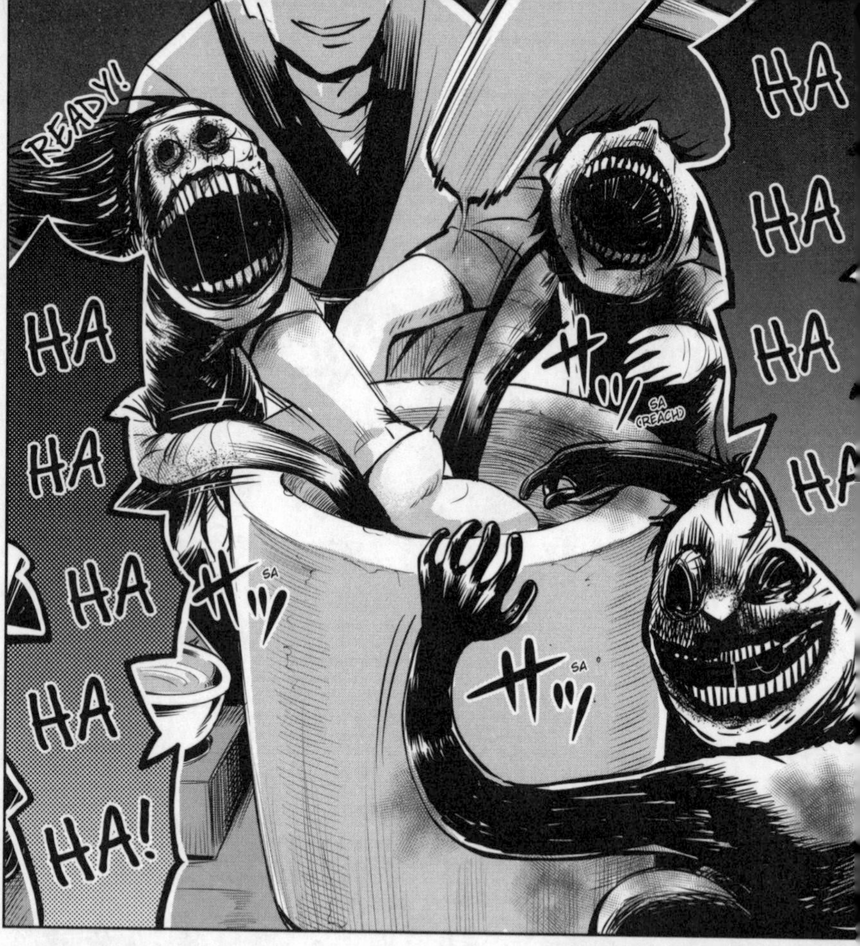
HA
HA
HA
HA
サッ
SA (REACH)
READY!
サッ
SA
サッ
SA
HA
HA
HA
HA
HA!

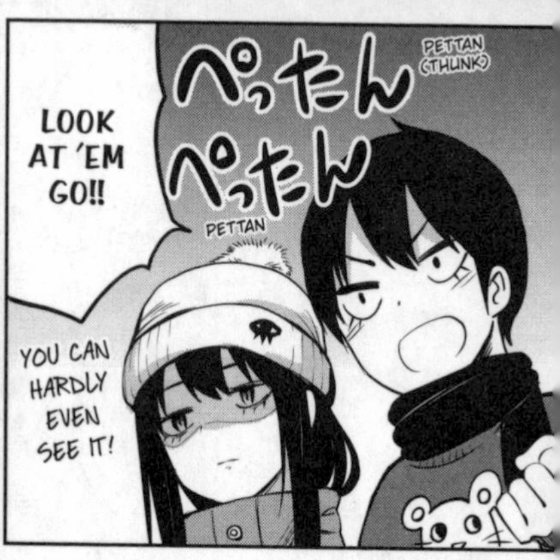
ぺったん
PETTAN (THUNK)
ぺったん
PETTAN
LOOK AT 'EM GO!!
YOU CAN HARDLY EVEN SEE IT!

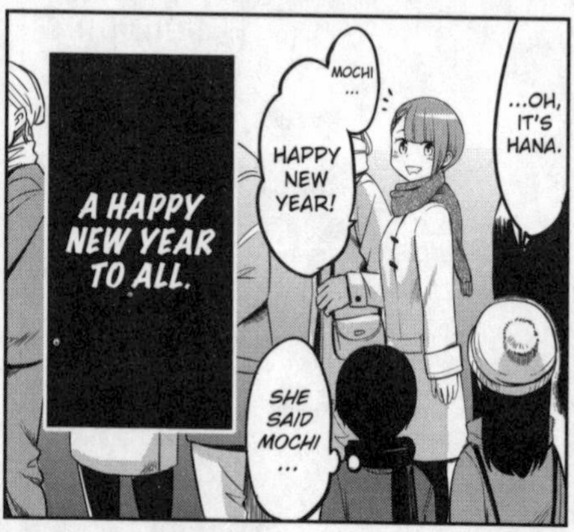
...OH, IT'S HANA.
MOCHI ...
HAPPY NEW YEAR!
A HAPPY NEW YEAR TO ALL.
SHE SAID MOCHI ...

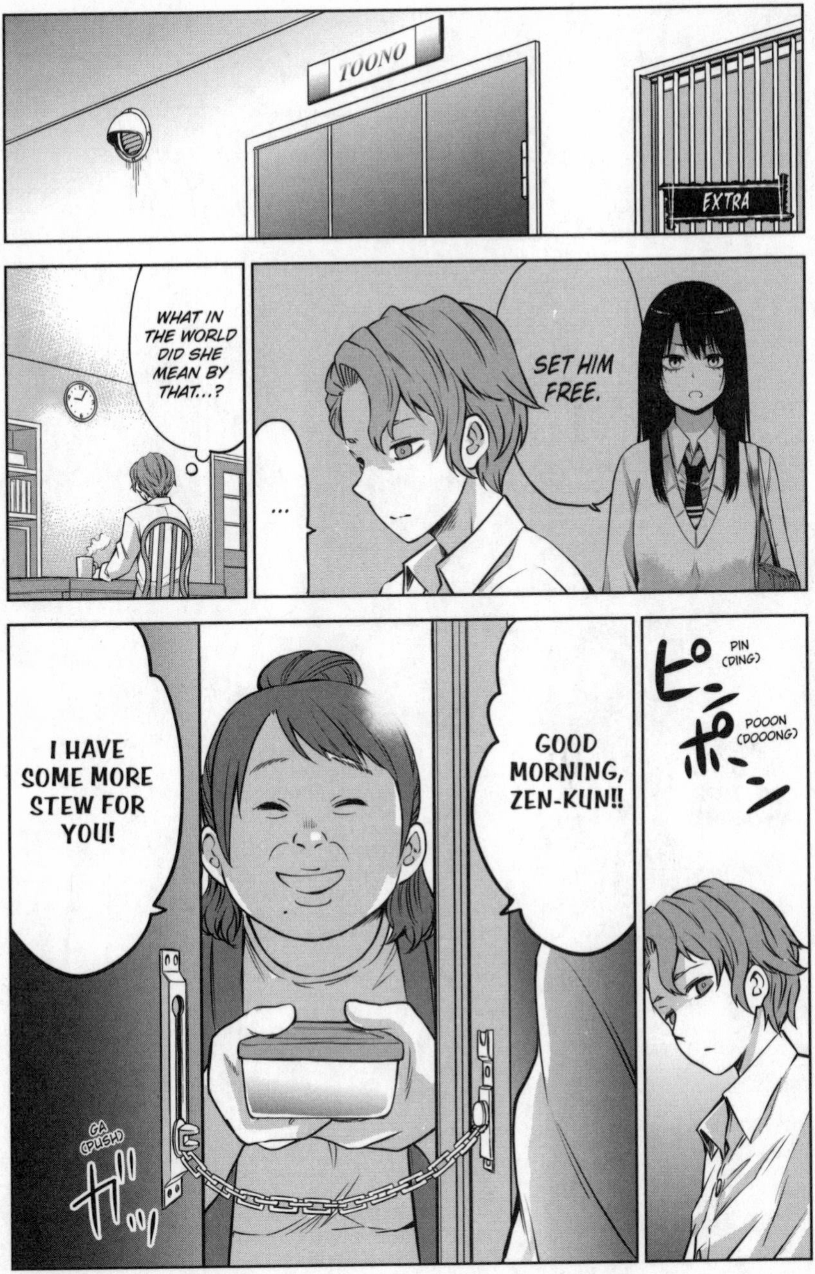
TOONO
EXTRA
SET HIM FREE.
...
WHAT IN THE WORLD DID SHE MEAN BY THAT...?
PIN (DING)
POOON (DOOONG)
GOOD MORNING, ZEN-KUN!!
I HAVE SOME MORE STEW FOR YOU!
GA (PUSH)

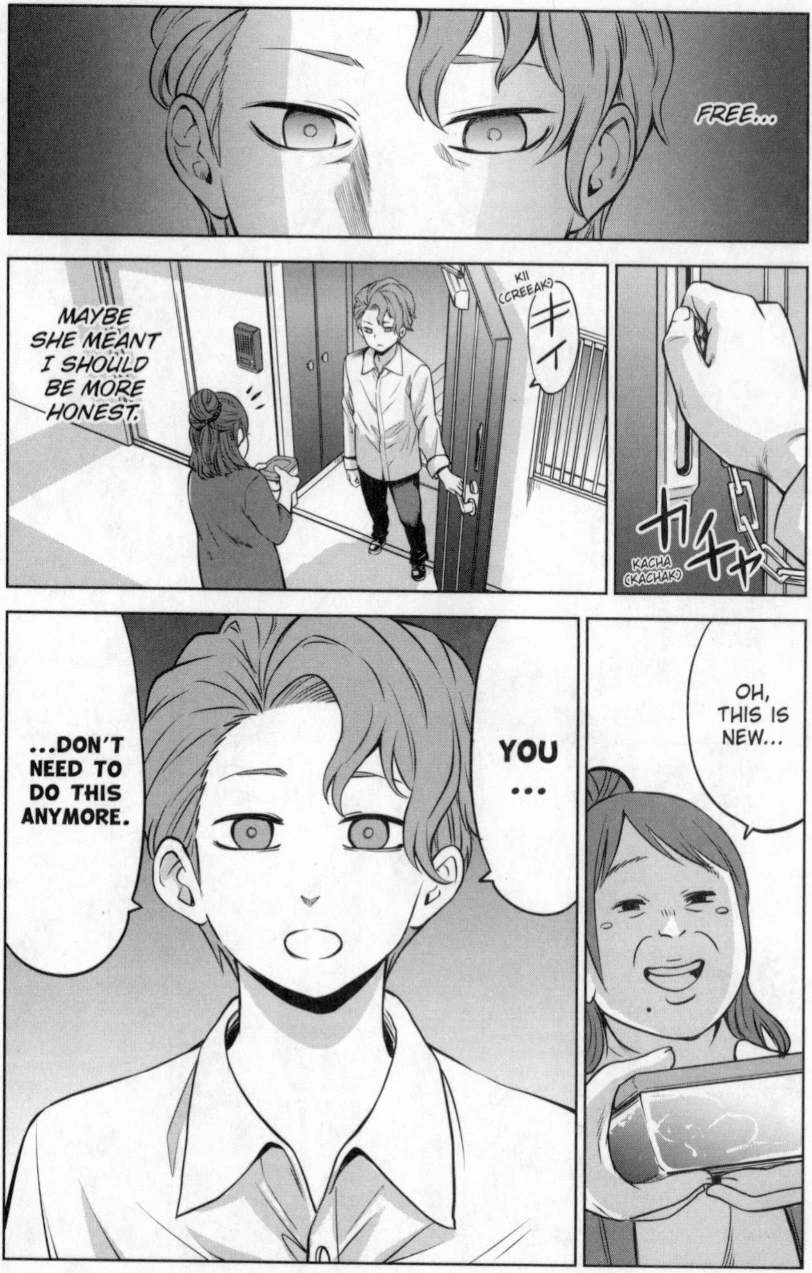
FREE...
カチャ
KACHA (KACHAK)
キイ
KII (CREEAK)
MAYBE SHE MEANT I SHOULD BE MORE HONEST.
OH, THIS IS NEW...
YOU...
...DON'T NEED TO DO THIS ANYMORE.

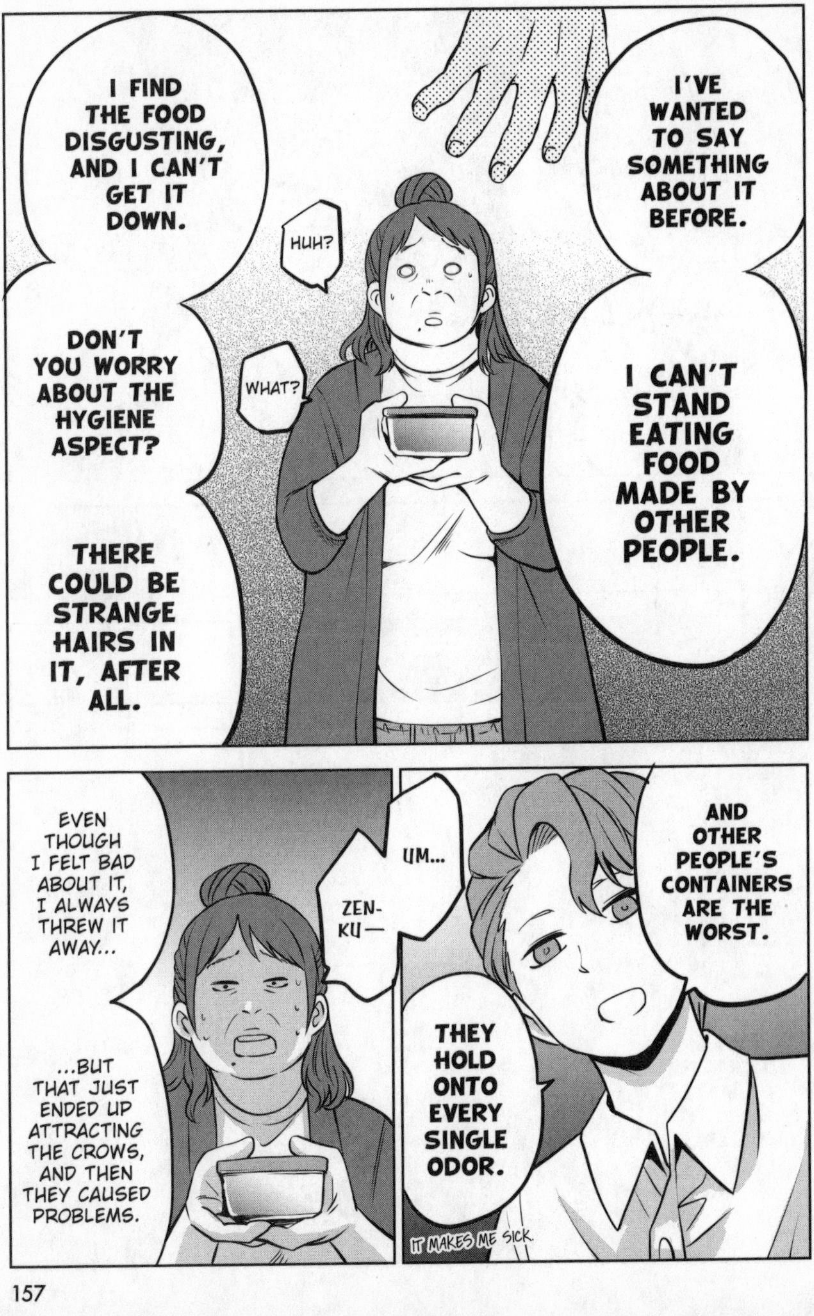
I'VE WANTED TO SAY SOMETHING ABOUT IT BEFORE.
I CAN'T STAND EATING FOOD MADE BY OTHER PEOPLE.
HUH?
WHAT?
I FIND THE FOOD DISGUSTING, AND I CAN'T GET IT DOWN.
DON'T YOU WORRY ABOUT THE HYGIENE ASPECT?
THERE COULD BE STRANGE HAIRS IN IT, AFTER ALL.
AND OTHER PEOPLE'S CONTAINERS ARE THE WORST.
THEY HOLD ONTO EVERY SINGLE ODOR.
IT MAKES ME SICK.
UM...
ZEN-KU—
EVEN THOUGH I FELT BAD ABOUT IT, I ALWAYS THREW IT AWAY...
...BUT THAT JUST ENDED UP ATTRACTING THE CROWS, AND THEN THEY CAUSED PROBLEMS.

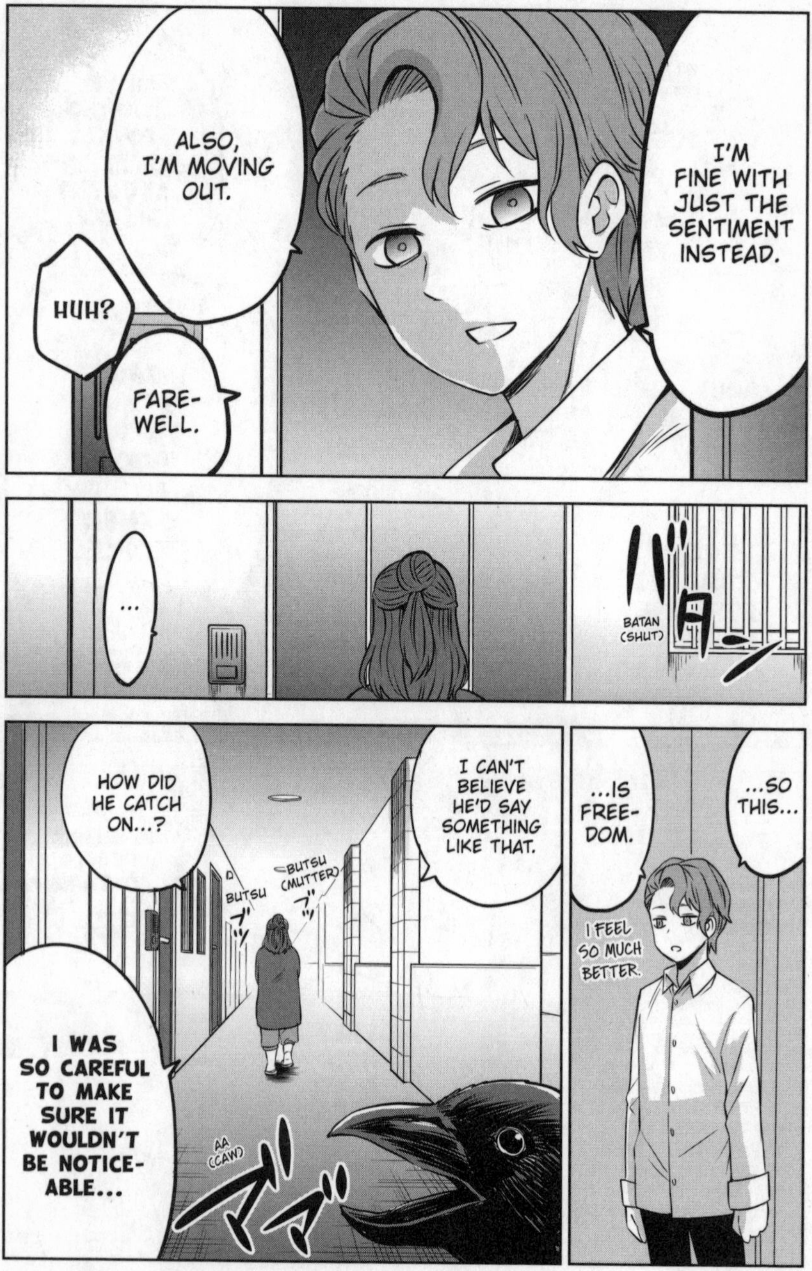
I'M FINE WITH JUST THE SENTIMENT INSTEAD.
ALSO, I'M MOVING OUT.
HUH?
FARE-WELL.
BATAN (SHUT)
...
...SO THIS...
...IS FREE-DOM.
I FEEL SO MUCH BETTER.
I CAN'T BELIEVE HE'D SAY SOMETHING LIKE THAT.
BUTSU (MUTTER)
BUTSU
HOW DID HE CATCH ON...?
I WAS SO CAREFUL TO MAKE SURE IT WOULDN'T BE NOTICE-ABLE...
AA (CAW)

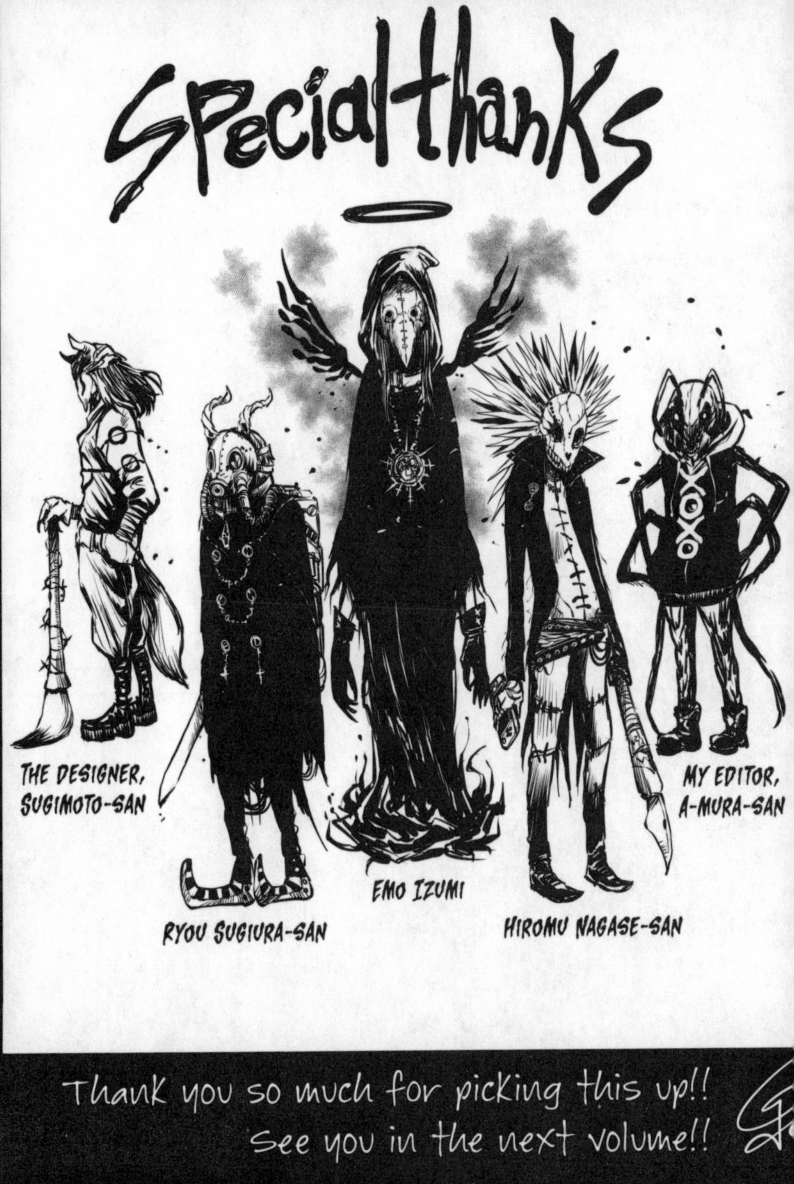
Special thanks
THE DESIGNER,
SUGIMOTO-SAN
RYOU SUGIURA-SAN
EMO IZUMI
HIROMU NAGASE-SAN
MY EDITOR,
A-MURA-SAN

Thank you so much for picking this up!!
See you in the next volume!!

I've never really written an afterword before...
I'm on twitter @izumi000

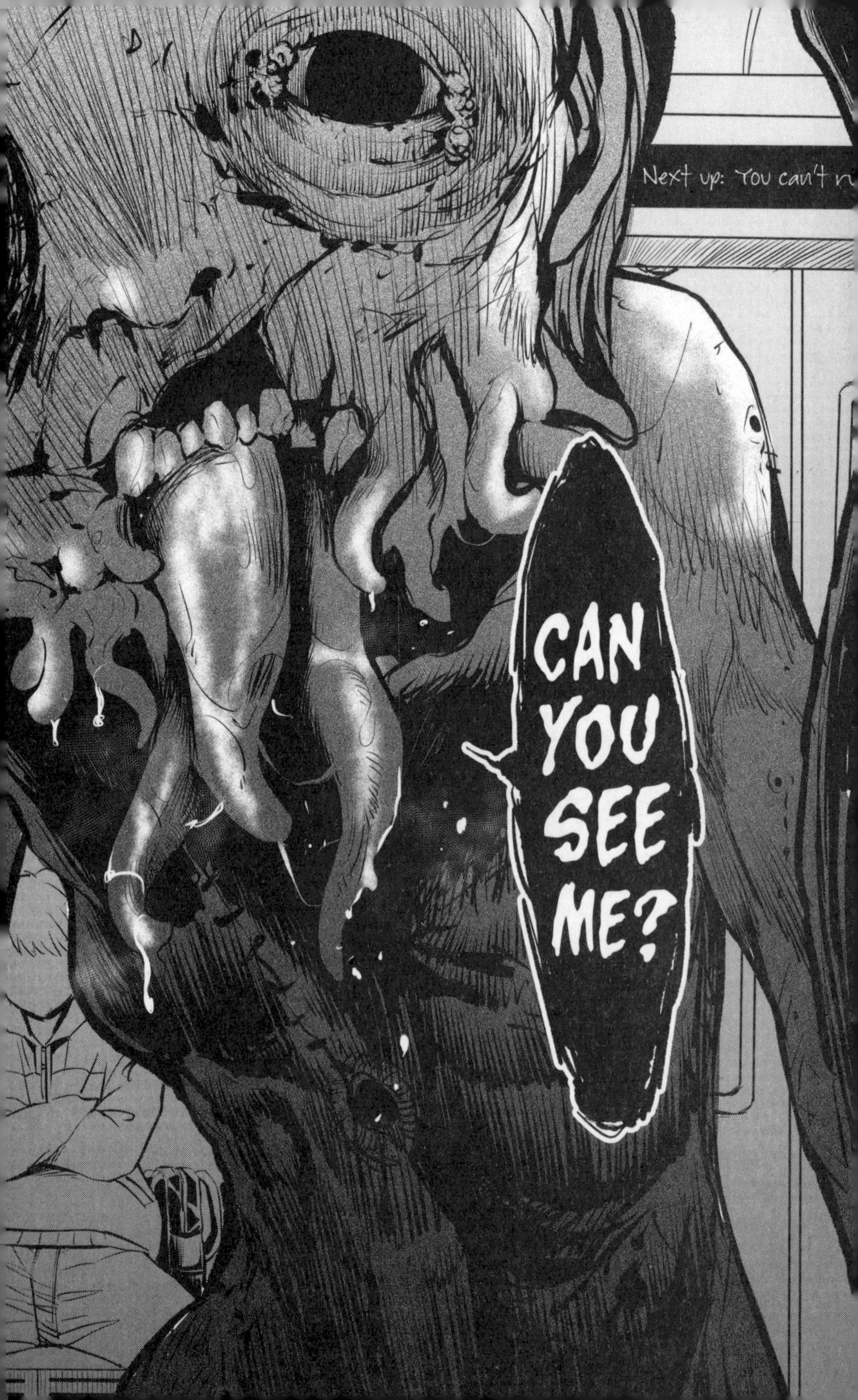
Next up: You can't
CAN YOU SEE ME?

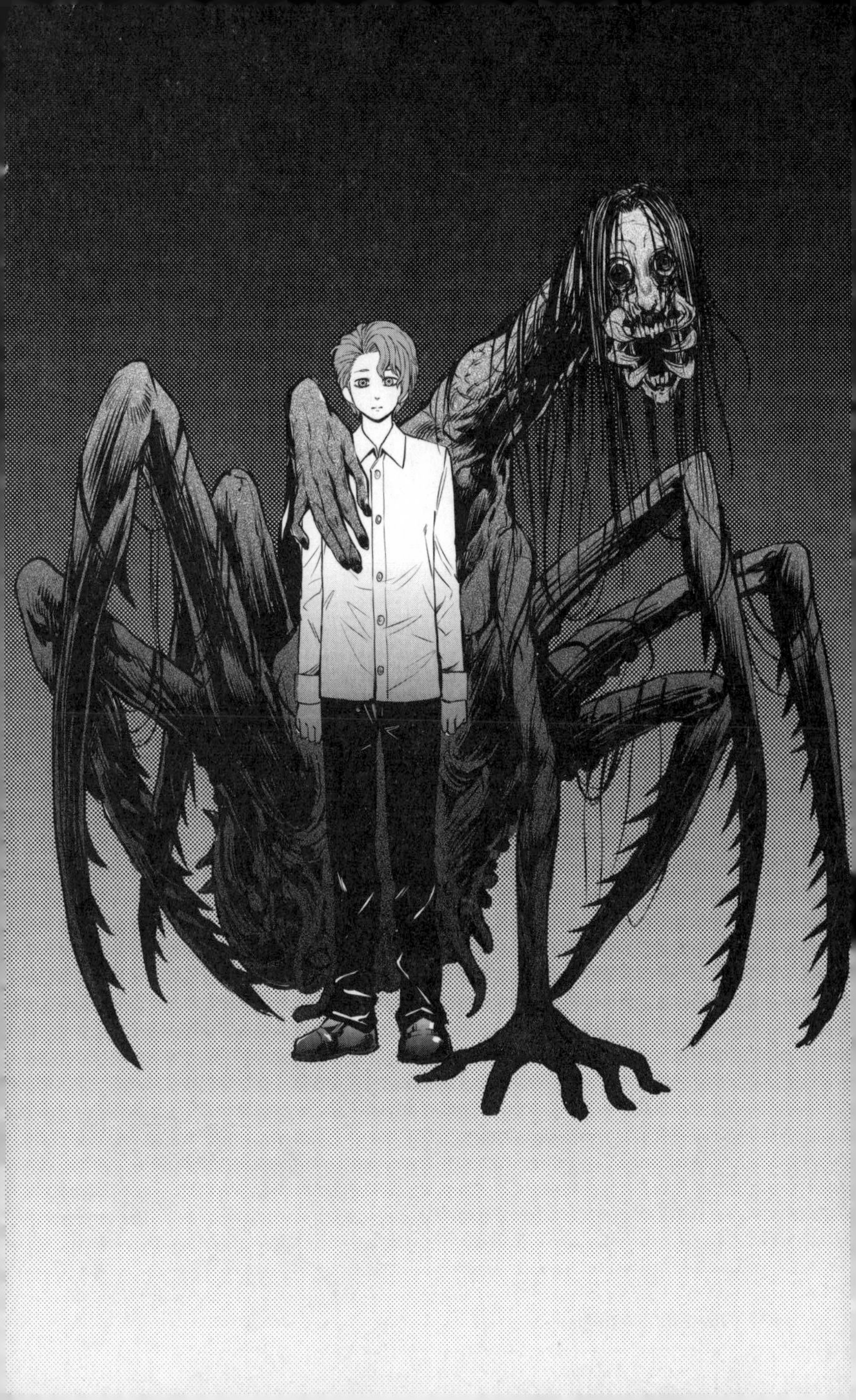

MIERUKO-CHAN 3

Tomoki Izumi

Translation: LEIGHANN HARVEY Lettering: ALEXIS ECKERMAN

MIERUKO-CHAN vol. 3
© Tomoki Izumi 2020
First published in Japan in 2020 by KADOKAWA CORPORATION, Tokyo.
English translation rights arranged with KADOKAWA CORPORATION, Tokyo, and Yen Press, LLC through Tuttle-Mori Agency, Inc.

English translation © 2021 by Yen Press, LLC.

Yen Press
150 West 30th Street, 19th Floor
New York, NY 10001

Visit us at yenpress.com • facebook.com/yenpress • twitter.com/yenpress • yenpress.tumblr.com

First Yen Press Edition: June 2021

Yen Press is an imprint of Yen Press, LLC.
The Yen Press name and logo are trademarks of Yen Press, LLC.

The publisher is not responsible for websites (or their content) that are not owned by the publisher.

Library of Congress Control Number: 2020944845

ISBNs: 978-1-9753-2431-5 (paperback)
        978-1-9753-2432-2 (ebook)

10 9 8 7 6 5 4 3 2 1

WOR

Printed in the United States of America